Christianizing the Roman Empire (A.D. 100–400)

Christianizing the Roman Empire
(A.D. 100–400)

RAMSAY MacMULLEN

YALE UNIVERSITY PRESS
New Haven and London

Designed by Nancy Ovedovitz and set in Bembo type by Eastern Graphics. Printed in the United States of America by Murray Printing Company, Westford, Massachusetts.

Library of Congress Cataloging in Publication Data
MacMullen, Ramsay, 1928–
    Christianizing the Roman Empire.
    Bibliography: p.   Includes index. 1. Evangelistic work—History—Early church, ca. 30–600. I. Title.
BR195.E9M33   1984   270.1   84-3694
ISBN 0-300-03216-1 (alk. paper)

10   9   8   7   6   5   4   3   2   1

Contents

Preface

My subject here is the growth of the church as seen from the outside, and the period is the one that saw the church become dominant, and Europe Christian.

I try to indicate some of the difficulties in seeing this subject clearly; also, the variety of factors at work in different strata of the population and at different periods; and last, the limits and possibilities in the sources, seen in a liberal sampling of their own words.

Because information reaches us in such unsatisfactory (at points, quite unusable) quantity and texture, and because it is drawn from such a great time span and such great numbers of lives and settings, I have not been able to arrange it all in a simple, straightforward story line. Simplicity could only have been bought at a great price in accuracy.

And, rather than add an inordinate amount of material on the historical background, I have chosen to take it for granted or leave it to three famous studies: Mikhail Rostovtzeff's *Social and Economic History of the Roman Empire* and A. H. M. Jones's *Later Roman Empire,* which together cover the whole stretch of time here studied; and Norman H. Baynes's *Constantine the Great and the Christian Church,* on the one event that needs signalizing, the first Christian emperor's conversion.

I hope, in spite of the difficulties I mention, that the account I offer will not be found too thorny by nonspecialists, for whom principally this book is written.

I am aware that general statements must rest on a broad evidentiary base, much broader than need be detailed in the text; and I can see also that my findings may at some points be at odds with what one might expect or with what has been suggested by others in the past. At such points I have felt obliged to lay out a great deal of evidence and argument. The bulky notes that result (though, in proportion, not so bulky as those of the three works referred to above), are meant mostly for specialists.

The choice of where to begin and where to leave off was made from straightforward considerations of historical significance. Had the church been wiped off the face of the earth at the end of the first century, its disappearance would have caused no dislocation in the empire, just as its presence was hardly noticed at the time. I think no one would dispute that—or expect any more exact measurement of Christianity's weight. Simply, it did not count. Three centuries later it had successfully displaced or suppressed the other religions of the empire's population. Much remained underground, and was to remain for a long, long time to come; but (again, not arguing terminology) the job was done. Among all leisurely great developments, *de longue durée,* this one of the period A.D. 100–400 might fairly be given pride of place in the whole of Western history.

E. R. McLaughlin, without realizing it, put me on the trail of a very useful bit of information; D. Fishwick, F. M. Donner, K. Berry, E. Patlagean, and T. Weiskel likewise, but of set purpose; and W. A. Meeks, with his usual generosity, read the whole typescript and helped me focus it. I am grateful to my learned, helpful friends. I thank R. Thompson for an extremely obliging offer of help not needed, after all. Lastly, I thank M. Anonyme for an item of information I use in an early chapter. He brought that, and fresh sheets and towels and breakfast, to the Left Bank hotel room where I wrote all but the final pages of this little book. He would find me in the morning already finished with at least an hour or two of work, since I could only use the daylight hours. The room was too ill equipped with artificial light for work after sundown; but I moved the table over to the window, indeed almost out the window, and there thumbed through my notes or contemplated the highly mysterious goings-on in the apartment house across the street. To my acquaintance's daily visits and our chats (for I knew almost no one else in the city) I quite looked forward, and always enjoyed them, before I had to turn back to the business at hand.

I

Problems of Approach

My object is history. It might be, but it isn't, theology. Accordingly, my view focuses naturally upon significance, the quality of weight that distinguishes historical phenomena from the (sometimes much more engrossing or at least more diverting) items of merely human interest that we see in the headlines of certain newspapers: "Mom Axes Babe" or the like. Significance, in its turn, indicates the degree to which many people, not just a few, are made to live their lives differently in respects that much engage their thoughts, not in respects they do not think about very carefully. Infanticide, though it violently changes two lives, ordinarily changes only two, or only a few. It does not count in history; and styles of greeting like "Hello" or "Good-morning" involve many people, but not in an action they themselves weigh seriously; so that, also, does not count for us. Significance must be compounded of both "many" and "much," in a sort of multiplicand of the two elements.

This is all elementary. Still, it needs to be said in order to explain the inclusion in my account of scenes not usually given much attention in books about church growth, scenes in which large numbers of persons are brought to a change in their religious allegiance, but namelessly—they are just ordinary folk of no account—and without great dramatic, further consequences in their manner of life. I think these scenes need to be included, along with Saint Augustine and a handful like him, because otherwise we would see only a church all head and no body, a phenomenon that affected only a few lives, a change without mass and therefore without historical significance. And *that* is the exact opposite of the truth.

In illustration, consider what Theodoret, bishop of Cyrus, witnessed during his long sojourn in that little compound that surrounded the base of Saint Symeon's pillar. The location is perhaps

1

forty miles east of Antioch; the date, in the second quarter of the fifth century.[1] Here on the pillar, day after broiling day, stood the saint, drawing to him by his great repute the most various visitors from the most distant places. Theodoret delights to record from how far they came.

> [Even the bedouins] in many thousands, enslaved to the darkness of impiety, were enlightened by the station upon the pillar. . . . They arrived in companies, 200 in one, 300 in another, occasionally a thousand. They renounced with their shouts their traditional errors; they broke up their venerated idols in the presence of that great light; and they foreswore the ecstatic rites of Aphrodite, the demon whose service they had long accepted. They enjoyed divine religious initiation and received their law instead spoken by that holy tongue (of Symeon). Bidding farewell to ancestral customs, they renounced also the diet of the wild ass or the camel. And I myself was witness to these things and heard them, as they renounced their ancestral impiety and submitted to evangelic instruction. Once even I was in the greatest danger: for he himself (Symeon) told them to approach to receive a priestly blessing from me, declaring they would draw the greatest benefits therefrom. But, in a most savage way, they gathered at a run, and some snatched at me from in front, some from behind, others at my sides; and those a little removed, following on top of the others and reaching out with their hands, seized my beard, or took hold of my cloak. I would have suffocated under this enthusiastic onrush of theirs if, by his shouts, he (Symeon) had not put them all to flight.

This is a rare moment: we see as in a little snapshot the actual day and hour in which, as the bishop understands it (and so must we), a mass of new adherents have been added to the church. Behold the kind of bulk, as it may be termed, or weight, or body that gave the church historical significance—at least in this eastern area of the empire!

We know something of these folk—not much, but more, perhaps, than Theodoret, who could not speak their language and had never ventured into their homelands. They had indeed come far, for their inscriptions cannot be traced to any point less than 250 miles distant from him (that is, not north of Palmyra). Their usual haunts lay even farther to the south, in the Djebel Druse.[2] They wandered like wild birds over a vast expanse, recording themselves only on the rocks of the desert. A male deity, Dusares, guarded them; a female, Allat, and other deities also. The only real pictorial evidence of their religion shows a festival honoring a goddess, most likely Allat (and

Theodoret's "Aphrodite"?). Their prayers reveal their preoccupations: "O Allat, grant security!" "O Allat, grant vengeance!"—for the conditions of their life were incorrigibly vulnerable and hazardous.[3]

There is no chance whatsoever, in my mind, that those among them who touched the bishop thereafter returned to the desert without returning to their desert ways—no chance that, in renouncing their little household icons, they also renounced the pillaging of their enemies and the avenging of their own dead. They may never have understood Symeon (still less, Theodoret); for he wanted them to seek a blessing, while they wanted, rather, a transfer of supernatural power from Theodoret, as if he were a talisman. That view Jesus had found, too, in the backlands of Galilee nearer to the bedouins' home.[4]

The question then arises whether these bedouins had really joined the church. With that question we must also decide whether our object is history or theology.

The choice has already been made—arbitrarily, the reader is entitled to say. But what started this discussion was my wish to understand how the whole empire was converted; and in a conventional sense (the sense to be found in all the ordinary history books), populations exactly like the bedouins in the degree of their spiritual change are certainly counted as converts—are and *were* counted. It will be clear in later pages that contemporaries of authoritative opinion saw the process in that same light. In anticipation, Saint Augustine may serve, reporting how pagan rebels by conversion bought their lives from a merciful emperor in 394, for "he wanted them made Christians by the occasion";[5] or the fourth-century church councils may serve, announcing that the laying on of hands alone suffices for the salvation of nonbelievers, without any instruction being needed;[6] or we may note the words of Saint Hypatius, in Callinicus' account, exhorting a pagan to "fulfill your promise to God and become a Christian" upon the spot, after a miracle.[7] Earlier still, in the apocryphal Acts of John, the usual Greek word for conversion is applied to spectators of a miracle, who declare, "[There is but] one god, [the god] of John. . . . We are converted, now that we have seen thy marvelous works! Have mercy upon us, O God, according to thy will, and save us from our great error!"[8]

The process we are tracing, of the slow but gigantic growth of a community of believers, seems thus to have had at its heart a psychological moment that might have been, though it was not always, quite uncomplicated; and that fact belongs by right, and not by later development, to the whole long process of ecclesiastical maturing. From the very beginning, Jesus' disciples followed him instantly, without instruction; new adherents, by supernatural actions, were won to instantaneous belief, or trust (πίστις, "commonly mistranslated, 'Your faith' . . . ," with implications of doctrine, as has been pointed out).[9]

Non-Christian religious loyalty bore the same character. For the moment, let a single illustration suffice: a votive stele put up in a Saturn-shrine twenty miles from Carthage in A.D. 238, where we read that the priest, "advised in visions and commended by the divinity of Saturn, . . . made good on his promise and dedicated this offering, for trust [or belief, *fides,* in Saturn] assured and health secured."[10] For both the Christian and the non-Christian, in such scenes the essential and, so far as we can tell, the only thing believed in was some supernatural power to bestow benefits.

There is an obvious connection between simplicity of belief and rapidity of conversion: the simpler the set of ideas with their attendant feelings, the shorter must be the period of transition to the new. Which is not to say that much longer, complicated transitions may not also have had their abrupt moments, like Saint Augustine's in the garden near Milan. The point is worth stressing because the more richly intellectual and dramatically interesting conversions naturally hold our attention best, and are most written about. The work to which readers wanting to learn about the subject of this book are most likely to turn indeed assumes that conversion cannot exist at all except as adherence "body and soul," and that, since such adherence was "prescribed by authority" within the church, "there was therefore," in the world of non-Christian beliefs, "no possibility of anything which can be called conversion. In fact the only context in which we find it in ancient paganism is that of philosophy."[11]

Arthur Darby Nock—for it is he who offers this view—here chooses a focus for his discussion that is, if not theology, at least not history; for he excludes from his attention the bedouins of the eastern deserts and their like in every province and century—and therefore, the overwhelming bulk of the Christian population. Underlying his view is the fundamental assumption that religious belief does not deserve the name unless it is intense and consuming. Against this can be set, from among a million demonstrations to the contrary, discoveries made by church workers in regions and in a period where we would assume particularly deep and well-instructed religiosity: Saxony and the neighboring parts of Germany around 1600. Once out of the upper-class circles, however, and even in a time of bitter theological rivalries to concentrate the greatest possible attention on the faith, the vast bulk of the population are found to have been largely or totally ignorant of the simplest matters of doctrine, rarely or never attending church. They were devoted instead to "a vigorous religious subculture . . . beyond the theologian's grasp, the preacher's appeal, or the visitor's power to compel"—that is, they were given over to "soothsayers, cunning women, crystal-gazers, casters of spells, witches, and other practitioners of forbidden arts."[12]

"Given over," it is fair to say—but not "body and soul." Therefore, in Reformation times an adherent might have been made out of the belief (πίστις or *fides*) that cunning women and spells actually worked and bestowed benefits. "Christian" Germany, as it certainly would be called in all conventional historiography, appears to have melted into the secular and even the non-Christian without clear demarcation. It serves as a reminder that we who observe long-distant periods on their own terms, freeing ourselves of theological presuppositions, must be ready to recognize and to treat as religious history an almost unmanageably broad range of psychological phenomena, of which the most historically significant need not have been at all intense or complicated intellectually.

But the boundaries around my subject are in danger of dissolving completely, to leave it without fixed lodging in the infinite continuum of human thoughts and doings. I should delay no longer in offering *some* definition. Let me declare Christian conversion, then, to have been that change of belief by which a person accepted the reality and supreme power of God and determined to obey Him.[13] Whether actual, entire, and doctrinally centrist obedience resulted would depend on cases. It would depend on cases whether the change lay half on the surface and in conduct, or produced an exclusive loyalty, or was warmly or little felt. As we have seen, however, the church itself interpreted the initial process very loosely, without, of course, abandoning the duty to perfect it thereafter. Moreover, as we will come to see in later pages, our definition—a device only of convenience, after all—becomes impossibly inconvenient in any discussion of the post-Constantinian world. We can worry about that at the proper time.

The church's duty to perfect its converts was carried out in quite remarkable fashion by schools of instruction, weekly lectures offered authoritatively from pulpits, and other pastoral devices familiar to everyone. They included also a close control over publication and dissemination of facts and opinions that dealt with church matters. Secular literature from the pagan past, Christian readers avoided, or they struggled in their conscience to justify it or not to read it too much. A long story there, and often told. The non-Christian setting of the church, except as it bore directly on church affairs, was ignored in Christian historical accounts ancient and, for that matter, modern.[14] Hostile writings and discarded views were not recopied or passed on, or they were actively suppressed; and, by the overwhelming authority of Eusebius, the father of church historiography, matters discreditable to the faith were to be consigned to silence.[15] His intent appears nowhere more clearly than in the solemn introduction to his eighth Book, where he must show how his coreligionists responded to the Great Persecution. Some had fallen.

> But it is not for us to describe their miserable vicissitudes, as things turned out, just as it is not a part of our our task to leave on record their faction-fights and their unnatural conduct towards each other, prior to the persecution. That is why we have decided to say no more about them than suffices for us to justify God's Judgment. . . . We shall rather set forth in our whole narrative only what may be of profit, first, to our own times, and then to later times.

Various consequences follow. We may, for instance, be misled about the proportions of piety and indifference within the empire's population. We would not expect to find, in the millions of words of the chief sources for our own subject—in Origen, Eusebius, Ambrose, Augustine, and the rest—such candor as ecclesiastical visitations offered in their reports on early Reformation Germany. There would be no profit in that. On the contrary, and in particular, and very much as still today, we expect to be offered a picture of widespread interest in the church, of coherent and powerful argument for its doctrines, of eager acceptance of them, radical changes in way of life resulting, and, in sum, the kind of spiritual community in the process of development that every churchman across the earlier centuries of Christianity wished most to see around him.

Very much the same distortions can be found in even the best of modern attempts to describe how the church grew. In Harnack,

Nock, and Bardy, I have already pointed out what seem to me to be examples of such distortions.[16] They may be called idealizing, like those of their sources: idealizing in the sense of discovering in the record of early conversions the same qualities that their sources wish to emphasize. And these are not the qualities of bedouins.

There is also a second type of distortion to beware of: the anthropologizing. Especially in the last generation, discussions of ancient religions are likely to make use of parallels drawn from scientific studies of still or recently living societies. It is, for example, almost obligatory to mention Polynesian "cargo" cults. But there are real difficulties in the way of this approach.

If we were to take Simon Kimbangu as one of those helpful parallels, we might trace his career from the moment of his being divinely empowered to go out and preach, in 1921, in the Belgian Congo: his first application of his powers to the healing of a child; its being miraculously saved from death; his continued healings; his growing fame, which he used as a platform for his preaching; the remarkably rapid spread of the gospel; the determination by the authorities to arrest him; his peaceful surrender to them; and his death as a broken man still in prison thirty years later.[17] His story might alert us to points in the evidence from antiquity which deserve special attention; but, naturally, we have acquired no new information. Kimbanguism may, further, be aligned with similar movements in Africa and elsewhere, and the similarities may be framed into general statements; but those, too, can be heuristic, nothing more. They certainly supply no reason for saying that ancient conversions "must have been" motivated in such-and-such ways, simply because those are the ways that have been observed in certain living societies.[18]

It is each context in its entirety and uniqueness that must govern any explanation. Within that, whether a historical parallel fits well and therefore supplies *likely* explanations, cannot be determined from the top down, so to speak, by measurement against abstract suppositions.

But really, nothing is more difficult to control than our sense of what is *likely*. If we distrust the human sciences and judgments rendered "scientifically," shall we turn instead to our own life's experiences? Here enters the last source of distortion, which I might term the "generalizing." It arises from a person's addressing our present subject, for example, as one particular slice of "religion" altogether, or of "Christianity" altogether. But he already knows what those

two things are. He has known all his life. If he then studies conversion in some given place, let us say fourth-century Antioch, he feels
safe in conjecturing that, even for some persons declared Christian,
"it was no doubt important to gain salvation; but it was important
no less, as long as one were at the scene, to enjoy fully the good
things of this life. It was this Christian people who filled the hippo-
drome and theater and, perhaps, followed the parades for Bacchus
and Demeter, in (the emperor) Valens' time. The festival was public,
why miss it? *But true Christianity is something different. It is essentially
the life of the Spirit,* the desire for union with God."[19] Perhaps so, today; yet the historical conclusion must be shown to arise out of the
minds of the people being studied, not out of generalizing.

Or again, generalizing may conclude that all forms of religion
have one common structure: so a person's shift of allegiance toward
Christianity need have involved only the exchange of one theology
or theodicy or liturgy or system of morals for some other that was
seen as preferable. Perhaps no one today is likely to make so strange
an error, but it is not hard to find it in older authorities otherwise de-
serving of great respect.[20] Granted, some variations of the generalizing fault are hard to avoid. Even to be recognized, they need a certain
degree of detachment from our own ways. We ourselves naturally
suppose, immersed as we are in the Judeo-Christian heritage, that religion means doctrine. *Why* should we think so? In fact, "that emphasis is most unusual as seen from a cross-cultural perspective."[21]
Among actual alternatives in the early centuries of the era, it is little
attested, very little. The opposite, the unchallenged right of anyone
to say or do or believe anything he wanted about any deity he addressed, so long as it was not aggressively hostile to other beliefs, is
easily shown in a thousand proofs.[22]

Yet again: it may be assumed on "general" grounds (but really because we have in our own culture a certain established view of asceticism) that pain sought out to please god is good and shows devotion,
while pleasure sought out for the same reason is bad and proves in-
sincerity. For example, ancient Isiacs "possessed a moral system
purer, more elevated than that of classical Roman religion. Who did
not feel his soul shaken with feelings of admiration as he watched
those votaries of Isis plunge thrice into the frozen Tiber and, shiv-
ering with cold, creep about the temple?" But some non-
Christian spectators saw it instead as madness;[23] indeed, so did some

Christians, before Saint Anthony had established new modes of worship.[24]

Of course, a great deal depends on one's point of view. We have the founder of the Society of Friends reporting how "I was commanded by the Lord to pull off my shoes. I stood still, for it was winter" but obeyed and then walked for miles barefoot into, and around, and back out of the town of Lichfield in England; whereas Aelius Aristides, for doing the same thing in Turkey, is judged by us to be "a brainsick noodle," at best "a very interesting crank."[25] Is there too much detachment in this judgment? But, of course, it was so very long ago. "Time," as the hymn says, "time makes ancient good uncouth."

Enough of preliminaries chiefly useful to myself as guidelines. They may be summed up in a few words: the adhesion to the church that turned it into a dominant institution is to be traced and understood as much as possible from the ancient evidence, and with the least possible coloring imported from other worlds.

II

What Pagans Believed

The subject of this book is something that happened to pagans, of course, and to the Roman Empire, not to the church and the Christians. The latter are already converted. It is in the non-Christian world where the action lies that chiefly interests me: the action of coming over. Accordingly, it is non-Christians who must be most carefully examined, as if by some pollster of public opinion.

Perhaps I should begin by sketching the broad outlines of the acceptable in religion. Within them any change of loyalty must surely be sought; within them, surely, Christianity must operate. It is, for example, clear in Christian apologetic (that is, propaganda, from which a number of pamphlets survive) that no audience addressed directly or indirectly would have been attracted by deviant sexual behavior within whatever religious community was being advertised. Incest wouldn't do, nor polygamy; and religious communities that did in fact experiment in those areas found themselves handicapped in their missionary efforts. Similarly, human sacrifice and cannibalism both (and often conjoined in a sequence) were talked about commonly as ingredients in religious rites. Human sacrifice, at least, was to be found in the past of the Etruscan, Roman, Punic, and Celtic populations. But that was all over, in the centuries that concern us.

The religious views most easily recoverable from the non-Christian Roman world do not, at any rate in some respects, strike a modern reader as alien or outlandish. In part, that results from our choice of witnesses: the ones most conveniently got at are those represented by their writings, or quoted or addressed in formal literature. They belong, then, to an elite who think in some respects like ourselves: Apuleius, for example, or Plutarch. They are distinguished by at least some years of education beyond the ABCs, therefore they had possessed at some point money sufficient to free them from the necessity of full-time labor. It was not out of the question for a man (never a woman) to earn the necessary money and leisure out of a working-class background, or something not much better: Lucian did it and so did Saint Paul.[1] But it was unusual to *want* to. The overwhelming majority of the elite as just defined (themselves no more than a tenth of the empire's population) belonged to a quite stable upper class.

Their religious views we might suppose began with, or logically rested on, ideas of immortality. Homer portrayed man as having a soul, and Elysian Fields to go to after death. Plato taught of life indestructible. When you hired one of the town's eloquence professors (never a priest) to speak at the funeral of a loved one, he followed the book, the conventions of his culture, even literally a little handbook on speechification composed for the more customary occasions. He would work himself up to a passionate pitch, according to the rules of his art, and then, perhaps with a catch in his voice at the most effective intervals, extemporize a bit: "for it is not unsuitable on these topics also to philosophize," referring to Elysium, "where Rhadamanthus, Menelaus, Achilles, and Memnon reside. And perhaps, better, he [the deceased] now lives among the gods, traversing the heavens and looking down on life below. Perhaps, even, he is reproaching those who mourn for him; for the soul is related to the divine, descends thence, but longs again to mount to its kin—as Helen, the Dioscuri, and Heracles, they say, belong to the gods' community. Let us therefore sing praises to him as if to a hero, indeed as a god let us bless him!"[2] Hollow comfort!—that your loved one might be chosen by Olympus to enjoy the same divinization as Heracles! But that was the best hope in those long post-Homeric days. Something similar, indeed a good deal less hesitant and shifting a view, appears in a highly wrought essay on consolation by Plutarch. He and others mention, too, immortality through Dionysiac initiations. Verse epitaphs of the richer sort refer to an afterlife in Elysium or Hades; so, possibly, does the Dionysiac imagery on carved sarcophagi. But there are also explicit denials of any afterlife in various authors, as well as indications, overwhelmingly dominant in grave inscriptions and grave practices, that life was either thought to end in death or to linger only as a miserable little spark or spirit in the tomb. It is difficult to adjust our own ideas to an ancient world so rich in variety yet so impoverished in the very beliefs that mean so much in the Judeo-Christian heritage; but we really must acknowledge that the empire before conversion had radically different views of that subject from our own.[3]

Moreover, among the upper classes serving as our focus at the moment, if there was more speculation about an afterlife than you would find among the masses, it was framed in very refined terms. Such life belonged wholly to the realm of the divine: therefore it lay beyond deformity, pain, or any other burden of mortal existence. Resurrection in the flesh appeared a startling, distasteful idea, at odds with everything that passed for wisdom among the educated.

Divine realms included the Blessed, the Happy Ones, gods and heroes, all in Olympus. Olympus was a Greek idea, however, and a most antique one. It is hard to find any reference to it outside of self-consciously cultivated circles, international and widespread though their culture was. Other realms lay both above and below Olympus. The highest was ruled by some figure, perhaps very abstractly conceived, that Plato had envisioned and descendants in his line of thought had elaborated over centuries, a figure without corporeal qualities, needs, or susceptibilities, perfect in every respect: One God, maker of heaven and earth. All other beings could be seen as mere expressions of his will: in short,[4] monotheism.

Other circles besides the highly educated approach the idea of monotheism, one suspects, by working through the language of flattery or abasement until terms of address like "All-Highest" or "One and Unique" were encountered—encountered, but not meant literally. Or approach was made to it through attributing to the chosen deity one function after another and one home after another, in hymns of salutation, until there was nothing left for the rest of the pantheon: "You are the force that binds the waves, You are the Savior of all cities," and so on. Again, because of people's narrowness of curiosity and loyalty the beliefs of some neighboring region or city might have no reality; and such indifference could be simply accepted: "all men do not worship all gods, but each, a certain one that he acknowledges."[5] Or, last and most commonly, monotheism was approached through conceiving the world above us as pyramidical, rising to an apex in a single point; and that point is "more 'god,'" in Orwellian fashion, than the others. I will come back to this last conception a little later.

The lower parts of the pyramid, pressing upon everyday life and even within human reach and control through application of special spells, were the demonic. How could these two worlds be told apart?

The answer lay in behavior: inhabitants of the daimon-world were less good (or they might be positively baneful) and less powerful than gods—hence manipulable through magic. A daimon might be discovered in the form of a mad dog or an old man, causing plague or riot; it was a daimon that one invoked to skewer an enemy or inflame an unresponsive love. In combination with belief in mere chance or Fortune, non-Christians, and for that matter Christians also, in substantial numbers, could thus solve that ancient riddle, Whence Evil? For they could ascribe no wrong to divinity.[6]

It followed in their logic, or at least in their practice, that no deity could inflict wrong on another. In Homer's day, perhaps, things had been different. That was long ago and mere myth. Only the Christian propagandists recalled it, to raise laughs, or eyebrows, against their rivals. Living worshipers in the world we are considering instead entered a shrine of Isis to put up a vow or an altar to Aphrodite, and the priest let them. They worshiped Mithras in Hadad's temple. West or east, wherever one looked, there reigned a truly divine peace and undisturbed religious toleration.

From divinity all good might be received: foreknowledge, safety in risky doings, good crops, and (attested above all else and especially signalized in various points of cult) good health. Such were the universal expectations, so far as we can judge, outside of Judeo-Christian circles. The idea that any sort of day-to-day service or perpetual allegiance was owing to divinity had little currency. Neither was there the least uneasiness about the self-interested nature of worship. You only made offerings, or promises of offerings, in order to gain favor from powerful beings. In exactly the same way, very poor people brought very poor little presents to a great man when they came to call—as petitioners, or potential petitioners; so it would be well to insure a kindly hearing in advance.[7] The relationship appears continually. "For your cattle, for them to be healthy," very much as one gives them vitamin shots today, "make this sacrifice to Mars Silvanus. . . . If you want, you make this vow each year"—so, Cato the Elder (*Agr.* 83). Or, more up-to-date, the graffito on a wall in Rome's port city, "Hermes, good fellow, bring me profit!"[8] If book-learned circles were made uncomfortable by the view that god could be inclined to trivial ends or swayed by sheer din of entreaty, they too nevertheless subscribed to the need of divine help for larger purposes. "If the security of the empire lies in sacrifices there [in Rome], then we must suppose that performing sacrifices everywhere yields benefits, the greater beings in Rome conferring the greater benefits and those in the country, and in other cities, less; but anyone of sense would welcome even these latter." The tone of calm rationality here is not unrepresentative of non-Christian thinking,[9] and it is of course confirmed by much argument back and forth between Christian and non-Christian propagandists: both sides insist that history has (or has not) been kind to Rome because (or in disproof) of Rome's obedient centuries of hecatombs.

Christians did not renounce benefit from their own prayers: quite the contrary, "to people who are zealous in those [Christian] beliefs," so proclaimed a Christian monarch among his subjects, "all good things in abundance are accustomed to fall, and whatever they set their hand to will answer to their highest hopes."[10] In the world we are studying, there was nothing to be ashamed of in needing and asking favors from heaven. On the other hand, too crudely contractual a worship may have had the wrong feel to it—clearly there could be no equality between what men might offer and gods might grant —and the profit-motive, when it showed in a holy man's conduct, destroyed his credibility. We would expect just that, and it appears explicitly in the satires of Lucian, for example, or in Jesus' handling of magicians. The anti-Christian publicist Celsus, in second-century eastern provincial cities, encountered "those who have learned from Egyptians, who sell their revered teachings in the middle of the market-place for a few obols, and drive demons out of people and blow away diseases and call up spirits."[11] Such men were only out to cheat you.

So we arrive at the desired point, where one person is advocating a set of religious beliefs that at least *he* would call "revered teachings," while his audience listens and rejects, as here, or listens and accepts, that is, becomes converted. The point of action lies near the center of the region chiefly interesting to me, where Saint Paul traveled, to which I must add for my study a sector of North Africa within a couple of hundred miles of Carthage, and parts also of France up the Rhone valley. All this is the area in which the church made headway first and most strongly. Herein also originate most of our witnesses to the nature of non-Christian cults.

The very rapid sketch in the preceding pages has been offered as a reminder of the sort of expectations and prejudices that any new, revered teachings were likely to encounter. The audience most easily described is found, of course, among the highly educated. But within that group was a certain ex-consul Rutilianus, later provincial governor, who fell for a great religious hoax: the cult of Glycon. Or was it a hoax (as its annalist Lucian says) any more than any other faith? More than Mithraism?—which may be a second instance of a new invention within the period of my study. And was Rutilianus, any more than Aelius Aristides or George Fox, "brainsick"? Does he not, rather, point to the last preliminary caution one should accept —namely, that human beings are simply born into different degrees of religiosity, degrees distributed regardless of education or social class, and that no survey of a civilization's prevailing views is complete without allowing for the full range of individual interpretation, from the very "cool" to the very "hot"?

The ordinary, near the center, is best sensed by returning to the word "acceptable." Open challenge by Lucian to the cult of Glycon—visiting its chief priest, poking around its shrine, asking questions with a grin on his face—brought his life into danger. Mockery would get you lynched, anywhere. At the other extreme, mockery was thought to be fairly earned by people who believed too much, too easily, or too foolishly. Plutarch's essay "On Superstition" may stand as representative (he himself was a religious man).

To our surprise, perhaps, the state stayed out of the picture. Jews —alternately privileged and persecuted—and Christians were exceptional, the latter seen as atheists. Evidently they talked freely and from an early date about their "atheism," in the sense of denying the true divinity of all but their own god, and they talked with irrepressible conviction; for their persecutors by at least the mid-second century were reacting to them in that sense.[12] Theirs, however, was no crime per se; for sacrilege punishable by law referred to actions not so much against piety as against property (temple-robbing).[13] Nor was atheism illegal on the municipal level. Cities had their special guardian, patron, and/or resident god(s); and, since the season or even the exact date of certain widely known rituals was accommodated in many different cities, they could form a sort of religious calendar out of all the more popular cults.[14] Election of priests and priestesses for the older-established cults was also likely to be public.[15] But none of this structure of worship was defended by legislation. Only the capital of the whole empire, itself unique, had gods that an ardent patriot might think of as identified in any special way with a political entity. In the dying days of open opposition to Christianity, the leader of the faith in Rome spoke out sternly against holy virgins abandoning their vows: he recommended punishment "in view of the state's requirements," *reipublicae utilitatem . . . considerans*.[16] On the other hand, the emperors themselves pressed no special religious views on their subjects, who no doubt waited with curiosity to see which deities would receive the publicized favor of each new ruler.[17]

Does it not all appear, in review, a very spongy, shapeless, easily penetrated structure of beliefs? From the throne—occupied every decade or so by the particular favorite of some different deity —down to the marketplace of some individual town in which might be seen both the thoroughly skeptical Celsus or Lucian and the thoroughly credulous customers of the latest wizard, the empire seemed positively to invite a sharply focused and intransigent creed—if only to round out an embrace that was so infinitely tolerant.

III

Christianity as Presented

By contrast, Christianity presented ideas that demanded a choice, not tolerance; and while some lay easily within the bounds of the acceptable, others were a lot harder to swallow.

To the possibility of a new deity and new cult, no opposition arose. Besides the wonderful Glycon, who came down to earth in the form of a prophesying serpent, a number of beings with human form began to be worshiped during the period of our study, after they had finished their span of days in the flesh. We cannot say of them that they "died." They were placed in the category of the superhuman called "heroes": the philosopher Plotinus, the priestess Ammias serving near Thyatira, and so forth.[1] Inspired messengers risked being mistaken for deities themselves: Saint Peter or Apollonius, for exampel, or, later, the bishop of Antioch.[2] We must remind ourselves, of course, of the spectrum of temperament and the degrees of exposure to a diversity of ideas, already emphasized. It was not a world in which absolutely everyone trembled on the edge of believing absolutely anything.

That the deity presented was sole and unique likewise raised no difficulties. Something close to monotheism, by one approach or another, had long been talked about and attracted adherents among Greeks and Romans alike. That He should be envisioned as a monarch enthroned on high was familiar; that He should have his angels and other supernatural beings to do his work, just as Satan had *his* throngs—that was familiar too. So we have a Christian describing "'Adonai the All-High seated above cherubs and seraphs,'" —at which the non-Christian listener inquires curiously, "'What are cherubs and seraphs?' Acacius answers, 'The agent of the All-High God and attendant on His lofty seat.'"[3]

A gulf opened, however, over the word *god* as distinct from *dai-*

mon. The latter, we have seen, was a second-rate being in degree of authority, as in morals. Like a dog, you could whistle him up to do your dirty work for you.[4] Non-Christians observed the customs of terminology unconsciously or, when pressed, consciously: Jesus, said Celsus, was presented as if he were a Great God, whereas he was not so much as an ordinary one, nor even a daimon (these were the three ranks, of which there are also less explicit indications in other writers of various sorts).[5] Such definitions are not found very often because there was little call for them—before the Christian attack.

That attack was sharp and consistent. It followed from Jewish practice. Saint Paul is at pains to emphasize and control his usage, referring to "the so-called 'gods,'" "'gods' that are not in their nature'"; Eusebius speaks of the "mis-named 'gods'"; and a triumphant champion of the church erected an inscription at Ephesus that begins, "Destroying the delusive image of the demon Artemis, Demeas has erected this symbol of Truth, the God that drives away idols, and the Cross of priests, deathless and victorious sign of Christ."[6] In a host of passages, it is explained by Tertullian or Origen that daimones, not gods, had produced all the miracles, oracles, epiphanies, signs, and even benefactions of any sort that constituted the whole divine history of the non-Christian world since time began.[7] So a campaign of demotion was under way.

More sharply still, the real God was pictured as being at war against all rivals, ranged with his angels in combat against Satan. Saint Paul issued a summons to join the struggle to defeat the powers of darkness. It was a duty, preached later too, by many another, like Justin or Tatian. Such a view "impiously divides the kingdom of god and makes two opposing forces, as if there was one party on one side and another at variance with it" (it is a non-Christian speaking here, of course).[8]

That a divine being would extend his wrath even beyond this dualism and send down suffering upon human beings simply for their failure to offer him regular cult seemed an even more blasphemous idea.[9] As Livy put it, "people even attack the gods with headstrong words; but we have never heard of anyone on that account being struck by lightning"; or again, we have Libanius pointing to the gods as examples to ourselves, by reason of their "forgiveness to those who daily slander them, whenever any of their affairs go amiss."[10] Still further: punishment in *after*life received hardly a mention in non-Christian debate. That may have been partly because of disbelief in resurrection of the flesh, but no doubt more because of the general disbelief in immortality of any sort at all.[11]

"The living God," by contrast, "the God of vengeance, the jealous God who has need of nothing," was the master whom Saint Paul is said to serve and to preach to a non-Christian audience. With that introduction, he summoned them to turn from their past neglect of Him and His wishes. In the summons, or in the contrast drawn by preachers between men saved and "those without faith called still 'the children of wrath,'" or again, in the pagan Celsus' knowledge that Christians "believe in eternal punishments" and "threaten others with these punishments"—in all this, we can hear the spoken message of the church.[12]

If we stop here a moment, however, to assess the various familiar ways, so summarily recalled, in which Christianity differed from the general context of opinion around it, the one point of difference that seems most salient was the antagonism inherent in it—antagonism of God toward all other supernatural powers, of God toward every man or woman who refused allegiance, and (we shall see) of those who granted their allegiance toward all the remaining stubborn unbelievers. It was not the church's liturgy, nor morals, nor monotheism, nor internal organization (when these things were correctly understood) that seemed to non-Christians much different from other people's or at all blameworthy. At least, there is no evidence for anything of that sort.

We should not attach much weight, either, to certain special prejudices found in special groups: among the literate elite, for example. They were provoked that crude views crudely written down, as they saw it, should be impudently assigned a great value by crude people. But more than one churchman eventually came round to a similar opinion. As to Christians' everday neighbors, whose ideas of social entertainment were inextricably rooted in festival practices (even if those were no more than superficially religious), they felt offended at being snubbed. Surely that was natural, at times, too, historically important, the chief cause of suspicion, dislike, and readiness to persecute. But beyond these well-known reasons for hostility, Christianity did present a kind of polarization to its audience at various points in what may be called pagan theology—a polarization that pricked or alarmed the observer.

We are now at a juncture where I must stop to confront a most important question: What *did* Christianity present to its audience? For plainly the process of conversion that interests me took place in people's minds on the basis of what they knew, or thought they knew. It is useless to consider in the process all the things *we* know, which might have been discovered by a convert after he had picked up some further instruction and further experience of the new faith. Accordingly, those and only those precise impressions must be isolated which were manifestly and for certain transmitted by members of the church to persons outside, and through which Christianity worked its spell.

Anticipating this question, I have woven into the comparison of Christian and non-Christian views only matters (but not all matters) directly attested in our sources. The sources are very limited in number. Indeed, they offer only a few scenes from the canonical or apocryphal Acts, plus the Apologists (so far as they actually did reach beyond church circles), plus certain snatches of conversation in martyr-acts. But when we are told, for example, that martyrs in that dreadful amphitheater of Carthage made signs to the noisy crowd in reference to their own approaching ordeal, "You, us; but God, you," we can assume that the doctrine of divine punishment was known to that audience. This seems a certain inference. On the other hand, I don't think we can assume any general knowledge among non-Christians regarding, for example, the cause of divine wrath. For how would they have learned more? Why should they care?

As a preliminary, it has even to be established whether much curiosity was attested about other people's religious beliefs. The contours of that question, like others we have looked at, are largely fixed by individual temperament. It is, however, striking to discover, through a good, long immersion in the evidence for ancient religion, how much there is to be found on practice and how relatively little ancient comment or discussion exists about that practice. I suppose the disproportion is mostly due to the unimportance of dogma. In any case, Christians often show themselves ignorant of non-Christian views which are well known to us or would have been to a traveler; and, more to the point, non-Christians generally did not know much about Christianity.[13]

Writings originally directed or later offered from within the church to an audience beyond did not include, of course, any pages that are now canonical or, for that matter, apocryphal; for those pages were rather for internal consumption. At best, the occasional outsider who investigated them was an enemy, like Celsus or Porphyry. That leaves nothing but Apologetic literature for a wider readership. On the basis of a statement by Tertullian and on general probability, however, the experts today are generally agreed that that literature likewise served chiefly for internal consumption. And there was little enough reading of any sort, anyway. Three quarters or more of the population were illiterate. Points of contact and media of communication that we take for granted in our world simply did not exist in antiquity.[14]

We are thus thrown back on face-to-face encounters as very nearly the only kind of meeting-point through which a knowledge of church teachings might be gained. In due course, I will return to these meetings, to see what might have happened when they occurred; here I must take note only of the information conveyed. It was exiguous: monotheism, to begin with. That was taught, and God was compared, in familiar fashion, to a monarch with his companies of servants about him; and contrast was drawn between Him and mere imitations, the daimones that passed for gods by animating idols and so forth. Word was spread of divine wrath and punishments, the more readily imagined through being leveled at evildoers resurrected in the flesh; while immortal delights were also known to await the blessed. The very stark blacks and whites of this whole crude picture of Christianity, and the very unsteady focus on the role of Jesus, are most striking.[15]

To this picture remains to be added a very much fuller kind of instruction, long and patient, gained by a few individuals. I defer that subject likewise, for a moment. What we already have before us, however, even if it appears stark to a point almost unrecognizable, sufficed and more than sufficed for conversion—which, after all, is the target of my inquiry. It sufficed because conversion in the sense specified above, and within the non-Christian world, did not require doctrine of the least elaboration, nor a divine biography, nor very much more than the certainty that truth was being proposed for acceptance, not some silly or wicked fiction. That much being fixed, all else followed. It followed for Marcus Aurelius, describing the foundations of his own beliefs, as it did for the stupidest stable-boy.[16] Rather to expect that non-Christians would be converted *both* to new convictions *and* by new means, is too much—and beyond that, quite needless. It was rather their general instinct, I suppose, as it is generally everybody's instinct, to make the least possible tear in the fabric of already held beliefs, when obliged to admit some urgent novelty. At any rate, we do in fact see them acting along exactly those lines.

The fact appears first in an earlier period than my chosen one, in New Testament scenes. "The gospels represent Jesus as attracting attention primarily as a miracle worker, and winning his followers"—or, in other terminology, producing conversions—"by miracles. The gospels do so because *he* did so."[17] Their purpose in preserving the record was also conscious: "These [manifestations] have been recorded *in order that you may believe* that Jesus is the Messiah, the Son of God" (Jn 20 : 30f.). Likewise in the next generation, the Apostles' success in winning recruits arose from their deeds, above all, in healing. "Although laymen in their language," says the very educated bishop Eusebius, "they drew courage from divine, miraculous powers."[18] Even Simon Magus through miracles made converts—meaning persons ready to obey him out of the conviction that he was a supernatural being (Acts 8 : 11).

These passages force a choice, in our modern world a rather uncomfortable choice, between two possible interpretations. Either we must suppose the laws of nature to have been really and truly suspended, or we must try to accommodate the record within interpretations "scientific" but as little Procrustean as possible. Of the two alternatives, the first seems to need a great deal of discussing and defining and adjusting to. Why so much? The answer lies in our own encumbered imaginations. We cannot easily divest ourselves of our great knowledge and superior reasoning, so as to think more nearly like the people of the Roman Empire. They, however, took miracles quite for granted. That was the general starting point. *Not* to believe in them would have made you seem more than odd, simply irrational, as it would have seemed irrational seriously to suppose that babies are brought by storks.

Such ancient views seem to us very well in their place. When we read in Herodotus or in Livy, for example, that divine beings appeared on Greek or Roman battlefields to help our heroes, we can quite easily accept the credulity of the account. That is how we would describe it. It doesn't bother us because it lies at such a distance from ourselves. But when the same ancients confront scenes of significance to our own beliefs, then it is troubling to find them still so different, and, of course, vastly more troubling to confront the central question: whether the miracles really occurred.

Even within our period of study that question concerned non-

Christians as well as Christians. The latter, after no long stretch of generations, looked back to earlier times as being in essence somehow capable of producing events that were no longer possible.[19] Or, on the other hand, rather than thinking ancient miracles real because the miracle-workers were formerly a better species, people might suppose them worse, even fakes. "Jesus the Swami" (γόης in Greek, a swindler holy-man who practices only deceits but fools people successfully) was a figure once familiar in non-Christian attacks, just as worshipers of Apollonius the Divine once had bitterly to dispute the accusations leveled against him.[20] It should not be forgotten, either, that people are capable of keeping nature and its laws and ordinary life in one compartment of their minds and something quite different in another: Galen the true scientist, for example, who believed in centaurs and yet didn't.[21] Accordingly, believers may have had their cake and eaten it, too.

Last, we may suppose that it gave pleasure both to relate and to hear wonderful stories, because such is human nature; and that pleasure can be increased, at least till the point of incredulity is reached, by exaggerating the wonderful. So some real happening at the base of an account may be reconstructed by shrinking the account down to the physically possible.[22]

But the problem, of course, will not leave us alone. It must be confronted every week at Sainte Anne de Beaupré or Lourdes or Monserrat. It recurs in the story of William Wade Harris—not remote, at least no more so than the miraculous stupidity called the First World War—who in 1914 came forward in receipt of divine powers to preach God's word and heal the sick. His mission was extraordinarily successful along the Gold Coast. He was able "to drive out demons and spirits, the enemies of god. . . . These powers gave him an advantage over the missionaries because he showed his power over the spirits and did not ask people to act on blind faith. He completely discredited the old gods as he introduced his God. . . . The Harris converts had only to take a step—a substitution of God for the former pantheon of gods and spirits, and an observance of God's taboos in place of theirs."[23] A few refused, or thought Harris himself was god. An up-to-date observer possessing a higher education described him as "a harmless maniac," just as we have heard Kimbangu, Aelius Aristides, and George Fox so characterized. But to most of his countrymen, Harris truly had God within him, and only by that power was able to heal the paralyzed and even to raise the dead. Attesting this, there were clouds of witnesses, most of them still alive when I was born.

To doubt their account of what they saw—to doubt that Harris, or any saint, or Jesus himself truly suspended the laws of nature —could only be theology, good or bad. To doubt that Asclepius worked miracles back then would likewise be theology. And to worry too much about whose miracles were real, the pagans' or the Christians', is surely to prepare oneself for belief in one or the other, and therefore for theology also; for by what else but true divinity can nature's laws have been suspended?

The problem of presentation is a very old one. Consider it at the juncture most central to the story I am concerned with: Constantine's conversion and (or by?) the fiery vision in the sky. "Whether that appearance of the cross of light was only a subjective experience or whether it was objective reality the historian cannot decide," as one of the best of them confesses, a half-century ago or more. And he cites contributions to that debate receding another fifty years into the past. "Still less," he continues, "can he determine whether it was a God-granted miracle; to answer such a question the historian must turn philosopher or theologian."[24] Quite right. Therefore in these pages I report as faithfully as I can what people of that ancient time believed. On their beliefs they based their actions. Beliefs and actions together are realities. The historian who sticks to *those* sticks to his last.

IV

Points of Contact, Modes of Persuasion, before 312

Eusebius, the great first church historian (3.37), recounts how, around the turn of the first century in the province Asia, there were "many . . . who amplified the Message, planting the saving seed of the heavenly kingdom far and wide in the world, . . . evangelizing . . . with God's favor and help, since wonderful miracles were wrought by them in those times also through the Holy Spirit. As a result, assembled crowds, every man of them on the first hearing, eagerly espoused piety toward the maker of all things." The scene is easily expanded from Saint Paul's writings, with their accounts of his own "signs, marvels, and miracles" matched against his competitors. Unlike the latter, the "super-preachers" as he calls them, he relies "not on plausible, clever argument but on manifestations of the Holy Spirit and of supernatural power."[1]

There was, however, in Paul's day and in the time that Eusebius describes, a lot of coming and going also of inconsequential visionaries, evangelists, and fakes, of whom Peregrinus is a late descendant in Palestine (he is described by Lucian) and of whom we shall also hear, toward the end of this chapter, in other eastern areas.[2] Celsus may have similar types in mind (or perhaps he was caricaturing Christians) when he speaks of "many, who are nameless, who prophesy at the slightest excuse for some trivial cause both inside and outside temples; and there are some who wander about begging and roaming around cities and military camps, and they pretend to be moved as if giving some oracular utterance." These in turn blend into an even more miscellaneous population of visionaries, doomsayers, sorcerers, and the like, all in touch or actually filled and brimming over with divine powers.

25

Powers which must be seen to be believed, naturally. The population and religious expectations that encouraged the pullulation of such wandering wonder-workers could discriminate and tell the fakes from the genuine. There was a good deal of discussion about how to do that, in Christian Apologetic writings and elsewhere, too. For most purposes, however, it was enough that the wonder-worker should merely work his wonders. Then he gained credit. Otherwise, not.

At Ephesus, so told the Acts of John, the Apostle encountered unbelievers but, with miracles of healing, won them over. More effectively yet, in the very temple of Artemis himself, he prayed, "'O God . . . at whose name every idol takes flight and every demon and every unclean power: now let the demon that is here take flight at thy name . . .' And while John was saying this, of a sudden the altar of Artemis split in many pieces . . . and half the temple fell down. Then the assembled Ephesians cried out, '[There is but] one God, [the God] of John! . . . We are converted, now that we have seen thy marvelous works! Have mercy on us, O God, according to thy will, and save us from our great error!' And some of them lay on their faces and made supplication, others bent their knees and prayed; some tore their clothes and wept, and others tried to take flight."[3]

I don't think the explanatory force of this scene should be discounted on the grounds that it cannot have really happened, that it is fiction, that no one was meant to believe it. I suppose instead that it was quite widely believed in the second and third centuries with which we are concerned at the moment; and I assume that its substance, mostly in oral form, led on through belief to conversion. Why not? Such wonderful stories were most reliably reported. In his essay on the martyrs of Palestine (§4.14f.), Eusebius recounts how one of the victims of the persecution in 305 was killed by drowning; how the port town where this happened felt a distinct tremor of the earth shortly afterward; and how the body of the victim washed ashore. To this extraordinary sequence "every inhabitant of Caesarea can testify," so he assures us. He uses the present tense of people among whom he was living at the time, and he emphasizes how remarkable but how unchallengeable the whole thing was and is. At such a sign it could be seen how God "threatened all men with terrible wrath," and before it the whole town "confessed the one and only God of the Christians." That is, they were converted.

But to return to Ephesus: reasons for believing whatever an apostle (or, by implication, any later evangel in the same heritage) might say are obvious in the description just quoted. Listeners were and should have been scared half to death. Divine power had a terrifying, high-voltage quality that split and blinded. There might be some fate even worse to come, beyond the grave; and, while you were waiting, you had to consider the unpredictable wrath of the prophet himself, well able to blast you like a bolt of lightning.[4] There was no refuge to be sought from that. He had shown and you had seen—or others like you had seen, and believed, and the report was now here before you—that even a being supposed to be great, such as Artemis of Ephesus, proved less great than the other one that was preached. It had been demonstrated head-on in the riven altar.[5]

Driving all competition from the field head-on was crucial. The world, after all, held many dozens and hundreds of gods. Choice was open to everybody. It could thus be only a most exceptional force that would actually displace alternatives and compel allegiance; it could be only the most probative demonstrations that would work. We should therefore assign as much weight to this, the chief instrument of conversion, as the best, earliest reporters do. True, "historians . . . of the church have declared that such phenomena (of divine confrontations) 'are more problems of crowd psychology than of Christian piety.' In so doing, they have declared the study of exorcism, possibly the most highly rated activity of the early Christian church, a historiographical 'no-go' area."[6] But we have Justin boasting "how many persons possessed by demons, everywhere in the world *and in our own city,* have been exorcized by many of our Christian men"; Irenaeus asserting that "some people *incontestably and truly* drive out demons, so that those very persons often become believers"; Tertullian issuing the challenge, "let a man be produced *right here before your court* who, it is clear, is possessed by a demon, and that spirit, commanded by any Christian at all, will as much confess himself a demon in truth as, by lying, he will elsewhere profess himself a 'god'"; and Cyprian once again declaring that demons in idols, "when they are adjured by us in the name of the true God, yield forthwith, and confess, and admit they are forced also to leave the bodies they have invaded; and *you may see them,* by our summons and by the workings of hidden majesty, consumed with flames."

Jesus' authority (ἐξουσία) over the fiercest infestations of satanic power, making them do whatever he wished by a mere word of command, he passed on to his disciples, with instructions to use it.

They did. Exorcists by title became early established in the churches. Eusebius says theirs is "an office of special labor." Rome itself still had twenty-two of them at the turn of the fifth to the sixth century. The institution had taproots in Judaism, exorcism was of little account otherwise; but in Christianity it found an extraordinary flowering and produced that string of decisive, specific assertions just quoted. They cover experiences of roughly the mid-second to the mid-third century.[7]

By then, the author of the Acts of Peter had dramatized a Christian's superiority over merely demonic power through a sort of "shoot-out" scene in the very forum of the capital, after a great deal of braggadocio and confrontational theatrics in previous days, and statements for the press, and in the presence of a highly interested crowd. By then, too, in faraway Pontus, the story was circulating of Gregory the Wonder-worker's exploits in a demon's temple: just by routinely saying his prayers there, where he had taken shelter from the dark, he made it forever uninhabitable by its former owner.[8] And there are less grandiose tales of his powers as well, in the salvation of the possessed (below, p. 60).

The manhandling of demons—humiliating them, making them howl, beg for mercy, tell their secrets, and depart in a hurry—served a purpose quite essential to the Christian definition of monotheism: it made physically (or dramatically) visible the superiority of the Christian's patron Power over all others. One and only one was God. The rest were *daimones* demonstrably, and therefore already familiar to the audience as nasty, lower powers that no one would want to worship anyway.

It is important to bear in mind the full consequences of these scenes. Where they persuaded, they produced a special loyalty. For stories of wonders wrought by other deities certainly circulated as much, making believers in just as large numbers (if we total up the new devotees of Sabazius, Jupiter of Doliche, Mithra, and so forth during the second and third centuries); but these new devotees were thenceforth not lost to paganism. They only focused a particular conviction and gratitude on one more god. Christian converts, by contrast, denied the name and even the very existence of all those gods, from the moment of believing.

On occasion, exorcisms are specified as the cause of conversion—in Ephesus, as we have seen, in Palestine, Italy, Africa, or Gaul.[9] Persuasion lay in the simplest of facts: "In religious usage, a miracle is an event in which one knows one is dealing with God."[10] So the yielding of North African droughts to Christian prayer also induced a shout from "the populace, hailing 'The God of Gods!' "[11] In Palestine, where the wonders of healing by the young Hilarion "were on everyone's lips far and wide, the people flocked in to him from Syria and Egypt, so that many believed in Christ."[12] And Eusebius, in the passages cited above, mentions unspecified kinds of miracles in the command of the subapostolic missionaries and later, in his own day, the miracle at Caesarea. The various bits and pieces of evidence gathered in the preceding pages constitute, to my knowledge, the sum of our information on how *groups* (not individuals) turned to the church, prior to the opening up of toleration—that is, before A.D. 312. (I exclude only the more doubtful reports of Gregory the Wonderworker, on which see below, chap. VII.) In every case the motive underlying the giving of allegiance was to avoid the horrors of divine punishment or to gain the benefits, in this world if not in the next, that were promised to loyal adherents. This is just what we would expect if we reviewed what is known of non-Christian habits of belief in the second and third centuries—or, for that matter, reasoning back from figures like Kimbangu and William Wade Harris.

Is it necessary to distinguish between moments that gained single individuals for the church from moments that won over large or small groups? Is there a special sort of crowd psychology at work in the scenes preserved for us or, for that matter, in those producing adherents to non-Christian deities? I refer to some wholly pagan conversions in the first chapter (notes 10 and 25). But no differences appear in the way people reason and respond. The only purpose served by the distinction is to explain better the *rate* of change we are observing. In the whole process, very large numbers are obviously involved. For reasons that will appear shortly, it would be hard to picture the necessary scale of conversion if we limited ourselves to contexts and modes of persuasion that concerned only single individuals talking to each other. If the evidence for steady evangelizing in private settings, however, is combined with the evidence for successes en masse, the two in combination do seem to me adequate to explain what we know happened.

There remains a single odd factor: the role persecutions played in conversion. "The blood of martyrs watered the churches and reared up many times as many champions of piety,"[13] so it was said back then, and often has been since. But exactly how did this work? The only clue (aside from the negative one, that public suicides might appear simply mad)[14] lies in the account given of the Carthaginian prison guard's change of heart as he observed the conduct of a group of his prisoners: "he began to make much of us, realizing there was a great *virtus,* a miraculous power, in us," until in the end "the guard of the prison now believed."[15] The manifestation of something supernatural was needed, somehow. Thereafter, we have no indication of the path of his thoughts.

The martyr Justin has been supposed to be the clue to the connection between martyrs and conversions, in describing how he witnessed the indifference of Christians to death. But of the two possibilities that might occur to anyone at such a sight—the martyrs' madness, or their complete, considered certainty about *something*—Justin evidently inclined to the second; and that set off a train of reflections which may or may not have had anything to do with his conversion. Most likely not.[16] Tertullian a little later asks rhetorically (*Apol.* 50.15), "At the sight of it [that is, endurance of pain and death] who is not profoundly troubled, to the point of inquiring what may lie behind it all?" Inquiry, he continues, leads to joining the faith. But just how and why, he does not explain. I assume that here in such junctures, as in the others that are better described, it was the report of wonderful acts that ultimately authenticated the Christian message.

Justin's conversion he tells us about in some detail at the commencement of a little Apologetic tract, the "Dialogue with Trypho" (§2f.) of the mid–second century. I use his description to turn now to conversions reported of single individuals. He had once longed for true "philosophy," evidently meaning a short road to positive certainty about god, the right paths to happiness, and all manner of logical reasoning. In his longing, he sought wisdom from a Stoic first; next, a Peripatetic; next, a Pythagorean; afterward, a Platonist. Then finally he was argued into the true philosophy by an elderly Christian whom he met strolling by the seaside. It is hard to know what to do with this account, in the light of its parallels. The latter are numerous, either because the intellectual experience described is thoroughly human and natural, or because it is a cliché so long established that its various points flow from the tip of the pen almost of themselves.[17] Which, then? Or both?

I am inclined to suppose a mixture of both. Further, it speaks for the genuineness of the mental process outlined (which does not seem in itself in the least improbable) that we should have from Tatian at about the same time an account independent of the more stylized parts of Justin's recollections, yet in other respects similar, and convincing. "I came to my faith," says Tatian, speaking of the Scriptures, "through the unpretentious style, the artlessness of the speakers, the clear explaining of Creation, the foreknowledge of what was to happen, the excellence of the precepts, and the single ruler over the whole universe."[18] Tatian's plane of approach is wholly rational, wholly disciplined. But he goes on, referring to all the fancy education that represented the summit of his culture, "And my soul being taught of God, I have learned that [Greek] writings lead to our being judged and condemned, but that these others put an end to our slavery." Like Justin, he had surveyed all he could gain from his teachers—up to a certain point. Then the clouds broke and he saw yet farther.

His contemporary, the satirist Lucian, invents the same round of studies for young Menippus, taking him from one great source of wisdom to another, testing every school. At last, in despair, he quits them all for an answer found outside their world entirely.[19] The story, until its end, is just like Justin's; but it succeeds as literature because it has a cliché as center or point of parody. Later, like Menippus, the real Plotinus traveled about in his youthful years of study from one instructor to another, as his biographer recounts; the young Hilarion likewise outgrew his local schooling and so was sent to Alexandria, there to be converted; and the no-longer-young Ammonius "applied himself to thinking and philosophy," as his biographer says, "and so made an instant conversion—to lawful loyalties" (i.e. away from the church; for it is a non-Christian writing).[20] There is no saying, however, out of our tiny corpus of evidence, what aspects of church doctrine in practice worked to attract non-Christians especially, or what especially worked to drive them away.

The few glimpses we have surely reveal real as well as fictional people. The real pilgrimages are a little too closely modeled on the fictional, granted. We shall encounter more of them later. Their type nevertheless existed, as it still exists today. They do seem somewhat too self-conscious: that of Origen, or example—a man of overwhelming and uncompromising intellectuality. Yet he cannot be accused of the least brittleness of belief. He only deplores, lonely man! how "very few people are enthusiastic about rational thought."

A line later he adds, "As this matter of faith is so much talked of, I have to reply that we accept it as useful for the multitude, and that we admittedly teach those who cannot abandon everything and pursue a study of rational argument to believe without thinking out their reasons."[21] The division between men like Origen and the bulk of the urban population (to say nothing of the rural population) was not perfect. Justin, as illustration, notes and recommends for reflection among all non-Christians the terrifying or dreadful element in Scripture.[22] That was prominent before the eyes of the least cultivated converts. And one of Origen's students, Gregory the Wonderworker, while under his direction perhaps, or shortly after leaving him, wrote a dialogue on a standard school topic, the impassivity of the divine; he and his non-Christian interrogator in the dialogue circle around the question asked, both gentlemen of leisure and learning; but this is the same Gregory who, in the same years and in the same settings as the dialogue, is preaching straight to the hearts and minds of as backward a populace as could be found in the empire, away in the hills of north-central Turkey.[23] That is to say, he works miracles among them for their conversion. The church leadership was aware of the gap between its gentlemen and the masses as a very important fact of life requiring conscious efforts to overcome if congregations were to attain any proper unity.[24] Modern studies, being free to indulge less pastoral preferences, often make much of one side of the gap and forget the other, which, after all, has left little mark on paper.[25]

But to return to our proper subject: we have taken our measure of the mass scenes and the quite narrowly intellectual scenes, trying to understand what is going on in them or, in more accurate terms, what are the thoughts and feelings that lead to a change of religious loyalties. What we have discovered is, as anyone might have predicted, entirely in accord with long established—that is, non-Christian—patterns. It remains to translate what we have found into a historical event, of however long-drawn-out development. But it is just here that more puzzling problems arise. How did it ever happen that the church could grow at such a rate, so as actually to predominate in occasional little towns or districts by the turn of the second century and, by the turn of the fourth, to have attained a population of, let us say, five million?[26]

The rate of growth is puzzling among both the intellectual elite and the masses. The former certainly included many Christians to equal, not necessarily the power of mind of Origen, but the suavity and cultivation of Octavius (the imaginary Christian who worked a conversion by eloquence and reasoning, in Minucius Felix's Dialogue). That did not make them a very effective force for the spreading of the faith. As non-Christians did not read Christian writings, so, for different reasons, they did not spend much time in converse with Christian intellectuals. Indeed, it would be hard to instance a single match for the interested acquaintance that sprang up between Origen and a member of the imperial house, the empress Mammaea.

Or rather, we can find a match, but a manifest failure. Cyprian in the 250s in Carthage was sought out by a man of the strongest interest in religion. His name alone is known, Demetrian. He kept coming back to the bishop for renewed conversations. The bishop expected them to be opportunities for Christian instruction; his visitor was to listen to him patiently; instead of which, Demetrian disagreed, he offered counterarguments, the meetings grew heated, and at last Cyprian terminated them in a stream of abuse, which he then published: he had "held in contempt your howlings and railing," your "ignorance," "dementedness," and "mad rage." And he concludes from scripture (Prov. 26 : 4), "Answer not a fool according to his folly" (*Ad Demetr.* 1).

It would be hard to imagine a more vehemently encountered or less adroitly handled opportunity for teaching. There is, however, no reason to suppose it was any more ordinary or representative than Octavius' in Minucius' Dialogue. We must rather suppose that encounters of any sort at this level, successful or unsuccessful, were always rare. The reason was social. The church before Constantine had only a tiny share in what was at all times a tiny segment of the population, the elite; and the setting usually assigned to its leaders is the catechetical schools, to which were admitted only persons already converted.[27]

As to the vastly broader ranks of ordinary people: how well could they be reached when it was so often dangerous to give evangelizing speeches in public? True, the persecutions were few and far between; government was limited, clumsy, and quickly exhausted in its operations; perhaps even the numbers it actually got hold of and put to death were "only a few, from time to time, and very easily totalled up."[28] Still, the news of their fate would be known and would influence conduct through their region. From the turn of the second century—that is, from around the beginning of my period of study

—the mentions of missionary effort (never abundant) taper off. In the latter part of that century, summing up experiences in some eastern province, Celsus reports that "if anyone [Christian] does still wander about in secret, yet he is sought out and condemned to death." A generation later Christians could be described as "a tribe obscure, shunning the light, *dumb in public* though talkative in the corners." That sums up experiences in North Africa and perhaps other western areas. Confirmation can be had from the best census possible of preachers known and recorded anywhere in our sources. They hardly exist. There is only Polycarp around Smyrna, Gregory the Wonderworker around Neocaesarea, unspecified activity of unspecified location and date by nameless persons in Egypt and perhaps in Syria. That adds up to a fact recognized also in the abstract: that, after Saint Paul, the church had no mission, it made no organized or official approach to unbelievers; rather, it left everything to the individual.[29]

We do have a third-century description of teachers circulating in one certain eastern district, just where is not known. I return to them, very briefly, in the last chapter. Their like is otherwise attested only in Origen (as I show in a moment) and their mission is directed only inward to the already converted. In that respect they lie outside my focus; and the same is true of the much earlier itinerants mentioned in the Didache (11–13), a book of instruction compiled perhaps at the turn of the second century. Finally, the traveling teachers of the province of Asia in that same period deserve mention—again, only briefly. They are "the brethren" that Saint John speaks of in one of his letters (3.7.9), "taking nothing from pagans." He praises their spreading of the word; so perhaps they did not address only their fellow Christians. Their activities and province place them among the "many . . . who amplified the Message," in Eusebius' pages, from which I quoted at the outset of this chapter.

To continue my survey of the very scanty evidence about preachers in the second and third centuries, Origen at one point in his great work of rebuttal takes issue with what Celsus says (3.9) about itinerant evangelizing, "If all men wanted to be Christians, the latter wouldn't want them any more." They are a prickly lot. Origen replies, "that this is false appears from the fact that Christians, so far as lies with them, neglect nothing that would spread the word everywhere on the globe. Some do the work of fanning out not only to the cities but to villages and cottages as well." He goes on to say that such preachers take little money, most of them, even where several persons may have clubbed together to supply more than their actual needs. Granted, because rich and distinguished Christians "nowadays offer welcome to them on account of the word," some are drawn into the work by hopes of social climbing. "But at the outset when it was really dangerous for teachers in particular, one couldn't reasonably suspect anything of that sort." To judge from these remarks, Origen is quick to correct Celsus but actually able to instance in his own time only teachers among the already converted, that is, among persons eager to house and reward them. His account fits with the other third-century mention I just referred to.

During most of the period I speak of, from around A.D. 100 to 312, Christians as such avoided attention. The fact is well known and easily illustrated. They can hardly be blamed for that, out of common prudence. Even where they were most numerous and presumably most taken for granted, there were many among their neighbors ready and willing to cite them before a hanging court. So Pliny discovered. They avoided on religious grounds also those occasions when their neighbors gathered for a good time, in private or community celebrations. From their own meetings, if by chance a stranger entered, he was not to be expelled; but, as a limit on this tolerance and evidently after testing him, "if anyone does not love the Lord, let him be outcast," with a curse added to make sure.[30] A prickly lot, just as Celsus said. They didn't marry non-Christians, or were at least taught to think it a sin.[31] It happened anyway, of course, and the strictures were a little relaxed in the fourth century. Still, and in sum, the church before Constantine seems to have kept itself to itself in its divine services and marital policies, as in its schools. We cannot find in these institutions any adequate explanation for its growth, whether or not they may have produced an occasional convert.

The answer to the central question of my inquiry, What made adherents to the church? is often sought in the social and psychological rewards experienced by its members. As to the psychological, the only indication of their nature that I know of must be sought in Cyprian's letter to his friend Donatus (§3f.), where he tries to describe his state of mind before and after conversion. "When I lay amongst the shades and gloomy night," he recounts, in a long and highly wrought passage,

tossed on the seas of this proud age, driven about in uncertainty and with wandering steps, ignorant of my own life, a stranger to truth and illumi-

nation, I supposed it a hard thing indeed in consideration of my way of
life at that time . . . for anyone to be born again, or that he might be inspired to a new life by washing in the waters of life. . . . 'How is so great a
conversion possible,' I used to say, 'whereby in a trice and swiftly we
may shed what has hardened by inborn lodging in our very substance? . . .
When does a man learn thrift who has grown used to great banquets and
bountiful feasts? Or someone who has stood out resplendent in his costly
clothing of gold and purple—when does he humble his costume to the
plebeian and unadorned? The man who took delight in consular office
and high honors cannot be an inglorious private citizen, and he who was
attended by crowds of dependents . . . thinks it a punishment to be
alone. . . .' Often I revolved these matters in my thoughts; for in how
many errors of my past life was I not entangled, from which I did
not believe I could be freed. . . . But subsequently, when by the aid of the
life-bringing waters the stains of my earlier life were cleansed away
and light from above was shed upon my purged and purified heart, . . .
straightway and in a marvelous manner uncertainties became clear, hidden things were opened up, and dark things illuminated.

A difficult passage, this, to bring to bear on conversion. There is
no indication that the rewards experienced by Cyprian were known
to him before he joined the church, and thus drew him in. Still, they
may have been promised him by other Christians, just as he now
promises them to someone like Donatus. We are bound to ask, however, how many people in the Roman world were really tortured by
the domination in their lives of too many brilliant parties, too much
gold and purple, and too onerous a public position, very much as we
are bound to ask what sort of audience the Stoic moralists addressed,
when they too offered very similar reflections on an excess of this
world's good fortune. What we must remember is the size of the historical phenomenon we confront: a matter of millions.

As to any social reward in conversion, there is a question even
more serious: our sources never speak of any such element in the
process. Beyond that, none shows how it could have been very well
sensed before entrance into a congregation. In addition, as has just
been shown, congregations of worshipers as such seem to have had a
rather repellent shell around them. And that fits with the sense of
We-They that runs throughout accounts of the persecutions.

Where, then, could believers make contact with unbelievers to win
them over? Surely the answer must somehow lie where the Christians themselves direct our attention—among those endless driv-
ings-out of demons, for one thing. For another, in quite obscure set-

tings of everyday. We should listen also to non-Christians who describe them; and first, to Celsus.

> Their [the Christians'] injunctions are like this: "Let no one educated, no one wise, no one sensible draw near. For these abilities are thought by us to be evils. But as for anyone ignorant, anyone stupid, anyone uneducated, anyone who is a child, let him come boldly." By the fact that they themselves admit that these people are worthy of the God, they show that they want and are able to convince only the foolish, dishonorable and stupid, and only slaves, women, and little children. . . . Moreover, we see that those who display their trickery in the market-places and go about begging would never enter a gathering of intelligent men, nor would they dare to reveal their noble beliefs in their presence; but whenever they see adolescent boys and a crowd of slaves and a company of fools they push themselves in and show off. . . . In private houses also we see wool-workers, cobblers, laundry-workers, and the most illiterate and bucolic yokels, who would not dare to say anything at all in front of their elders and more intelligent masters. But whenever they get hold of children in private and some stupid women with them, they let out some astounding statements as, for example, that they must not pay any attention to their father and school-teacher, but must obey them; they say that these talk nonsense and have no understanding, and that in reality they neither know nor are able to do anything good, but are taken up with mere empty chatter. But they alone, they say, know the right way to live, and if the children would believe them, they would become happy and make their home happy as well. And if just as they are speaking they see one of the school-teachers coming, or some intelligent person, or even the father himself, the more cautious of them flee in all directions; but the more reckless urge the children on to rebel. They whisper to them that in the presence of their father and their schoolmasters they do not feel able to explain to the children anything, since they do not want to have anything to do with the silly and obtuse teachers who are totally corrupted and far gone in wickedness and who inflict punishment on the children. But, if they like, they should leave father and their schoolmasters, and go along with the women and little children who are their playfellows to the wooldresser's shop, or to the cobbler's or the washerwoman's shop, that they may learn perfection. And by saying this they persuade them.[32]

Drained of its venom, what remains in this brew is, to our taste, quite innocent: the church's teachings were offered most often to the unsophisticated or uneducated, and by people of low standing in the community. They were two sorts, wanderers and workers. So much, our other sources generally confirm.

The wanderers, we have already encountered and largely discounted since they focused their efforts on those who were already
friends and members of the church, not the pagan masses. Of course
Celsus, in his contempt for any sort of low fellow, may lump together such itinerant Christians—who in his day were not very sure
of their welcome in the churches, either—with other kinds of non-
Christian preachers. There were Cynics, for instance. Cynics made
their living by begging, and in return they spoke in marketplaces to
the crowds, offering moral exhortation and social criticism. They
gave people something to talk about and were popular for that reason, like the editorial page in a newspaper. But their popularity by
no means extended to the upper classes. They could be told from the
uniform of their calling: dirty long hair, beard, dirty long cloak, a
staff, and a little knapsack.

A closer match to the kind of person Celsus described is met with
likewise in an eastern province (see above, n. 2), in the earlier second
century. "A certain man from the lands called Gallic . . . had learned
both the Greek language and loquacity, and made great use of this,
and was dubbed a sophist. He used to do the rounds of cities and
market towns, gathering crowds and revealing evil to them and
sniffing out iniquity. Beyond that, he was a most clever deviser of
spells and skillful at magicians' tricks, claiming powers over life and
death; and he exercised such an attraction over people that many
throngs of men and women came to him. The men, on the one hand,
he convinced that he could compel women to yield to them, and he
made the reverse promise to the women. This he used to demonstrate, while only preaching it clandestinely. He was a teacher of
evildoing above all others, and gathered lethal poisons."

With this, we approach Celsus' reference to Christian wonder-
working (scandalous "trickery," above, p. 38). But there is a suspicious tone here. It springs from social prejudice easily sensed in the
description: scornful, and not very clear, because, like Celsus, the
writer does not want to get too close to the trash he describes. We
have to confront that fact, because for us it is most important: it pre-
vents us too from drawing close to what was a predominantly lower-
class religious movement. Christianity after New Testament times is
presented to us almost exclusively in pages addressed to upper-class
readers. And they preferred to keep a good distance between themselves and their inferiors.

Next, giving much more detail and the impression of really knowing what he is talking about, Celsus describes a second type of person likely to spread the word of Christianity: the worker in the city's most despised and little skilled occupations. We are reminded of Saint Paul, combining hand-work with talking ("preaching" would suggest a big audience in a big place, and that is not the picture that generally emerges from either scripture or Celsus). The scene of action in Celsus' pages is a room of lowly artisans, or a nursery or servants' quarters in some more substantial home. In Paul's experiences, the mistress was sometimes a believer, too; in Celsus', the master was not. Origen in his long reply disputes none of the outline Celsus gives. His interest focuses, rather, on the value of what these lowly folk were recommending.

Celsus also spoke of that value. He began the quoted passages with an attack on it. From the earliest times it had been a charge commonly directed against the church that its doctrines had gained credence only with a public unable to tell truth from nonsense. They were believed in only by children, slaves, and especially women. Ardent credulity was presented as a weakness characteristic of the sex, pagan or Christian.[33] "They are carried about in their rounds of the temples, offering sacrifices, consulting oracles, parading about every day with begging priests, dervishes, and the old crones that haunt the altars and meddle in marriages." Was there any truth in such a picture? Women, except at the absolute top of society, did in fact enjoy far less access to advanced education and wide reading than men; and women, except at the very bottom of society, had far less liberty to stir about in the towns and gain a wide experience than men; so their capacity for critical discrimination would be less well developed. Moreover, there was often a great age difference between women and their spouses, which would encourage the perception of them as "mere children." For all that, their influence over their husbands and children need not have been less once they themselves had come to some conviction on a matter of religion.

Urban households and groups that were poor, or at least not rich, were obliged to live right on top of each other. Their crowding necessarily exposed them to ideas from their neighbors, even if their wish was for some degree of privacy; and the larger the city, the closer the crowding. A particularly striking example is the meeting-place Christians bought or leased in the western basement rooms of a building in Rome, now Santa Prisca, toward the start of the second century, adjoining which were other rooms already in use by a non-Christian group. For two centuries the two precincts appear to have been separated only by a door,[34] until the non-Christian in A.D. 400 was destroyed and filled in. Similarly, cemeteries were sometimes shared by non-Christians and Christians.[35]

And there is the outburst by an Apologist,[36] "We live together with you in this world, including the forum, including the meat-market, baths, shops, workrooms, inns, fairs, and the rest of commercial intercourse, and we sail along with you and serve in the army and are active in agriculture and trade." What he describes finds confirmation in a third-century text: Christians "have won riches and renown among pagans . . . they are absorbed in business and wealth and friendships with pagans"; and one Christian in particular appears in a Phrygian inscription as an itinerant professional athlete, venturing as far as Italy while being simultaneously (though only honorifically) citizen of many cities in his homeland and a member of his own city's senate and Elders Association. But it was not unusual for Christians to serve in real, active civic magistracies, too. Church councils had to reflect on the problems raised by such service.[37] In their secular lives Christians thus appear not to have been in the least ghettoized.

Contradiction between their tolerated omnipresence, on the one hand, and their isolation and persecution, on the other, is easily resolved. *As Christians,* declaring themselves in that role to the public, preaching, holding meetings, or the like, they were very little in evidence. They preferred to keep apart, and to keep others from approaching. But simply as neighbors, they were naturally everywhere. Being excluded from the normal social gatherings,[38] their points of contact with non-Christians lay quite inevitably at street-corners or at places of employment, or in the working quarters of dwellings, just as Celsus says (and in no contradiction with our exiguous church records).

In such settings, if the subject of religion arose, it would be the aspects commonly most talked about; and, given the concentration of ancient religion on the relief of sickness or deformity,[39] an exchange of views might most likely begin with the wonderful cures wrought by this or that divine power. Of all worships, the Christian best and most particularly advertised its miracles by driving out of spirits and laying on of hands. Reports would spread without need of preaching throughout all the places so contemptuously catalogued by Celsus.

Testing to see if I can imagine in some detail a scene that conflicts with no point of the little that is known about conversion in the second and third centuries, I would choose the room of some sick person: there, a servant talking to a mistress, or one spouse to another, saying, perhaps, "Unquestionably they can help, if you believe. And I know, I have seen, I have heard, they have related to me, they have books, they have a special person, a sort of officer. It is true. Besides and anyway, if you don't believe, then you are doomed when a certain time comes, so say the prophecies; whereas, if you do, then they can help even in great sickness. I know people who have seen or who have spoken with others who have seen. And healing is even the least that they tell. Theirs is truly a God all-powerful. He has worked a hundred wonders." So a priest is sent for, or an exorcist; illness is healed; the household after that counts as Christian; it is baptized; and through instruction it comes to accept the first consequences: that all other cults are false and wicked, all seeming gods, the same.

The subject of this chapter cannot, however, be left at such a scene. For beyond such points of contact and persuasion, after the first shock of belief that led to a person's cry, "Great is the God of the Christians!" there lay initiation in many other possible degrees. Historians who think in terms of millions of people, and indeed contemporaries within the church, might well accept the bare moment of that cry as the making of a Christian. But everyone knows that a great depth of further experiences remained to be tested in the church: of membership in such a close group as second- or third-century congregations were likely to afford; of daily life governed by a more insistent moral standard than could be found in any other, non-Christian, association; of introduction to an ordered system of beliefs commanding history, cosmology, metaphysics, ethics. There would be temperaments that specially responded to the challenge of these experiences, no doubt. There would be many a Lucius of Apuleius' novel, many an Aelius Aristides, many who, being once recruited to the church, went on to explore and grow within it more fully. They could attain what Festugière, Nock, and others (see above, chap. I) would call "true" Christianity. They could report about it with all the more conviction to others like themselves. Their words would strike an answering chord and incline their listeners to belief. No doubt. But no reports of this sort are attested. We cannot reasonably turn these "many," then, into the thousands and thousands—to say nothing of millions—of persons that make up the whole of our story.

Here is a warning to anyone who attempts a historical reconstruction, as I have done. The explicit record at important points fits badly with what are, to ourselves, entirely natural expectations. The record and the expectations I have tried to compare in this chapter; but we must, of course, favor the former.

V

Constantine as a
Friend of the Church

The conversion of Constantine radically and quickly changed matters. It had quite enormous consequences. Like all great events, however, being great both because of the number of lives it affected and the seriousness with which its effects were viewed by the victims (or beneficiaries) themselves, it must be assessed slowly, layer by layer.

If we begin at the top, we have before us a piece of evidence for the dossier of conversions itself: a relatively well-reported account. The emperor at a sticky point in his career had a dream that could be interpreted in the light of his necessities. It showed him what he must do to defeat his enemies, and it identified the supernatural power that would ensure this good result. Revelations in the non-Christian world normally came through dreams, not prayers; Constantine had had a similar revelation earlier that produced his first conversion; and there was nothing novel in his response to the second one. He followed out its directions, conquered his enemies, and bound himself—whether in gratitude or out of fear or to ensure further benefits he does not say—to his new Lord and Master.[1] The train of his actions pursued the same path as that followed by others we know of; the train of thought may be followed, too: If you, Lord, can do so much for me, you will have proved that you are Lord indeed, and you will have made me your servant forever.[2]

Being converted, in the sense being used here—that is, to acknowledge a certain god as supreme and determine to obey him —had special consequences when an emperor was involved. But their special character lay more in their proportions than in their essential nature, when they are compared to those that might result from the conversion of any great senator-millionaire. It meant pa-

43

tronage, the building of a very lavishly decorated place of worship in the capital by Elagabalus, for example, in honor of a Syrian deity. The ruins survive.[3] But we do have great difficulty in knowing what is conversion, in emperors, and what is just the choosing of a favorite.

However deep or shallow its wellsprings, imperial preference was not at all influenced by strategy. Constantine himself, for years after A.D. 312, continued to pay his public honors to the Sun. They were paid in coin of the realm—rather, *on* coins, in the form of images of the emperor shown jointly with Sol; but other coins showed the Chi-Rho sign; so it was known that both compliments were acceptable to Constantine.[4] The bargain he struck in those years, familiar in history as the Edict of Milan (A.D. 313) neither increased toleration in his own domain nor guaranteed it in that of his rival, Licinius, in the east. On the political plane, which is what J. B. Bury and others have looked at, it is therefore quite mistaken to conclude that "Constantine's revolution was perhaps the most audacious act ever committed by an autocrat in disregard and defiance of the vast majority of his subjects."[5] It wasn't that, nor can the great majority of his subjects have seen it that way. Its immediate effect on them was nil.

The distinction needs to be drawn in this way between the emperor's favor, freely shown, out of his feelings toward the church, and his favor shown in order to gain political advantage; for, further, it governs the kinds of inducements and therefore the kinds of response that make up the whole history of conversion post-312. The same distinction must also take us off on several pages of detour; for it needs to be reconnoitered and walked around and looked at from several angles.

Consider first the most obvious target of political analysis, army loyalty. It was that which determined who won, and what might be the major changes of direction, in ancient as in modern history. Did Constantine's troops fight better for him in 312, or his enemies worse, because of his adherence to the Christian God? No, no one has thought so, among modern historians of that event—not at all, because the historians all know and agree that the army on both sides had never drawn more than a handful of its recruits from Christians, and those few had, by 312, been largely weeded out again during the persecutions.[6] For Constantine's troops, then, the job of fighting must have been somehow seen as separate from religion.

Everyone is agreed, too, that conscription turned by preference to rural areas, coincidentally the least likely to have been touched by missionary efforts. A priori, it follows that a non-Christian army in A.D. 312 through normal processes remained overwhelmingly non-Christian still at the end of the century. Even the best reasoning must occasionally yield to fact; and it is no doubt a fact, even though reported by Eusebius—devout, obliging, panegyrical biographer of Constantine—that the emperor did some evangelizing among the Palace Guard and gave Sundays off to his coreligionists in the forces generally.[7] The troops could thus have been non-Christians on enlistment but Christians subsequently. However, Constantine's missionary efforts were evidently very limited. We may add, though no one of course can assess, the effect on the troops of simply knowing that he himself was of the new faith.

A capital error, however, leading to or showing all sorts of fundamental misunderstandings about the empire and its normal operations, is to suppose that after A.D. 312, specifically, on "Oct. 28, 312, the army of Constantine became officially Christian."[8] Evidence that there was widespread in the empire a sense of lawful norms in religion, other than mutual respect among all faiths, that these norms were customarily to be enforced by the chief officers of the state, or even that some vaguer kind of religious guidance was to be sought from the ruler, cannot be found so early in the century. The gradual appearance of such views must at any rate be looked for in the relations between the monarch and the church, not for many decades between the monarch and religions of all kinds.

Constantine, then, was not expected to change the faith of his men "officially," and made no great effort in that direction; but he and his remaining rival in the east, Licinius, could not avoid some statement on the subject—it seemed to be, after all, a moment only of hiatus in the persecutions. So they issued one of many most ambiguously worded calls, in those decades, for piety "toward the divine and holy" (or similar periphrases).[9] Believers of every persuasion could certainly swallow *that*.

Equally anxious not to give offense, the men in the ranks were accustomed to shout monotheistically, in choral invocations of divine help and approval: "they called god as witness, in their usual way, that their leader" (here, Julian, the ardent non-Christian) "was invincible"; and he replied that "god and myself are your leaders"; but the same nameless power was invoked for the troops' encouragement by a Christian commander, or they initiated the invocation themselves, "the whole assembly . . . calling god" (or "God"? the capital letter does not reveal itself viva voce) "as witness in the usual way, that Constantius" (ardent Christian) "was invincible."[10]

Meanwhile, the tracing of these habits of declaration has taken us from A.D. 312 to the 360s, and into various moments in the interval. Except for the brief years of Julian (A.D. 361–63) the emperors had all been "officially" members, and even very involved and vigorous members, of the church. Did that make any difference? Shouts and speeches aside, what really were the army preferences in this half-century?

Bishop Theodoret, a long time after the event, imagined a speech by the (actually, rather waffling) new emperor Jovian to his army: "'I am unable,' he tells them, 'being a Christian, to rule over such men or be king of Julian's army, instructed in wicked doctrines. For such men as those, bereft of divine providence, are easy to conquer and over-ready for defeat, and created for an enemy's enjoyment.' The soldiers, when they heard these words, shouted back as one, 'Have no misgivings, O Emperor! Do not let slip the leadership over us, as if it were something bad; for you are ruler over Christians, raised in pious doctrine. The older among us enjoyed instruction from Constantine, and those who came afterward shared in the teachings offered by Constantius. He has been dead only a little while—not enough for the settled destruction of persons misled.'"[11]

The notion here of soldiers converted by Constantine's speeches but still serving in arms forty years afterward is a little hard to accept; also the notion of conversion (in my sense) being wrought by speeches at all. We shall return to that problem later. But even after the date of this address by Jovian, we have the one breach of toleration certainly recorded: a moment when three legions in the east support a (non-Christian) pretender with "the invocation of Jupiter, as soldiers do."[12] A year or two earlier, we find an army happy under, certainly loyal to, the non-Christian Julian. Its members accepted quite casually the notion of sitting down (more accurately, lying down) to dinner with comrades who were not of their own faith, and corporately joined their commander in his piety.[13] Was that only to enjoy the gigantic cookouts that accompanied Julian's enthusiastic rendering of cult? He himself knew that material rewards might win converts—even if very doubtful ones, in my terminology.[14] And evidently it was only the Christians who were likely to make much fuss about loyalties anyway.[15]

There is, in summary thus far, an easy case to be made for a live-and-let-live tradition within the armed forces, against which the Christians predictably but not very strenuously made their objections felt.[16] How else could it have happened that, after Julian's abrupt death when the army turned to the choice of a successor (it had become their traditional right to make that choice), they first settled on a pious pagan? But he was too old, so they turned to Jovian the Christian.[17] And who were "they" anyway? Two little coteries of high officers, we are told. The one was made up of men of Gallic origin; the other, of particular favorites of Constantius, all Christians.[18] Therefore Julian himself had chosen to keep on under his own command, undisturbed, the enemies of his own faith.

The natural explanation for Julian's conduct must be the fact that faith counted for nothing, or not much, in the high command. To test the explanation, we have a considerable dossier of careers matched with religious preference, over the fourth century. It is a dossier indeed full enough, regarding more than a dozen of the chief posts from Constantine to the end of our period, to yield statistical statements. The one to begin with, perhaps, is the most general of all: that up to Gratian (A.D. 375–83), paganism was "the norm" among holders of the praetorian, Egyptian, and city prefectures, the three most prestigious governorships (proconsulates), and the posts of Master of Soldiers and Count of the East.[19] Even adding in the incumbents of the last quarter of the century, Christians barely outnumbered non-Christians (140 to 128) and, at that, only within the provinces longest exposed to evangelical effort (77 to 52) in the eastern half of the empire. One striking fact appears: that of the seventeen incumbents in Julian's reign, all but three were his coreligionists—his three Masters of Soldiers. Which suggests that, in that particular responsibility, talent was what counted, not faith.[20]

Turning back to our point of departure, the weight of religion in Constantine's day, we have noted that two-thirds of his government at the top were non-Christian. His rival Licinius made special efforts to get rid of Christians in his own immediate entourage, so we are told; but we know he missed some.[21] His chief officer up to the very end was the praetorian prefect of the east Julius Julianus, whom the victorious Constantine, far from punishing in any way, immediately made consul.[22] No appointment carried greater prestige.

Commemorating his victory in 324, Constantine's mints in his new eastern domains issued coins showing him spearing Licinius (portrayed as a nasty dragon) with the staff of a little battle flag. On the flag was the Chi-Rho, or Christogram ☧. The same sign on the same banner appears abundantly on both his western and eastern coinage a few years later. Its intended audience is designated in praise: "The Glory of Our Armies," or "Victory for Constantine the Emperor"; and his sons adopted the same symbolism. But it was so empty of religious meaning by the 350s that it could be displayed by a non-Christian, the pretender Magnentius, in issue after issue for years.[23]

Our point of inquiry has thus been turned all around and subjected to various questions from various angles. Were coreligionists given a monopoly in office by an incoming emperor in this half-century up to the mid-360s? No. Did great military commanders elect a coreligionist as emperor? No. Did emperors or their men use good clear language when they called on divine aid in the camp, and did the symbolism of victory that they used for advertisement in army settings have a clearly religious meaning? No. The negatives all prepare us for the final question, whether the political history of this period can be written in religious terms at all. The answer is surely no.[24]

So much depends, as Paul Veyne has pointed out,[25] on seeing clearly the kind of role in which the foremost actors in the drama of concern to us defined themselves and meant to act. There was, we must recognize, no leader of jihads, Saint Louis, or duke of Alva in Constantine's mind. There had been none before him in the empire's past. There were, rather, quite stupendous acts of generosity shown by great men toward meritorious dependents: Hadrian's completion of the temple of Zeus at Athens, for example; Septimius Severus's religious building in his birthplace Lepcis Magna; the jewel of a temple that Elagabalus built and personally opened to worship in his capital.[26] On an unofficial level, the physical facilities for non-Christian worship in every city and, for that matter, in most rural settings as well, were regularly given as a present. Sometimes the benefactor was a community; far more often, indeed normally, it was a very rich local man or woman.[27] In hopes of attracting their generosity, such persons were also asked to serve for largely honorific terms as chief officers (however named—"priests," most often) in religious associations. Religious associations were common, especially but not only in the eastern provinces. An inscription from the countryside in the Roman Campagna records the names of four hundred and more Dionysus-worshipers in a congregation headed by the wife of a consul. In Syria, congregations are most typically found in kin-groups, assembling in their own shrine but equally dependent on their wealthy members to meet their building costs. And entirely secular associations of great and universal popularity, whose headquarters served for a monthly get-together and banquet, also chose a presiding deity and housed it, by someone's kind generosity, in a suitable apse, chapel, or tempietto. Good examples are known at Rome's port of Ostia.[28]

The role of patron, then, permitted Constantine in his new faith to have "quite enormous consequences," as I termed it a few pages back. It was, moreover, part of his conversion to want to yield obedience to his newfound deity, as best he understood what was wanted. If at first—indeed, at various points throughout his reign —he demonstrated quite eccentric ideas about Christianity,[29] he was on safe ground in thinking that a good Christian should make tangible contributions to the fabric of cult, and that no harm could be done in requiring Christianity's rivals, wicked and misguided folk that they were, to foot the bill.

Best known are the extraordinary number, size, and grandeur of the basilicas with which Constantine enriched the church in Rome, many of them also assigned great endowments of land and other wealth, others in Aquileia to the north, Trier, Antioch, Nicomedia, Jerusalem, Constantinople, Cirta, and Savaria.[30] In some now-lost decree, he exempted church lands from taxation;[31] he ordered provincial officials to make available materials and labor for construction; set up a system of gifts of food to churches, grain allowances to nuns, widows, and others in church service;[32] excused clerics from shouldering onerous, sometimes ruinous, civic obligations, indeed, saw that they were given regular "contributions" from the fiscus; and, in short and in sum, "presented the churches with many things."[33] Overnight, it seemed, he created "a Christianity whose bishops and clergy had had their social horizons blown wide open by finding the open-handed Constantine in their midst."[34]

As to the means of paying for all this, and incidentally enabling the mints at long last to produce an abundant gold currency, there survives a description in one of the ecclesiastical historians.

> It appeared to him [Constantine] necessary to teach his subjects to give up their rites; and this would be easy if he could first accustom them to despise their temples and the images contained therein. In considering this project, there was no need of military force; for the Christians serving in the palace carried out their instructions among the cities with the imperial

proclamation. The population kept quiet out of fear that they themselves, wives and children, might suffer if they offered opposition. The wardens and priests, deprived of the support of their majority of the populace, proffered their most precious treasures, even those [icons] called Heaven-Sent, and, through themselves, these objects emerged from the sacred recesses and hiding places in the temples . . . and became public property.[35]

Tremendous wealth in precious metal, so it is agreed on all hands, accrued from these measures, beginning in A.D. 331, and flowed into the imperial treasure.

The fear inspired in his subjects, needing no armed force in supplement, is easily understood. The empire had never had on the throne a man given to such bloodthirsty violence as Constantine.[36] He could hardly control the tone of his proclamations. For instance: "The inhabitants of Egypt, especially the Alexandrians, were accustomed to offer cult-worship through eunuch priests. Constantine issued a decree that every species of androgyne should be exterminated as a sort of monstrosity"—that is, subjected to summary execution—"and that no one henceforward should be seen contaminated with such impurity."[37] This was a ban that only followed in the train of several others against the making of eunuchs (forbidden from humane, not religious, considerations, in the past). It was joined by a ban on cult acts performed for purposes of learning the future. That, too, was nothing new, a safety measure taken by the emperors, very much as modern chiefs of state object to the bugging of their cabinet sessions.[38] The 320s and 330s did not, then, see the forces of law or the police enlisted under the banner bearing the Chi-Rho—indeed, the regime had announced from the start, as its explicit policy, that everyone should respect everyone else's religion.[39] But it was easy to see what the emperor really wanted; easy, too, to calculate the costs of countering the will of so angry an autocrat.

Constantine was a quarter-century on the throne as a Christian monarch, the first ever. In so long a reign, though its Christian years had begun without the least intent to propagate the Faith, his violent energies were gradually and to some degree drawn into a more truly Christian posture of active aggression: error, he saw, must be confronted and given its right name, and those who counted as his co-religionists must all pull together, "lest the Highest Divinity should be aroused not only against the human race" (bad enough, one would think) "but even against me, myself."[40]

The tone of Constantine's pronouncements by the 320s had become sharper, even when he was talking about non-Christians. I cite some illustrations elsewhere.[41] But of far greater importance, and the chief reason for that enormous impact he had on the rate of the church's growth, was the set of his measures making his favor explicit and official: first, toleration decreed; second, money or its equivalent assigned in such forms as tax exemptions and grand buildings. And even these benefactions, here rapidly sketched, constitute only the topmost layer of his part in the history of conversion.

VI

Nonreligious Factors in Conversion

Layers of impact: we look first at the impact of money, which cannot make converts in the sense I have been using; but it can certainly constitute a most important element in a mixture of motives. It can—if we accept conversion known only by external signs. And that is just what churchmen did, generally. I have supplied many examples of how they judged allegiance (Saint Augustine, for one, at chap. I, n. 5, or n. 27, below; Pope Gregory, n. 18; or Theodoret, above, at p. 2). It would be arbitrary to insist on a stricter definition of "Christian" than did the church itself.

To keep a church going, money was in fact nearly essential—essential for a community to develop some specialization of functions and some degree of independence so as to survive as itself. In Rome, as one certain account shows us, the thought of losing the support of a rich friend was terribly upsetting to the congregation.[1] He had been their regular source of gifts and provided lodging to the head of their community (a head whose claims were now challenged as false and wicked). Again, at the other end of the whole long development of the church that we are surveying, we have the campaign between two North African congregations to secure for themselves their share of the good things in life. In the town of Tagaste, where the very rich Albina was staying with her son Pinian, their hosts complain that they have received none of her wealth as yet; while in the neighboring town of Hippo, the citizens stage a riot right in the church and come to the edge of violence, all because "they hoped to possess in their midst—not for the sake of a priest but for his money" (i.e., Pinian, if he would accept election and prove a generous benefactor)—"a rich man and one who felt himself above such wealth, and a handsome dispenser of it." The complaint comes from Albina. To whom Augustine replies, "In truth, all such jealousy" (between congregations) "boils up only against the clergy, especially bishops, whose authority is seen to bulk the largest and who are thought to use and enjoy church property as if they owned it themselves."[2]

It was such considerations of a material sort that often appear to have been decisive in the selection of late Roman church leaders — like Synesius, not really a Christian, or like Saint Ambrose, not even a priest, both of whom were correctly judged to be of the right circles, eloquence, vigor, and place in the world to provide strength at the summit of the community.[3] They might be expected to attract the favor of the emperor toward the building of a new cathedral or even to pay for it themselves.[4] For there was a very great deal of effort and capital to be poured into ecclesiastical construction of all sorts in the period I am dealing with. A story that so decisively changed the locale of greatest circulation and civic pride in literally hundreds of towns in the space of a few generations ought really to be told someday.

Constantine's sons continued and extended their father's gifts to the church — gifts of exemptions from taxes and inheritance rights "and ten thousand other matters, as he [Constantius] reviewed them, through which he supposed he might bring his subjects over to the faith." His motive is reported by a historian a full century after the event,[5] but it brings out the significance of the present topic. Emperors had cash gifts to make, too, ad hoc; so might a bishop, to reward someone for coming over from the ranks of unbelievers.[6]

On the pagan side, things were different. Money was hard to find. Julian in his brief reign tried to undo some of his predecessors' measures and to restore the finances of non-Christian congregations; so did the pretender Eugenius, very briefly, in A.D. 392–94; but the renewed and restless pillage of a once glorious non-Christian Establishment — with all the claims of temples on local taxes, the temple-estates, the investments set aside by devoted or boastful donors to pay the priests and cover the costs of worship — all this accumulated fat of centuries of piety was essentially torn away. There can have been nothing much left by A.D. 400.[7]

The costs of pagan worship could be very considerable. Fancy offerings like an ox required a city's purse; private offerings you had to save up for, and then you sent out invitations to the feast. In the lands of Carthage or Damascus, or for the Rider-Gods of Thrace or the Arval Brethren in Rome, worship meant eating, eating meant friends and family.[8] Their presence or the presence of your fellow citizens at great holy days gave support to your faith. Within the immense chaos of non-Christian religious practices across all the provinces of the empire, a great deal of the lonely, or at least the alone and private, is attested; but a great deal, too—and important for all sorts of religious feelings—was communal, festal, and expensive. Facilities were expensive, the materials of entertainment involved some cost. Therefore the structure of most non-Christian cults could suffer real injury from the denial of financial support.

Around pagan shrines it was not uncommon to find a dependent population. In good times, to which Libanius looked back regretfully in the later fourth century, the temples stood open, "and there was wealth in every one, a sort of common resort for people in need."[9] The kind of generosity he remembered at its grandest appears for us in the second century, in proof of the boundless ambition of mind of a provincial millionaire, "which he would, for example, often turn to the sacrificing of a hundred oxen to the goddess (Athena) on a single day, banqueting the Athenian citizen populace at the sacrifice, tribe by tribe, clan by clan; and whenever the Dionysus-festival came around, in which the image of Dionysus descends to the Academy, he would provide drink in the Ceramicus for the city residents of all sorts, including aliens, as they lay on couches of ivy leaves."[10] How delightful! Of course, all this was easily brought to an end.

Or placed under new management. Judaism taught concern for poverty (and who outside that tradition in the ancient world would have been recorded on his tombstone as "a lover of the poor"?).[11] The tradition carried forward within Christianity. As the pagan temples closed, the churches opened: the Basilica of St. Peter in Rome, for example, as setting for an enormous banquet for the poor provided by a senator in commemoration of the anniversary of his wife's death; or the Basilica of St. Ambrose in Milan, where the bishop preached on the need to succor the less fortunate.[12] Julian was right to see this transfer of function to his rivals as important to their success. "It is generosity toward non-members, care for the graves of the dead, and pretended holiness of life that have specially fostered the growth of atheism" (i.e. Christianity).[13] Therefore he was right in his plan to make temples even more active centers for relief of the poor. However, that project came to nothing.

"Those [pagans]," said Ambrose, "think their ceremonies cannot subsist without their getting money for it."[14] Was this true? A good argument can be made that he misunderstood the real facts out of his wish to make the pagans look cheap; a good argument, also, that the state's financial support was seen by the pagans as part of a solemn bargain with the gods, not as a nice bit of change in their pockets.[15] I will return to this point at the end of the chapter. But the bishop of Milan, when he turned to struggles entirely within the Christian community, played an even more than usually strenuous role in the affair of the *deposita,* church funds, of the orthodox bishop of Ticinum. They would otherwise have been stripped away by the heretic emperor Valentinian II. Ambrose intervened and supported his fellow bishop, resisting until in the end, "the authority of divine law being explained, at last and with difficulty the emperor gave in to our reasoning."[16]

Another heretic emperor, Constantius, in 356 came to loggerheads with Athanasius, bishop of Alexandria. He sent Count Heraclius to the city to announce in public "by proclamation that, if the emperor was not obeyed" and popular support (non-Christian and orthodox alike) promptly withdrawn, the whole people of the city could expect "the termination of their grain-dole and the overthrow of their idols," along with other dire measures. The threat worked on the non-Christians, also on some of the bishop's working-class followers. He refers to them quite scornfully.[17]

Such masses underneath a bishop, however, were an essential element in his influence with secular authority. Once again turning to Milan, there, in A.D. 386, the heretic empress Justina, guardian to her son, was harassing the orthodox of the city; and when they grabbed a priest of her persuasion in a public square, she aimed a general fine of some tremendous sum of gold at the Merchants' Association. They boldly "replied they would give twice or thrice that amount if need be, provided only that they might continue in their faith."[18]

Last, in A.D. 394, the triumphant emperor Theodosius turned from the battlefield where non-Christian arms had been defeated and addressed the stubborn center of non-Christian loyalties, Rome itself. He had before him a delegation of senators come to his palace. He made "a speech calling for the abandoning of the error [in his terms] that they once espoused, and the adoption of the Christian faith, the good word of which brought acquittal from every wrongdoing and impiety"—a speech for conversion, in sum, and from the very throne. Yet it availed nothing. The senators could only talk about their ancestral heritage. "Theodosius then replied that the Treasury was overloaded by the costs of cult and sacrifices, he wanted to abolish them, and he did not concur in these practices. Besides, military necessities required the cash."[19] Against reasons of state, naturally the senators could put up no argument.

Theodosius assumed that people, at any rate some people, could be turned into coreligionists with his party and himself simply because it would cost them too much money to refuse. He was right, if he can be allowed his own notions of what was involved in becoming or being a Christian. At the very outset of the Christianizing of the monarchy under Constantine, Eusebius noted and deplored "the unspeakable hypocrisy of those accepting the church and adopting the facade, the deceitful name of 'Christian.'" He gave the cause as "fear of the emperor's menaces," which we have seen mentioned already.[20] As a Christian, however, and if otherwise well enough connected, you could line up to receive some of those confiscated estates.[21] You could qualify better for imperial appointment, too, since there was a clear if not very aggressive preference for Christians in office; and office was sought for material reward. The ranks among which moved the men successful enough to have left a mark on our records all opened up great opportunities for personal gain.[22] You could even win a new and improved municipal charter for your hometown by informing the emperor that it was now (he would be glad to know) completely Christian. So the port city of Maiouma told Constantine, who renamed it Constantia.[23] It was, in sum, manifestly profitable in worldly terms to declare yourself Christian; and Christians believed that the motive was widely at work among at least the governing classes, on whose conduct their opinions are occasionally reported.

A few careers of plain turncoats or trimmers can be traced;[24] better, broad trends in appointments to the top ranks, military (see above, pp. 45ff.) or civil. As we have seen, the hold of Christians on them broadened steadily, right through to the end of the fourth century and a few years beyond. Some apparent converts were moved by their alarm; "others, envious at the honor in which Christians were held by the emperor, deemed it necessary to follow in the emperor's path."[25] So much, and so visibly, might be at stake: the uniform of service that opened every door, privileges of public conveyance, lodging in provincial palaces, and all the world bowing and scraping before you.

Saint Ambrose and, later, Saint Augustine devote a good deal of attention to insincere conversions. They show that people who were already Christian did not want to betroth a daughter to a non-Christian or let him into local office, and would try to do him harm, or at least withhold help of any sort.[26] The penalties for not subscribing to the religion of the new Establishment by this time, from A.D. 380 or so, were thus being felt throughout the upper levels of society and, of course, much more sharply among the more vulnerable folk. They yielded a natural harvest. But all converts were to be accepted—"that they are false is not for us but for God to judge."[27]

From the 360s on, there were also times when the man at the top, Julian or a pretender, was non-Christian. Such moments were few and brief; yet they, too, produced their evidently insincere "converts."[28] Ambrose recalls considerable numbers of Christians who, for secular advantage or convenience, were converted to non-Christian cults even under Christian emperors; and other sources or authorities indicate a steady trickle of loss to the church.[29] It is reasonable to guess that the bias in source-transmission has passed on to us more information about conversion or apostasy *to* the church than away from it. Still, it is obvious in which direction the current was flowing the more strongly.

The question arises here, whether the people we have been describing belong to our subject, at least as I have defined it thus far; for clearly their choice of conduct was not decided or necessarily much affected at all by their views regarding a god or gods. Here they are before us, impossible to pin down: neither in the church nor out of it, so far as anyone could tell from their inner convictions. If they had really made up their minds about the supreme deity (which hardly appears to be so), they were not much worried about obeying him; so, unless belief in God or the gods is to be simply lifted out of religion and put off to one side, they and the whole topic of this chapter might better be left to some other book, "Belief without God," or the like.

But the definition I have had in mind throughout the discussion thus far was from the start intended as a servant, not a master. I framed it as an aid to understanding how the church came to attain a dominant position over and against all other cults. It worked not badly so long as the material rewards in church membership were minor or nonexistent. Things changed after A.D. 312. Thereupon, people simply not of a very religious temperament were drawn to

the church, at least to its periphery, and constituted a numerous
though not very stable group. They were far too numerous to be ignored, nor did the church want to ignore them.

Their role is a little more important, too, than the purely numerical one of being counted by someone as Christians. They added to
the impressiveness and presence of the church. Thereby they played
a causal part in the inclining of others to a slower, more serious conversion. Though too ignoble to have ensured any record, the change
of heart that began out of mere imitation, fashion, and respectability
must surely be assumed to have been at work in the great burst of
growth that the church enjoyed after Constantine.[30]

That growth may be compared with another. I have in mind the
broad and instructive, if by no means perfect, parallel of Islam's subsequent spread over the regions longest Christianized: from Egypt
up through the Holy Land and Syria and across Asia Minor. Here,
throughout this vast area, the Islamic authorities, though exerting
little force in any direction, more often applied it to prevent conversions than to induce them. Christians, however, found themselves
without access to a court presided over by their coreligionists; they
were effectively denied high careers in government; they were generally looked on as second-class citizens; and they were penalized in
their pocket, mostly through special and heavy taxes but also, in
later times, through the loss of their corporate revenues and buildings. There were indeed, at the one extreme, conversions under du-
ress and, at the other extreme, conversions by sincere conviction; but
in the middle and very clearly predominant were conversions induced by a subtle mixture of social and material rewards. These latter, in effect, controlled the history of Islamization.[31]

VII

Evangelical Campaigns and Publicity, after 312

Constantine's intervention in the course of the church's growth brought not only tangible rewards to his coreligionists, as they were after A.D. 312. It also brought peace, for a moment. Non-Christians and Christians were to leave each other alone. The latter could now in safety follow their inclination to defend and actively advocate their religious views among unbelievers.

The nearest thing we have to a description of their activities can be found, not in the accounts of the time but in the story of Gregory the Wonder-worker in north-central Turkey (as it now is), during the 240s. We have seen him as a student of Origen's at Alexandria and as an author of theological works. But he was also effective as doer and preacher, and memory held fast for generations to the remarkable details of his missionary life, until Constantine's day, when they were written up in compendious form. Of this now lost work, the most trustworthy derivative is a translation into Syriac. There exist also much less trustworthy Latin and Greek texts. From these three texts a collection of incidents can be culled, in the confidence that contemporaries counted each of them as a fact, like a bad thunderstorm in the neighboring valley—a fact not seen with one's own eyes but reported altogether reliably.[1] It is on beliefs of this sort, after all, that everyone must depend to arrive at conclusions about the divine or about the neighbors.

Coming into the backlands of Pontus and on his travels sheltering for a night in a lonely temple (§5), Gregory passes the hours of darkness in prayer, as usual, and leaves in the morning. The temple-warden then turns up to set the daimon to work in *his* usual way, that is, by responding oracularly to worshipers' questions. But the

59

daimon will not enter his still-and-forever prayer-filled dwelling. He explains why to the warden. The warden runs after Gregory to fetch him back and get him to reinstate the daimon (for if the traveler can banish, he can surely recall). Gregory obliges, and the warden —Gregory's first convert in the territory and eventually his successor as bishop—draws the only possible conclusion: the being that Gregory worships is far more powerful than the one *he* had been worshiping. (There is an additional show of power, the supernatural moving of a rock, to clinch the matter.)

Similarly (§11), on another occasion, "when Gregory was standing teaching the people one day, behold, from among the crowd a young man shouted out in a loud voice," uttering some challenge; and Gregory exorcizes that demon likewise, saying, "'Not I is it that commands you but Christ who flung you with the swine into the sea [Mt 8 : 32]: Quit this youth!' And as the demon heard the name of the divine majesty, he cried out loudly, saying, 'Alas for me, for Jesus! Alas for me, on account of his disciple!'" And the devil himself (§11 and 13), being enraged by the territory conquered from him by the bishop, where once both countryside and chief city were in the grip of daimones (§3, and the daimon in the baths, §7), inspires a woman to defame him. She is a prostitute, and accuses him of being one of her lovers, but he exorcizes the evil spirit from her also (§11).

Gregory alters the course of a river to prevent further damage from spring floods (§7–8) and dries up a whole little lake that had become a cause of bad blood between two brothers (§9). Beneficent miracles—but when two Jews at the roadside hope to play on his sympathies and so trick a gift out of him, one of them who pretends to be dead is really struck lifeless suddenly (§4), and is revived only through Gregory's prayers; whereupon both Jews "straightway accept baptism and become monks." At the end, where there had been only seventeen Christians before, there are barely that number left who are not Christian, and in a neighboring town other converts are numerous enough to think they need their own bishop (§10, cf. §2). That appointment, like Gregory's own, is signaled and directed by various visions, thus securing the best candidate.

A mere blacksmith is chosen (and the point of the original account requires that he be a man of mean employ). In embarrassment, the narrative originally supplied him with a "true" identity, descent from a millionaire with seven hundred slaves in Italy, and later (by

Gregory of Nyssa) he is turned into a "philosopher." The second Gregory, author of the surviving Greek version, being of the highest, most cultivated class, could not imagine, or perhaps could not tolerate, divine election for the episcopacy falling on a person one would not ordinarily speak to on the street.

But surely we ourselves can accept the awkward truth, along with other matters made clear in the narrative. Clearly some very large part of the population, one region in the province Pontus, was won over to the church by Gregory the Wonder-worker in specific and identifiable decades—our only surviving account of any such event, however many others there may or must have been just like it. He succeeded perhaps in part through speaking publicly to groups. He is shown speaking like that, but confirming or instructing. No conversions arc said to result. Rather, and expressly, conversions result from his supernatural acts; and, by implication and by position in the narrative, they are presented as the cause of the whole grand picture of his success in his campaigns against demonic hosts.

The logic offered to account for the conversions he produced —that he or the divinity he invoked was of greater authority than the daimones, and that that power could both greatly help and greatly hurt one—fit altogether naturally with the logic described earlier (above, pp. 26ff.). No alternative equally natural suggests itself, and none is attested.

But such successes belong to rather more open scenes than Christians ordinarily enjoyed. Gregory's own career was interrupted by persecutions in the 250s, he and what may be called his "movement" had to go underground, and thereafter, until Constantine proclaimed toleration, episodes or campaigns of attack on the church recurred more frequently. What worked in a peaceful backwater town and region in the third century cannot have been representative of missionary activities in general, at any time from the end of the first century up to 313.

After that, the tested methods of the church could be more openly applied, in Gregorian fashion, by Saint Anthony in Alexandria or Saint Martin among the Gauls.[2] When the former made a rare visit to the city, "many [mad and possessed] pagans thought they would be helped if they only touched the old man, and fully as many became Christians in those few days as you would otherwise see in a year"; and Saint Martin was much talked about because he had "exorcized the slave of Tetradius, a former proconsul, and the owner, who was still a pagan, [therewith] became a catechumen and before long received baptism." The dislodged daimones would even say who they were—for example, Mercury (the Latin name by which the principal Gallic deity was normally called). That was the kind of theological demonstration that was irrefutable. I discussed its importance earlier. But in the relations of the sick, the mad, or the desperate with a real wonder-worker, there might well be an element of fear. Beyond the lesson that his conduct taught, visibly demonstrating and proving the truth of his central message, a kind of bargain was implied. Occasionally the bargain was explicit: acknowledge God or be punished. So an ascetic of Hermoupolis in Egypt reduces a procession of non-Christian worshipers to frozen immobility, right in the middle of the road, through spells; and they cannot regain the use of their limbs until they "renounce their error." Or you might defy the ascetic—in this case, Aphraates, in a Syrian city—and by no mere coincidence, straightway you died a horrible death. From that, people "realized the strength of Aphraates' prayer."[3]

In a tradition that reached back to its very roots, Christianity in the person of its most electric figures lit up the dualism they preached on the local level, as we may call it, before specific gatherings, and so dramatized Christian confrontation with the enemy—be it error or demons—through visible acts. Then the story went round, it grew, it was lovingly shaped, it became both an explanation and an exhortation. It showed how certain individuals had reasoned and then acted in real situations (even elaborated in later tellings); and it became a spring for action among its listeners.

In both ways, such stories supply the only direct evidence we have of the motivation that led to a change in religious adherence—evidence of the best sort, though certainly not in the abundance to be wished for: in the form, "So-and-So did thus-and-such, *and therefore* other people . . . ," or, "So-and-So believed such-and-such, *because he saw*. . . ." And our testimonies adduced are all reasonably close to contemporary. It might, of course, all be discounted on the grounds that the laws of nature could never have been really suspended, first, and, second, that no sane or candid person could ever have thought so. Therefore the true explanations remain to be sought among probabilities as they are seen in better-known situations. But, even if that first objection is sustained, the second still confronts overwhelming difficulties: for, beyond dispute, inhabitants of the empire by and large took it for granted that the laws of nature had always been and always would be continually suspended. They had come to terms with that fact, as they saw it; therefore they acted accordingly.

In the late fourth century the point made here is conveniently illustrated by a little poem of Christian propaganda. It is clearly meant to incline gentle readers to belief through the versified conversation overheard among three shepherds—a familiar literary form, of course, from Theocritus to Vergil. Buculus complains that all his sheep are dying; but Tityrus tells him salvation lies through the sign of the cross, and "no altar wet with blood" is needed; to which Aegon adds, "If, Tityrus, you should make good on these [assertions], without delay I'll serve true cult. I willingly would quit ancient error, for it is deceitful and empty. . . . For why should I doubt that the same sign may help men as well [as beasts] for all eternity, [the sign] by which the force of disease is vanquished?"[4] The reasoning is all explicit: it is miraculous healing that does and should produce conversion, even if the point of departure is one's sheep.

Being of the religion more in the sunlight than any other, toward the end of our period Christians could publicize their faith quite openly so as to reach non-Christians. The poet just quoted is a minor figure in this effort. Prudentius and others belong to it also.[5] Hymns for the same purpose, written in the hope of their being sung by nonbelievers, belong to the same period, though they have other obvious purposes inside the Christian community too.[6] There were tracts of aggressive debate addressed to non-Christians, to argue them down;[7] and the ludicrous piety of the prefect in the capital, Clearchus, "provided a lot of small plaques for the smaller Circus," on the occasion of imperial victories, showing "a hand stretched forth from the clouds with the inscription on it, 'God's hand puts the barbarians to flight,' and again, in another place, 'The barbarians flee God.'"[8] In Alexandria in A.D. 391, by whose instigation we are not told but in any case in the wake of the great antipagan riots, "busts of Sarapis which stood in the walls, vestibules, doorways and windows of every house were all torn out and annihilated . . . , and in their place the sign of the Lord's cross was painted in the doorways, vestibules, windows and walls, and on pillars."[9]

Mass media in antiquity were pretty limited. Such as they were, however, they belonged almost entirely to the church and its advocates. In the cities, at any rate, you heard the town crier roaring out the emperor's decrees, full of preaching (see above, p. 50); you might hear church music aimed beyond the church's congregation; there were various prominent uses made of didactic symbolism, notably the cross, in works of art or as graffiti. Finally, literature, so far as it was intended to persuade, was Christian. All these media we have seen at work openly, officially, and stridently, as became possible when Christians could at last emerge into the full sunlight of acceptance. We must make some effort to imagine how much more attractive must have seemed the alternative they offered to non-Christians. But we have no explicit proof of that consequence.

Of all the instruments of publicity favored in the empire, rhetoric was by far the most familiar. Within the church, it took the form of sermons in remarkable abundance: surviving are many millions of words spoken within our period of study and written down in Greek or Latin. Were any of these words heard by a non-Christian? There must have been a numerically negligible audience for the great orators from among those interested in oratory itself, not religion.[10] But Saint Ambrose specifically addressed non-Christians, either to explain and recommend points to them, or to discredit their own beliefs.[11] He knew whom he could expect among his listeners. And he congratulated the recently appointed bishop of Como on *his* success, where he (Ambrose) heard that "most of the city senators are already beginning to believe in your teaching and have received God's word through your instruction, *tuo magisterio*."[12] Evidently in Como, somehow, the bishop had gotten a hearing for his message.

Pulpit persuasion touched on a great variety of points—among them, for example, in a sermon of Maximus, the bishop of Turin, quite chilling references to the day of judgment. But then, there is no conversion without fear, says Saint Augustine.[13] And, turning from western cathedrals to eastern, there is John Chrysostom in Antioch taking pride that Christian meeting-places are not like Jewish synagogues: "for ours are not of that sort, but, rather, truly fearful and filled with shuddering. For within is the God that has power over life and death—so fearful is the place. And within, ten thousand sermons on eternal punishments, on the rivers of fire, on the poisonous worm, on unbreakable bonds and furthest darkness."[14] The casual visitor who was presented with such a tableau as this, like the tourist who confronts the west wall of the Sistine Chapel, certainly went away with something to think about.

Maximus of Turin, in the passage just quoted, goes on to appeal to his listeners for their active alliance: you may be good Christians yourselves, he says, but you must not neglect "your people; for there is hardly one of you whose fields are not polluted by idols, hardly any estate held free of worship to demons."[15] The obligation fell on the master, then. *He* must address himself to the non-Christians among his dependents. Episcopal eloquence thus set up echoes in settings the bishop himself could never reach.

"Many people," says John Chrysostom in Antioch, "have villages and estates and pay no mind to them nor communicate with them, but do give great attention to how the baths are working, and how the rates are set, and how halls and houses are constructed—not to the harvest of souls. . . . Should not everyone build a church, should he not get a teacher and make a congregation and, above all things, see to it that all are Christians?" And Augustine congratulates a particular large landholder of his acquaintance in North Africa in very similar terms.[16] Of another, he imagines everyone in the city saying, "That nobleman, if he were only Christian—not a pagan would be left! Men often say, 'Not a pagan would be left if *he* were a Christian!'" And the sense of what he describes, flattery or exaggeration aside, is quite right. Just as the emperor's servants followed his lead (though not always), so the slaves and tenant farmers and dependents of one of those counts or senators, or any rich man, were open to both pressure and persuasion from him. We have seen that casually mentioned at other points.[17]

Progress of the new faith within the body of older ones was channeled in one direction or another, or accelerated or retarded, by the whole network of relations within which each individual lived his life. When toleration was made official those relations of course changed. Consider the convert who was a slave in a non-Christian household. Insubordination! All sorts of problems! So, before Constantine, the church in Rome, and presumably elsewhere, sharply rejected such additions unless they had their master's support. Later it still insisted, through the arm of the state, that he should determine the religion of his slaves—that is (at this quite different juncture), the master should enforce their religious conformity by means of a good beating, or, if one weren't enough, "by progressively heavier beatings."[18] Here once more is the question: In what sense do you have a convert when he yields to mere force? We have confronted the problem before.[19] So long as one got the semblance of results, Augustine, for one, saw no difficulties. Neither did Saint Gregory somewhat later.[20] It is reasonable to take their views as representative of the religious Establishment overall as it had by then developed throughout the empire, because the same views are embodied in imperial legislation and accord entirely with that faith in violence that will be described in a later chapter.

In rural settings, too, the population with no land, or too little land to support independence, was really very much under the thumb of a big man. This was true in the second century. A letter of Pliny describes what the role of religious leadership involved on his own holdings, not only for the benefit of his tenants but also to accommodate big crowds of worshipers attending the holy days at a shrine that happened to be on his property.[21] In Spain in the third century there was a local custom according to which a landlord remitted to his tenants their costs for sacrifices, I suppose because the sacrifices were thought to be as much in the landlord's interests as anyone's.[22] But these benevolent times were pre-Christian. A century later, the emperors announced that they would confiscate the lands of any man who so much as allowed, even in ignorance, a meeting for prohibited worship on his acres.[23] Such an announcement, with introductory sermonizing of a highly colored sort, would be promulgated by being read aloud in public places at the most crowded times. The introductions to them have almost all perished from the record, but their flavor can easily be restored from the vestiges still surviving in the law codes and elsewhere, in references to the madness, contamination, poison, perfidy, monstrousness, polluted contagion, and so forth, that characterize proscribed religious views.[24] We must in that spirit supply similar explanatory fervor to the imperial laws we have just mentioned.

In assessing the psychological climate, the feel of those times, for the non-Christian population, account must be taken also of the topics in common currency. What items of experience were people talking about and passing on to their neighbors? What impinged on a person's settled universe of ideas, disturbing it and preparing him to question his previous beliefs and even to abandon them? What made news? The most likely items on the religious page concerned Christian holy men, miracles, exorcisms, healings, wonderful things. They concerned the emperor's laws read aloud in the town center, declaring all but Christian views to be entirely intolerable. They were oratorical displays in cathedrals for both everyday folk and the upper classes. For the latter alone, new publication of any ideologically aggressive sort likely to attract attention was Christian. The prevailing close social and economic relations did not allow non-Christian people to shut out this noise of Christian exuberance, this din of defeat.

VIII

Conversion of Intellectuals

In the latter half of the fourth century the church made conquests among many more, and more distinguished, intellectuals than in previous periods. They were, as Saint Jerome said, the last to be converted.[1] In the literature produced by the church in self-explanation and defense, they were for a long time unlikely to find what they ordinarily sought in books or what they were used to; nor were they, in the ordinary course of things—for example, in the classrooms and libraries of higher education—very likely even to learn of the existence of sophisticated Christian writings. As time went on, however, things changed. Augustine wrote his Confessions. Glimpses may be caught of other spirits in the process of development. These are of such high interest as human testimonies that they receive a disproportionate discussion in our own day— disproportionate as measured against the impact they had on the way others around them lived their lives. It will be sufficient, then, just to indicate the chief figures in a few pages.

Any account must pick up from such predecessors as Saint Justin or Tatian, described earlier. They grew out of a Greek world of rival philosophic schools. Each school offered its own answers to the perennial questions, each set of answers (or mixtures, or hybrids) was to be studied at the feet of this or that renowned teacher. Students formed a floating population, compared notes, and turned in doubt from one set of answers to another till they ended, it might happen, in a state of impatient cynicism about the entire search. There we find Menippus, in Lucian's satirical sketch; there we find the formidable bulk of Sextus Empiricus' writings. The alternative was to seek refuge from uncertainty in some superhuman authority. The agonies of doubt would thus end.[2] And so we have, growing within the empire in the third and fourth centuries, a taste for metaphysics of a kind that rather resembles revelation, a pursuit of knowledge that is really the pursuit and discovery of god. Among the population at large, indeed, it was assumed that someone with his nose always in his books could only be searching for divine truths—or, equally, demonic ones. To attain them one might just as well pass by books entirely and win revelations through an ascetic life instead. So an illiterate hermit might "philosophize" or a pious nun be called "philosopher."[3] Seekers after certainty in a life of ascetic practice or in a life of wandering and study till the Teacher was found, both belong by right to the later empire.

Once, Saint Basil tells us, he had been deeply engaged with higher learning. "I squandered a long period on vain things and destroyed virtually my entire youth in footling labor . . . , when, on a time, and as if from the depths of sleep, I arose and gazed toward the miraculous light of the Messiah, and so beheld the uselessness of the wisdom of the princes of this world."[4] Such was the certainty sought. To see it is to know it instantly, by an experience as much spiritual as intellectual. And in our tiny corpus of instances of such revelation, it came most typically while one was still young—young but reduced to anguish and desperation by a particular need unsatisfied despite many months, or even years, of inquiry. William James, in his Scottish lectures, opened to the public the phenomenon, long discussed among psychologists, connecting adolescence and conversion.[5]

In the eastern provinces, the chief point of resort for gifted students was Alexandria. Here, we chance on occasional conversions through intellectual demonstration, not by any miracle: for example, that of Saint Hilarion in his youth.[6] But for Prince Julian, the search had begun in faraway Cappadocia and ended in Ephesus; and for Victorinus it was Rome, in his old age.[7] The latter turned to reading the Bible very carefully, just why there is no record; went on to other Christian literature; and, out of the blue, told a friend one day that he believed. All his life he had been a rhetor, deeply read and a deeply religious man, even an evangelist for the cult of the gods.

In these same years, the mid-350s, Hilary, in exile from his bishopric in southern France, recalled his own development, from the philosophic views commonly held in learned non-Christian circles to Christianity. "Recalled" or invented? No clear answer is possible. The account in question, near the commencement of his treatise on the Trinity, is fashioned out of a rich reading in Cicero, Sallust, and, among Christian writers, Lactantius, Minucius Felix, and others. Doignon, in his monumental commentary on these pages, is surely right to treat them not as literally autobiographical but rather as a train of thought assembled entirely from the clichés of the author's culture. But he is right, too, in his caution: "il y a conversion et conversion." It cannot be shown to be impossible that some such "sober, pondering, logical" movement of the mind as Hilary relates did really underlie the elaborate essay he has given us.[8]

In any case, Hilary begins in rebellion. It is "unworthy, *indignum* (§2), that this life of ours itself has not been granted for some progress toward eternity," "unworthy, *non dignum,* of God that men should die" (§9). We must recall how elusive and rarely credited was the notion of immortality among non-Christians (see above, chap. 2, n. 2). Christianity offered something radically better, seen above all in John 11–14. Hilary, here as elsewhere, specifies his texts. Moreover, "most men, according to the general opinion, speak of god as existing but declare him to be uninterested and uncaring about human affairs" (§4). That view, too, we know to have prevailed among non-Christians: god contradicts his own perfection if he can be reached, touched, disturbed, or in any way changed from it by anything in this material world below. The philosopher that Gregory the Wonder-worker addressed had prodded him with the same point. Hilary, however, finds in scripture (§5, "I am who I am") a definition of divinity that fully satisfies him and enables him also to set aside any ridiculous anthropomorphizing. Divinity is not defined as male or female, or by more or less strength (§4). After further study of scripture, he can arrive, too, at a proper understanding of man's relation to God (§11 f.). In the end, all doubts are answered. "A steady faith spurns the captious, useless controversies of philosophy" (§13; compare above, n. 1), and "in that ease of its own safety the mind, happy in its hopes, reclines at rest" (§14).

Rest is set in contrast to the sharp anxieties he had suffered earlier.[9] His had been a tortured spirit. He had begun a search in a mood of rebellion against the indignity of death, likewise against the indignity he felt in prevalent ideas of godhead. His sense had been refined through readings in the controversies of the schools. It took on final definition in logical necessities, the *dignum*. And no set of answers met his need till, unassisted, he happened on the Old and New Testaments. Here was a progress toward conversion long familiar in the ancient world.

Even better known, and of course far more important, is the *peregrinatio animae* of the prince and later emperor, Julian. But it is not better known in the sense of its psychological origins or course. For that, the only trustworthy source could have been the man himself, and he reveals very little. He was a bookish, lonely teen-ager of strong will and strong intelligence. He read a lot, preco-ciously. Quite by himself and while under a sort of house arrest, however considerate it may have been, he came adrift, or cut him-self free, from the religious views in which he had been raised and by which he was carefully surrounded. Gaining freedom to move about, he then sought (and that much was evident to the outside world, which could report on the search) for further spiritual in-struction. He found it in the person of a certain Maximus of Ephesus, on the advice of another teacher, to whom he said (so we are told), "Goodby to you, then—and stick to your books. For you have shown me what I am looking for"—that is, not more learn-ing, but revelation.[10] To that he later added greatly, out of his life and thought. A considerable written record survives, and efforts have often been made to reason from the views he expounded in his reigning years till his death in 363, back to the views he must have settled on when he was nineteen. But this method seems to me not very sound.

A decade later, and at just the same age, occurred a famous con-version, that of Saint Augustine. It was, like Julian's, conversion to Wisdom with a capital letter, something beyond ordinary logical framing.[11] Augustine was introduced to it by figures, much like Maximus of Ephesus, with a wonderful physical presence, a pierc-ing, visionary glance, clearly in touch with supernatural sources of enlightenment. Over a space of years in their company, he tried to cure his tormenting uncertainty, studied under their guidance, at-tended their meetings, and listened to revelations by seekers in the congregation more successful than he.

But when he left Carthage and arrived in Milan, he underwent what Peter Brown well describes as a "final and definitive conver-sion."[12] Along the paths thus indicated he continued still to travel in later thought, distancing himself from his former coreligionists while at the same time seeking to bring them over to his own views. They must not reject him, for if they did, "before the Last Judgement, let them be made ready for their death."[13]

He had by then, in A.D. 386, passed through nearly fifteen years of intermittent spiritual unease and strain. He approached a condition of nervous breakdown, from which only the famous moment in his walled garden brought lasting relief. But, hearing over the wall the voice of a child at play chanting, "Pick it up and read! Pick it up and read!" he opened the Bible at random. There he found the message directed to his need. It was the end of his peregrination.

Few instants in the history of the church are more familiar. Enough to mention it. And its place in any account of conversion is equally obvious. But its special magic must not quite enchant us.

The object ultimately in view is the question, How did the church come to prevail over all rival cults, so as to become the dominant presence among religions of the empire? Granted, *within the church,* the impact of Saint Augustine was to be absolutely extraordinary. For that matter, the intellectual achievement of Julian within the non-Christian tradition also deserves notice. But none of that forms our focus. What, rather, did these two figures, or any of those we have reviewed in this chapter, contribute to the growth and bulk of the church *within the empire?*

Does their significance lie in what they tell us about a process?— the complicated intellectual process through which the young Julian and Augustine abandoned the beliefs of their family and upbringing in search of something that could better satisfy their spiritual needs? It was the same process through which Augustine at a second moment, Victorinus in old age, and Hilary at some point unknown in his life, turned in the opposite direction. But the process here, as in earlier centuries, seems to have worked in both directions (see above, p. 31). If our sources, as seems likely, have begrudged us a full report of the church's more notable losses, then perhaps the losses and gains were roughly equal. In quantitative terms, at any rate, the gain on either side is not significant.

The temperaments represented in our survey also belong to a particular type, "in every way very religious" (as one such person, a non-Christian, is described in a certain story).[14] More than that, they represented a very high degree of cultivation. They had read whole libraries; some were even professional intellectuals making their living out of their extended studies. By two separate qualifica-

tions, then, these individuals stood apart from their world, a number almost too small to measure.

Yet there may be some significance to be salvaged here: they
shared much with the ordinary convert. In addition to the special
intensity of feeling and complexity of thought that animated them,
they also responded to the church's promise of life after death. Terror before the threat of divine judgment they felt, too. And they
knew they had to choose. That logic penetrated their doubts, and
illuminates points of impact that were peculiar to Christianity.

IX

How Complete Was Conversion?

But consider again the scene in Augustine's garden: whatever made him think some divine message might be communicated to him through a child's prattle or in the random thumbing of a sacred text? Both modes of divination were alien to his faith. At the instant of taking the ultimate step in his conversion, he was still a pagan.[1]

Naturally. For Christianity had not developed its own particular way of doing everything. On many a corner even of religious life it had still to set its mark. Those corners, however, are of concern to us because they help to determine both the point at which a person could count as a convert and the historical impact of conversion. How broad a conformity to the practices prescribed by the church was needed to make one a Christian? And what difference did conversion actually make anyway in the various zones and areas of life? To these two questions we may add a third, rhetorically: What parts of life in a non-Christian community were *not* touched by non-Christian worship in the form of some patron deity presiding over one's place of work, one's artisan association, one's storeroom, one's betrothal or birthday, one's attendance at a spectacle, leisure promenades, and even the choice of an epitaph at the end of one's life—in sum, over everything? So disturbing and difficult must be conversion, or so incomplete.

Ambrose up in Milan (to begin with an awkward problem which that bishop faced) witnessed his congregation dancing during times of worship. (He seems to mean right inside the churches, but he does not supply details.) He was shocked. Such conduct was pagan. In southern France, the bishop Caesarius castigated "the wretches who dance and caper about before the churches of the saints themselves, . . . and if they appear at church as Christians, yet they leave the church as pagans—for that custom of dancing is still with us from pagan ritual" (he is writing some fifty years later than Ambrose). In the eastern provinces, Bishop Basil reproved the dancers in the very chapels of Caesarea. Other church leaders in Syria and the Levant tried to suppress dancing, or hand-clapping, or piping along with hymns or at weddings. And, returning to the west, in North Africa, Bishop Augustine encountered the same custom and spoke out against it. So everywhere we look we find the problem.[2]

But why *not* dance? What was the logic in banning it? Had not David danced? "Those actions [like David's] which are performed disgracefully, if looked at only as physical, are, when viewed through holy religion, rather to be held in respect." Thus wrote Ambrose.

Exactly—and non-Christians did hold them in respect and everywhere joined music and motion to their occasions of worship, often accompanied by pipe or castanet or little drum.[3] It was that conjunction or contamination that disturbed church leaders, not any particular logic. Unless, perhaps, they sensed a dictum of modern anthropology: "It is, primarily at least, out of the context of concrete acts of religious observance that religious conviction emerges on the human plane."[4] In other words, ritual gives authority to belief; and Christianity must not be seen to need anything of the sort from the pagan past.

But some ritual in and of itself was a thing enjoyable and important, which people were reluctant to give up. We have an illustration here: for, so far as we know, only on more or less explicitly religious occasions was there any music for a person to join, and get the pleasure of, in the empire of this period. Thus, to ban it was to impoverish life. The ban might be defied. Well, then, music could still be Christianized. And that process produced Christian hymns.[5] The church, considering how the boundaries around itself were defined, and to set it off from rival cults without too much reducing the rewards of life for those who were converted, had to take account of such practical considerations.

Non-Christians were accustomed, in North Africa, Syria, Italy, and so on, across a great scattering of localities and cultural variations, to drink wine at communal religious celebrations. That was only one aspect of religious parties. It was nice to sing, look in your neighbor's eyes, dance about, hold hands—and drink. Sometimes drink a lot. Ambrose and Augustine grew much disturbed at the thought of these vinous vigils on saints' days, when worshipers "take their cups to the martyrs' tombs and there drink till evening, believing" (and this is interesting) "that *otherwise they will not be heard*."[6] The function of festive conduct is thus made explicit: it is by no means only part of a good time; but it is non-Christian.

So intimately a part of life were the two joined aspects of sociability and effective supplication that, "when peace came to the church" (that is, in A.D. 313), "confused throngs of pagans wanting entrance to the church were held back because their feast days along with their idols used to be spent in an abundance of eating and drinking."[7] So intractable was resistance, however, that imperial policy, in extending its anti-pagan measures, gingerly walked around this very problem, so as still to permit "the cheerful gatherings of Our subjects and communal general happy mood" on festal days, to the very end of our period of study.[8]

Christianity in tolerant times gave rise to its own calendar of rejoicing, in which Augustine takes qualified pleasure; but Christians who attended often also attended the non-Christian celebrations too, which maintained their place in the civic year during his lifetime and much, much longer.[9] They can be traced in some of the great cities like Rome and Carthage, and are attested to or implied in a scattering of other centers as well. An attempt was made to terminate the Eleusinian mysteries next door to Athens, but the emperor's governor on the spot dissuaded him from "a measure that would, he said, render life unlivable for the Greeks." "Unlivable," of course, simply was a term to dramatize something vastly unpopular; but it was enough.[10]

At Antioch the non-Christian Libanius promised that patriotic hymns would be punctually sung at all of "the many festivals among us" pagans, a promise directed at the Christian Master of Soldiers and at Theodosius. Could the regime really forbid such welcome celebrations? Emperor-worship likewise, as is well known, continued in its more formal aspects: the appointment of provincial high priests, for instance, and the display of imperial images in the chapels of troop commanders and high civil officials. But there were popular manifestations of a genuinely enthusiastic kind that should have been intolerable but weren't.[11] How could Theodosius in his capital, even that self-consciously Christian monarch, officially rebuke the pious throngs that propitiated the statue of Constantine with sacrifices, lighted lamps, incense, and prayers (and expected this cult to ward off evil in return)? What minatory notice could he possibly take, from his ceremonial carriage, when crowds in a town turned out to welcome him, pagan priests at their head? Or when a no doubt highly nervous orator called him a god to his face, "What are you going to do," as the girl asks in *Oklahoma,* "spit in his eye?"

Confronting the need to survive, great political leaders rise above consistency. Or they are merely human, perhaps. When he was worried about an imminent war, Theodosius desired to know if he would win. Alas, he and his predecessors had stopped the mouths of all the oracles. However, the ascetic John of Lycopolis under different auspices was just as good—he prophesied all the time—and provided the imperial emissaries with just the reassurance or propaganda they required.[12] It has often been pointed out, and along much the same lines, that replacement had to be found for the comfort and healing once offered by pagan shrines,[13] whose disappearance had to be and was matched by new institutions from within the church. It was a question of essential functions in any civilized life, like the love of communal music and social gatherings mentioned a few pages back. As a result of irresistible pressure, and from nothing more mysterious than human nature, priests were asked for their prayers, ascetics for their magic touch, and martyrs for their intercession, by the sick and suffering of every province. That story, however, does not really concern my inquiry.

In one area, the church plainly offered too little: that of outpatient services and household medicine, as we may describe the whole matter of minor illnesses. So, despite its continual warnings, its members clung to non-Christian practices. Such practices could hardly be separated from broader religious beliefs—hence the concern of the church over the use of amulets to help a sick child and the like.[14] Probably the bulk of the evidence for recourse to magic among Christians in the fourth century, and later too, has to do with the cure of disease; but Christians in need of foreknowledge and unable to submit their uncertainties to John of Lycopolis in Egypt were in the habit of applying to the local seer instead. Any such resort came in for harsh but vain rebuke from ecclesiastical authorities.[15]

When the non-Christian Symmachus, however, wished his friend good health "by divinity's help," he may not have been assuming a shared religion between himself and the other. There was much they had in common in the vocabulary of religion; also, much religion that had become a part of people's unconscious behavior, quite denatured.[16] For that reason—really, no conscious reason—Julian crossed himself when he was scared, so went the story; while, on the other hand, a church deacon swore "by the divine and holy Tyche of our all-conquering Lords," the emperors.[17]

The tangible record gives the same impression of shared territory. For example, among the grave-goods of late Roman Egypt, very much the same things are found whether the burial be Christian or not.[18] In a Pannonian grave was placed a box ornamented with a relief of the gods, Orpheus in the center, Sol and Luna in the corners, but the Chi-Rho as well; elsewhere, in Danube burials, similar random mixtures of symbolism appear, with gods and busts of Saint Peter and Saint Paul all in the same bas-relief.[19] The Romans who bought cheap little baked clay oil-lamps from the shop of Annius Serapiodorus in the capital apparently didn't care whether he put the Good Shepherd or Bacchus or both together on his products; and the rich patrons of mosaicists in Gaul, North Africa, and Syria were similarly casual about the very confused symbolism they commissioned for their floors.[20] Stonecutters suggested identical funeral mottoes indifferently to their Christian customers and their non-Christian: "Sacred to the gods and spirits" sits atop many a Christian gravestone in Africa, but abbreviated and therefore little regarded; sometimes "No one lives forever," even "Enjoy life" or "Life is sweet."[21] These had been familiar sentiments for centuries.

As they had done in the past, Christians and non-Christians often shared the same cemeteries (though rarely around Rome itself). Archeologists and epigraphers are hard put to identify the religion from the fashion of burial.[22] That they should draw on each other's practices is hardly surprising since they not only died together but of course lived together, too. To that community of life and death, however, Christians came late, as aliens to cultural systems already fully formed around them. Those non-Christian systems, differing regionally, nevertheless shared to some degree a single, broad characteristic: they were pervaded in many and functionally significant parts by religion. Christian attack had, then, to be broadly directed. So logic prescribed; but necessity prevented. It was not possible, nor ever dreamed of, to assault and displace pagan customs of burial, farewell mottoes for the dead or good wishes to the living, decorative symbolism, music for weddings, social entertainment, and so on, across every conceivable activity. What was a way of life, but also intertwined with cult, therefore remained non-Christian very stubbornly and for very long.

"To allow a boy's hair to grow long on his neck is to make him feminine like a girl . . . , the result of pagan superstition," says John Chrysostom of Antioch. The connection in thought belongs to sexual custom, (Judeo-) Christian against the traditional upper-class Greek.[23] The latter, in the last quarter of the fourth century, still accepted male homosexuality, though with somewhat uneasy toleration. Pairing off two men to kill each other in an amphitheater as a spectator sport was likewise tolerated—indeed popular—but offensive to more refined non-Christian sensibilities as well as Christian.[24] Constantine is said to have aimed a flat prohibition against it—whether or not to any effect, no one can say. It certainly went on throughout the century, though gradually less attested. Against slaveholding, too, pulpit rebuke was directed, with no effect at all. On all three counts, did Christian leaders consciously try to change the way of life around them because of the logic of church doctrine? And similarly, against inhumanity shown by the rich to the poor, or against sexual indecency in theatrical performances, did the church fix new bounds around the daily life of its members, or did it merely make more explicit the old, prevailing values? These and similar questions will be answered when the impact of the church's ascendancy upon the way in which late Roman life was actually lived receives some serious study. For the moment it is not easy to trace the boundaries around behavior that marked a person as a tolerable member of the church and everything else as alien.[25]

Only a few steps from the palace in Trier, a non-Christian cult group was still holding its meetings in the last decades of the fourth century. The mosaic symbolism of their quarters indicates their beliefs—also their wealth, education, and no doubt their prominence.[26] To the palace in Milan came important emissaries in the same period to plead openly before the emperor for toleration toward non-Christian rites; and to the emperors in Constantinople, courtly orators like Themistius and Libanius directed explicitly non-Christian remarks, references, prayers, vows, and pious good wishes.[27]

Considering the taken-for-granted presence of so many non-Christians in government positions closest to the emperors into these very last decades of the fourth century, there is nothing unexpected about their being on free and easy speaking terms with their Most Christian Majesties. It is still less surprising that the Christian Establishment, as it may fairly be called at this point, should have extended its toleration to the way of life of such non-Christian notables—to their mosaics, literary tastes, choice of epitaphs, and so forth. The cultural ambiguities of the later fourth century, which I have been pointing out in the last few pages, are physically embodied in all sorts of transitional figures whose religion was evidently of no special interest to anyone, or not even determinable,[28] in this respect resembling the lamps and caskets of dubious decoration described above.

As to the army, whose religious affiliations I examined up to the 360s, its transition to Christianity thereafter seems to have been very gradual. A graveyard with Christian burials on the North African frontier, a pair of soldiers (one a Christian) doing guard duty in Syria—such random items prove very little. Even Egypt, relatively rich in documents, only tells us that you could serve in the army openly as a pagan far into the fifth century. (There is more evidence for the officers, but that may mean nothing.) As military recruits came to be increasingly drawn from barbarians living to the north of the Rhine and the Danube, or only recently settled to the south, the traditional religion of these folk took on greater historical significance within the empire. Generally they were non-Christian. Of course, they could have been converted.[29] A final flourishing of a pagan flag against Christian enemies was for a losing cause in the 390s; but it is surely significant that anyone in command would still choose to advertise his paganism and, by implication or by hope, his men's as well, through portraits of Hercules on their banners. Over their battle efforts other icons presided, too, of Jupiter specially posted on the hilltops. Their failure afforded welcome material to Christian poets and panegyrists.[30]

An army officer used contributions from other pious people to the shrine of Nodens to commission a handsome mosaic there. This was in Britain early in the generation following Julian's death. The shrine was then attracting a tremendous traffic of pilgrims.[31] Let the inscription serve to introduce the question, whether it was hard or easy to remain non-Christian in various settings over the last third of the century; for I suppose that religious loyalty needs at least some support from the surrounding community. If you were to notice that, recently, a great many of your comrades or neighbors were no longer attending the temple or that they seemed always to be attacking you for your own attendance, surely your comfortableness in your beliefs would suffer; beyond this social and psychological likelihood was the spiritual and theological fact that Nodens, or any god, induced belief through his efficacy, which, if lightly challenged, was seen to fade away. On the other hand, when a person of prestige and the habit of command set his name on a new mosaic floor for the god, and when you saw the precincts thronged on holy days with crowds from miles and miles away, you were bound to feel confirmed in your faith: Nodens really did exist and did *work*.

Accordingly, it is more than aimless head-counting to try to determine whether worshipers were numerous enough to provide each other with the communal affirmation that most belief for most people requires. It is rather useful and necessary to know that there were in fact dozens of British shrines besides that of Nodens still active as centers of worship in the latter half of the fourth century.[32] Granted, the record is almost wholly archeological: rebuilding, redecorating, abundance of small finds, and so on. But it suffices. On the other side, the evidence for British churches in the same period shows that they were few, small, and poor.

An island indeed, in those days! quite isolated from the pressures at the center of the empire (meaning the emperor's court, whether at Milan, Trier, Constantinople, or Antioch). Another island, Sardinia, remained almost wholly non-Christian to a far later date— likewise, all but the urbanized areas of Gaul, Spain, and northern Italy. But that last region's largest center, Milan, was half pagan.[33] Rome itself was more pagan than Christian until the 390s, when the balance began to change, perhaps sharply. Before that, the two sides might argue about the numbers of their supporters among the aristocracy but, if they were roughly equal, non-Christians nevertheless outweighed the Christians in wealth and position. It may be supposed that their households and tenants were of their own persuasion. They filled at least some of the traditional priesthoods, expressed a usual or even more than traditional devotion in their prayers inscribed on stone for all to see, and went through initiations publicly.[34] In the two port-towns of the capital at the mouth of the Tiber, pagan priesthoods were filled openly, not all from within senatorial ranks, and building went on at various pagan centers.

In late-fourth-century northern and western Europe, if we bear in mind that most people lived in villas, villages, and rural market-towns, non-Christians thus held out very strongly. That seems a certainty because, whenever this little-mentioned but greatly preponderant part of the population is for some moment illuminated, we glimpse only idols and temples and (as our almost invariably Christian sources lament) unregenerate superstition. The church in Italy and these provinces thus made up only a minority.

It was, however, the heir of A.D. 312, endowed beyond its own powerful resources in wonder-working[35] with the favor of the civil authorities. By direct or indirect operation, the latter counted for much: indirectly, by countenancing the use of force at the local level—for example, on Minorca, where a convert yielded to riots with the declaration, "I therefore am thinking of the danger to my life, and so off I go now to the church, to evade the death that otherwise awaits me"; directly, when the families of the losers in the civil war of A.D. 394 took refuge from the battlefield in churches, though themselves non-Christians, and the victorious emperor Theodosius let them redeem their lives by becoming Christians.[36] This was in northern Italy, ending the movement that had supported Eugenius. The two episodes throw into relief the strength of non-Christian resistance, to require such uncivil measures and at so very late a date.

Between the Roman nobility and North Africa the closest ties existed, especially economic. Here was a region of quite dense population and fine farming: the provinces of Proconsularis and most of Numidia and Byzacena. Much land was owned by senatorial absentees; high administrative positions were routinely held by representatives of great Roman families come over for their term of office. Perhaps North African non-Christians sheltered behind their influence. In any case, the better-known cities, from Carthage on down, appear to have had large and noisy non-Christian populations supporting priesthoods, temples, and a flow of funds enough to keep them all healthy—side by side, of course, with new ecclesiastical building, too, and plenty of friction between Christians and all other cults. Certain reported episodes in the history of these relations are hard to understand if the non-Christians are not thought of as the majority: for example, at Calama and Madauros, both in the Bagradas valley, where there was violence; less clearly, at Sufes and Carthage, likewise sites of rioting.[37] Over the region as a whole, the ratio of religious groups, one to another, cannot be closely determined. The evidence is too sparse, and within it there is too much of the Christian—hence the likelihood of distortion.[38] It is only safe to say, I think, that non-Christians made up a very large minority still at the beginning of the fifth century. Perhaps they constituted a half, given the number of centers still awaiting a bishop at that date.

In Egypt, history hardly seemed to happen outside of Alexandria. There, in the theater and the streets, non-Christians rioted against the emperor's hostility toward their beliefs in the 380s and 390s.[39] Until that time, they had enjoyed free access to their shrines and the regular schedule of their sacrifices—indeed, the city had served as point of repair for throngs of pilgrims.[40] Outside, the sources show churches and monasteries but also temples and processions: perhaps the numerical balance tipped toward Christianity in the 390s.[41]

Finally, Syria. Its capital, Antioch, in that decade was two-thirds Christian, by a reasonable guess.[42] Here (almost) Christianity had begun and boasted its longest turn and some of its most famous leaders. In the surrounding countryside, however, things were different. The peasants sent up their prayers to the gods, there were big temples drawing crowds, even whole towns that were non-Christian.[43] So far as one can form an impression of numbers at the turn of the fourth to fifth century, the entire Levant from the Euphrates south to Egypt was not much more than half converted.

Everyone is agreed that the church started as an urban phenomenon and continued in that tendency throughout our period of study; and scenes of change that surviving sources typically preserve show missionary impulses moving out from the centers to less populated areas, not the other way round. So everyone assumes, and surely they are right, that the countryside lagged far behind the cities in degree of Christianization. It is also agreed on all hands that a great majority of the empire's total population lived outside the cities. And, last, it is obvious that that majority is less reported in our evidence. It follows from all this that the Danube and north Balkan provinces, Cyrenaica, Asia Minor—in sum, vast parts of the empire that lie outside our range of clear sight—must be counted as less vigorously evangelized than the nearest parts better known: Noricum less than Italy; Mauretania less than Numidia. When that general supposition is added to the rest of my survey of percentages, the empire overall appears to have been predominantly non-Christian in A.D. 400.

That conclusion—call it a fact, if the reasoning seems clear and

fair—is of some interest immediately; for it immediately conflicts
with the impression that anyone might form casually from the
reading of ancient or modern histories of the later empire. Those
histories, of course, from several self-evident causes, tend to concentrate on ecclesiastical affairs. Thus they block off the light from
the specifically non-Christian (though not from all secular) affairs.
Even when adjustment is made for the resulting distortions in the
record, there remains some conflict between the actual achievement
of the state and what, likewise from casual reading, we would expect from nearly a hundred years of Christian monarchy. I turn to
this matter in the next chapter. It is enough to say here that the limits on success were set by the nature of late imperial government,
which tends to be credited with many times the power it wielded in
reality.

In any case, is the question of numbers the only one to be concerned with, or even the most revealing and helpful? I return to another question with which the earlier pages of this chapter dealt:
daily behavior, and the thoughts and feelings to which behavior
points. For it is possible that the *feel* of a community, judged by ob-
servable actions and conversations, might be Christian even if most
people in it were not; or vice versa. And that would be the result of
what I have called "noise," for lack of a better term. I mean the
readiness and capacity to attract attention, such as could be found
among Christians much more than among non-Christians. Thereby
the former seem to me to have enjoyed far more historical significance than their numbers alone could explain.

Noise is what you could hear "at a festival of the pagans," where
"the sacrilegious ceremonies were carried out . . . [by] a most unre-
strained, dancing mob on the street running right past the doors of
the church" of an African city in A.D. 408. Augustine was shocked.
Or you could hear it on the edge of Antioch a few years earlier,
"when the whole city together moves out to the suburbs . . . in one
of the notable pagan festivals called 'Olympic,' every fourth year,
celebrated in honor of Heracles' labors; and, in this, women by the
herds (so to speak) rush out with the crowds to Daphne to see the
contests."[44] Such are non-Christian beliefs caught, not at their
prettiest (our reporters are churchmen), but certainly in full vitality—beliefs equipped with a ceremony, a locus, a schedule, a divine
being, and an adequate company of people. Before A.D. 312 it
would have been easy to hear and see activities like this going on

everywhere in the empire; by A.D. 400 or so, it was very rare. And yet pagans still made up a good half of the population. An interesting fact, then: they existed, but they had been taught to keep quiet.

It remains for another book to explore further just what noise and silence might mean in the way of life of both pagans and Christians of the fourth and later Roman centuries. What effect did the two populations really exert on each other, the one by its ancient claims, the other by its jubilant publicity? Is it not striking to discover a pagan priest post-400 preaching to a pagan congregation on the raised, the purified, the allegorized and more edifying signification of pagan myth, just as if he were a bishop speaking to his flock? I know of nothing at all like this in untouched paganism earlier.

Such a phenomenon, however, was very unusual. Far more powerful was the influence exerted in the opposite direction. That produced effects upon church ceremonial, liturgy, costume, music, organization, burial, iconography, architecture, and so on and so forth. I refer to the beginning of this chapter for other signs of the process. But what else could be expected when the five million of A.D. 312 had to teach and make brothers and sisters of five times their own number in the space of a few generations? "As conversion progresses, the new religion becomes in its social dimension increasingly like the old. . . . In the long run, conversion gave rise to strong pressures that affected the course of development of the new religion."[45] Of course—and some day it would be interesting to explore in a large, synthetic way just how much of their past the converts of the fourth century carried into church with them and how much they left outside.

X

Conversion by Coercion

Increase in numbers of Christians from five to thirty million, let us say, in less than a century, constituted remarkable growth, a quintupling wholly through conversion (for there is no reason to think that Christian families differed at all from pagan ones in their rate of births or deaths). The increase was both cause and effect of the church's assertiveness. There are passages in Ambrose's sermons of exuberant congratulation to his flock on their swelling numbers and their need for larger quarters. Bishop Porphyry of Gaza near the same date bid his friends to have more faith, when they doubted the wisdom of building so extremely vast a cathedral. It would be filled, he said.[1]

Or did he? The Life of Porphyry[2] is the source for the anecdote. It is recounted by his deacon and devoted coadjutor, Mark. At least, there exists a rather substantial biography purporting to be by such a person, written in the first-person singular or plural, and containing many points of personal participation and reminiscence. From Greek, it was translated into several modern languages (the last was French, in 1930) and so comes to be routinely cited as real history by all sorts of fine scholars. There is a strong temptation to use it because it is so full, specific, and vivid. Paul Peeters, however, called attention to its copying word for word (or almost) quite considerable pieces from another work of a date so late that "Mark," according to his own chronology, could not have been alive to read it. Other proofs accumulated showing that the work was, in some respects anyway, and in some passages, a fake. Later, Peeters edited an early Georgian Life obviously related to the Greek, preceding it by a century or more, less elegant and less elaborate. But his commentary was technical, and he turned the Georgian not into any modern tongue but into Latin. The Greek Life, in French, therefore continues to be seen in the best circles.

Peeters persuades me that both the Georgian and the Greek versions developed out of a common source written in Syriac (the language spoken around Gaza); that that source dated to the later fifth or sixth century; and that the Greek is subsequent to that, most likely after the mid-sixth century, and departs more from its model, i.e., is even less reliable. Richly detailed glimpses of imperial circles and great names at Constantinople are all fake; specific important people—an archbishop, a governor, and others—are fake; and Mark and Porphyry themselves may well never have existed at all.

It is worth my while to say all this rather than pass by the biography in silence, because its inclusion might be expected in a book like this, and also because it contains anecdotes that can only have been built up from materials carefully chosen for the credibility they would merit among readers—readers familiar with whole libraries of accounts now lost to us (and the biography attempts to compete, so to speak, with the most accurately historical and detailed of those accounts). It should be possible, then, to learn about the general way things happened in well-known and recurring situations around the turn of the fourth century, even as they appear in a manifestly deceptive text.

And fortunately the selection of evidence from the Life need not be across a broad front. My interest focuses only on how non-Christians were won over to the church. Of this process there are a number of illustrations, which fall into two categories.

The first describes response to the miraculous. Bishop Porphyry, having been sent down to Gaza as the new incumbent in the 390s, finds a city very largely non-Christian (§4, 41, and 64), indeed, with eight different temples to eight different deities and villages around it that are entirely pagan (§17). The city is suffering from a spell of drought. When supplication even in the city's chief temple to Nonos brings no rain, Porphyry's prayers succeed better; whereupon "many idolaters believed in God and loudly called out, 'Great is the god of the Christians!'" (§17—here and elsewhere I cite from the Georgian text in translation, but only at points where the Greek text is closely similar). The episode is just such as Tertullian boasted of, down to the very words of exclamation; and they, in turn, are just such as non-Christians commonly did use to greet a miracle. More conversions are attributed to another wonder (§28) that saves a young mother in the midst of a difficult delivery, inducing from the witnesses the cry, "Great is the god of the Christians! There is no god but he!" (§31). This, however, was their part of a bargain they had made by which, if the woman's and the baby's lives were saved by prayer, they and the whole family would join the church (§29). Similarly, Porphyry offers the empress a male heir later, if she will build him a church (§42 f.) and holds out the prospect of calm seas and salvation from shipwreck to a ship's captain if he will renounce his errors (§56 f.). The same bargains, the same *do ut des,* the same heartfelt faith resulting, we have often encountered before (see above, pp. 4 and 13ff.).

On another occasion, the sign of the cross expels a daimon (whom the non-Christians call a "god") from his home in an icon—familiar feat; and men who had aimed abuse at the Christians are killed during their offering of a sacrifice by the collapse of temple columns (§61): "A number of idolaters see this miracle and straightway believe in our Lord Jesus Christ; and so, converted from superstition, they accompanied us to church and were baptized" (§62). That, too, is a train of cause and effect often seen in earlier instances (pp. 60–62) but also later, when an insincere Christian is divinely detected and dies a sticky death (§70), or a deluded prophetess challenges the bishop to debate but is struck dumb and dies on the spot before she can utter a word of her false teachings (§90); the bystanders are hurried off to baptism. The miraculous saving of three children and the divine branding of the saved, equally produce converts: "in awe at the sign of the cross, pagans were straightway made Christians" (§82). Porphyry's successes are in the tradition central to the story of the church's growth since the beginning.

There is also an element familiar only from the time of Constantine's reign forward: imperial cash gifts, some of them quite gigantic (§§40, 51, 53, 54, 75, 84, and 92). The role of material rewards in church growth I examined earlier. The Life here adds little about its effectiveness. Besides, it is only once explicitly linked to conversion, and then in the wrong way, that is, to non-Christian cult (§85).

What I have not yet mentioned, and what rounds out all the evidence on motivation that can be found in the Life, is the use of armed force. It belongs peculiarly to the closing decades of the fourth century. Intrigues and the pulling of the right strings in the capital that produce for Porphyry a high churchman's help, then a high official's, and then help still closer to the throne, until at last a letter is obtained from the emperor himself to be read aloud to the populace of Gaza by a commander at the head of his troops—all this may be pure invention (§§37–51, 63–75, and 99). But it fits the times. Its historical aptness will appear in a moment. Here I point out only the altogether predictable results. All Gaza's temples are torn down and burned and the city is cleansed of every belief but the Christian (§103). The most stubborn opponents, faute de mieux, are tied up, marched away to the provincial capital, severely tortured, and all killed *mala morte,* "a great number" (§99). Less stubborn folk repair to Porphyry's grand new church. There a question is raised about those "who had not left their mistaken ways of their free will but in fear and terror of the emperors" (§73), to which Porphyry answers "as the Apostle had: Whether falsely or truly, Christ is preached, and I rejoice in that.'" (Phil. 1:18). His views fit naturally in a tradition already well established (see above, pp. 57 and 65).

There we have the whole story of what happened (and, if really so, only by the inventor's good luck), or at least what certainly might well have happened, given the practices and common events attested in the period. It is beyond dispute that Gaza was very largely non-Christian before Porphyry's time, whereas, at the end, all local religious traditions had been entirely suppressed. The crude fact of the city's conversion is known (without any role for Porphyry) from other sources. But beyond miracles and money, the element presented to readers as essential to the final solution—the element on which I wish now to focus—is evidently force. Without that, pagan intransigence simply could not be overcome. And Gaza, I think, may be taken as a sort of model for the empire as a whole.[5]

The details of how, in that city, push came to shove, little provocations or collisions led to big ones, and many persons ultimately died, are of only heuristic interest. There is no reason to think they can be trusted. But, beginning with a near-fatal beating administered to a collector of church rents (§22), they do serve as a reminder that there were two sources of violence that might be brought to bear on religious disputes—violence from below or from above—and that the two might have quite separate histories. The emperor Arcadius is portrayed as quite unhappy about using compulsion (§41). He was, rather, concerned not to disturb the flow of taxes into his treasury and would obviously have preferred the local folk to do whatever they wanted without involving *him.*

Contrariwise, it could be an emperor who insisted on harsh action, while neighbors at the local level just wished to be left in peace. The latter situation can be seen very vividly in an African city in A.D. 303: "The community of Cirta, during Diocletian's time, is better known to us than any other in the Christian world."[4] There, the petty magistrates, Christian and non-Christian, cooperated to minimize suffering under the Great Persecutions, while the ranks above them tried to engage them in lethal conflict.

Given the differences to be discovered in the play of forces local and imperial, Christian and non-Christian, in different moments and places of the fourth century, there is some temptation to let it all go as a catalogue. But even that can advance our understanding. When looked at overall, a sort of beginning and end emerge. Naturally, the beginning belongs to the reign of Constantine, under whom pagans are reported to have lynched the deacon of a Lebanese city. Their subsequent horrible diseases make them an object-lesson to their coreligionists.[5] More trustworthy is the order of the southern Spanish bishops, assembled in A.D. 305, that "anyone who breaks idols and gets killed at it" does not formally count as a martyr; the provocation is too blatant.[6]

Apparently at a date not much earlier, there had been street fighting between Christians and non-Christians in Alexandria, at the other end of the Mediterranean. Eusebius makes bare mention of it.[7] But Alexandria had a history and a population unlike that of any other great center in antiquity, disturbed again and again by outbursts of mob action. They recurred under Constantine's successor in the east, Constantius (A.D. 337–61), whose struggle with his fellow-Christian, the bishop Athanasius, stretched out over decades and involved the whole city. Athanasius and his churches were at first attacked by the non-Christians in 341, thus aiding a different party of Christians—so he says, perhaps to raise doubts about the doctrinal integrity of his enemies. But in 356 the non-Christians supported him.[8] In 363 they killed Bishop George for repeated acts of pointed outrage, insult, and pillage of the most sacred treasures of the city. The emperor Julian, like Theodosius twenty-five years later, was talked out of harsh reprisals by his advisers.[9]

After mid-century, religious tensions in the east had evidently increased, for a while. Public displays of pagan piety might bring reprisal of some sort. They required courage. There were incidents of vandalism against non-Christian shrines in what is now central

Turkey in the 350s and early in Julian's reign; also in Syria (a bishop was lynched by pagans who had not forgiven his destruction of their city's chief temple.)[10] Some years later, Bishop Gregory of Nazianzus recalled that incident, justifying the destruction as having been authorized by the emperor. He must have been referring to some law no longer preserved, certainly of small effect. It is neither mentioned elsewhere among church writers nor invoked by other anti-pagan zealots. Indeed, we hear of no further clashes for twenty years or more. Through Constantine's measures to strip away temples' property, and his son's, to shut their gates, they had deteriorated badly—in some eastern areas, anyway.[11] But relations between Christians and non-Christians were, if unpleasant, at least not very bloody or dramatic during the years thereafter, up to the 380s. Had the reverse been true, we would know. Writers like Libanius and Sozomen had reason to present a full record.

The fact is surprising, for, whatever may be said against its persecutors, earlier, the church even quite undisturbed was not a good neighbor. Detestation of non-Christians, found in Constantine's edicts, can also be heard in the urgings of a recent convert under the reign of his sons:[12] "There remains only a very little for your laws to accomplish, whereby the devil may lie prostrate and overthrown before them, and the baneful contamination of a dead idolatry shall have vanished away. . . . Raise aloft the banner of faith! For you this is divinely appointed! . . . Need commands you, most sacred emperors, to exact vengeance and punishment upon this evil! This is prescribed to you by the law of the supreme deity, that Your Severity should follow up on all fronts the crime of idolatry."

A century later, passion still shook the bishop Theodoret when he recalled an apostate of the 370s, whose "entrails were destroyed by rot" as merited penalty for his betrayal, so "he could no longer discharge his dung through the proper parts; and his abominable mouth, organ of his blasphemy, became the part for excretion of dung."[13] Abuse traditional in ancient rhetoric and polemic, though most barbarous and repugnant to us, barely sufficed to express the feelings of a considerable sampling of church champions when they spoke of people whose religious beliefs differed from their own. Small wonder that their behavior should match their words in explosive animus!

It is important to make clear and vivid this trait of early Christianity. Otherwise its actions cannot be understood. And it is a trait not always given due prominence in modern accounts. On the contrary, Tertullian is more likely to be quoted, drawing attention to a quite different character among his coreligionists: "See what love they bear toward each other!" In support, their care of the poor among them is adduced, with abundant and unchallengeable testimony; even more remarkable, though less often noticed, is their care of the plague-stricken, whether or not of their own faith and at the obvious risk of their own lives.[14] Behold an ethic of love new, taught, and at work before one's very eyes!

But it could only be displayed from parity or strength, toward the like-minded or toward suppliant sufferers. It must never involve any cost to doctrine. Anyone who asserted wrong teachings, anyone serving the devil or his demons, earned instead an equally remarkable antagonism. In their official high meetings together, Christians thus could not keep their own disagreements within the bounds of civil language;[15] their continual quarrels required the intervention of the civil authorities; and all this was well known and noted by friends and foes alike.

Their behavior was not the result of toleration, of the lifting of the lid, of heady moments of release under benevolent rulers after 312. Two scenes from earlier times show a readiness for mortal animosity holding sway over great churches in the very moment of attack from outside. First is Carthage in 304, where the victims of a search of the city were thrown in jail, there to suffer from their wounds and chains but also from hunger and thirst; for the jail-keepers didn't feed you, that had to be done by your friends. A hostile crowd of Christians, however, set "whips and scourges and armed men in front of the prison gates in order, by inflicting serious hurt on persons entering or leaving, to prevent them from supplying food and drink to the martyrs."[16]

The second incident occurred the next year in another prison, this time in Alexandria, where the competing Egyptian church leaders found themselves confined together; and "when the archbishop Peter realized that Melitius and his party were opposed to his more humane counsels" (regarding Christians who had buckled under persecution), "filled as they were with excessive religious zeal, he [Peter] made a curtain down the middle of their cell, by hanging up a cloak, a blanket, a shirt; and he declared through a deacon, 'There are some who are of my view, let them come over on my side, and those of Melitius' view, stay with Melitius.'" After which, the two parties went on with their lives, their prayers, and the term of their incarceration, rigidly ignoring each others' existence.[17]

In the light of their doctrinal dualism and the intransigence, sometimes amounting to ferocity, with which its spirit was applied, Christians might have been expected to press their differences home with every device and force available. Moreover, if they are measured by their bishops (and a better yardstick is not easily thought of), close to half the population who called themselves church members toward mid-century must have belonged to some allegiance other than the one that ultimately prevailed: in other words, they were Arian, Donatist, or Meletian.[18] Sectarian rivalry was thus a very real thing, a spur to great exertions. Egypt especially, being split three ways, echoed to the shouts of partisans, the din of violence, and laments for those robbed, stripped naked, flogged, imprisoned, exiled, sent to the quarries and coppermines, conscripted into the army, tortured, decapitated, strangled, or stoned or beaten to death. The express object was to make converts. Force therefore aimed (or at least is advertised by the sufferers as aiming) often at bishops, monks, nuns, and other most easily identified adherents. Imperial officials and their troops played an extremely prominent role in all this—naturally, to account for the severity of punishments and loss of life; and it was a role played in numerous disconnected acts, from Constantine's reign beyond Athanasius' death in A.D. 373. Constantine's publicly proclaimed edicts against "Arius, wicked and impious" (A.D. 333), announce the cause and stimulate the contestants; he goes on to promise that "whoever hides them" (Arius' writings) "shall be condemned to death";[19] and the course of action that then followed was, as we have seen, entangled in deadly struggles.

Application of physical coercion to produce conformity of cult within the church of other eastern provinces outside of Egypt can be traced through various fourth-century sources and episodes. Perhaps the most striking is the law imposing the death penalty for celebrating Easter on the wrong day of the year (A.D. 382).[20] But the record does not really resemble that of Egypt. Why not? Explanation must lie chiefly in the character of the population, in their long-formed habits and patterns of community action. But there were also hidden feuds, political debts, partnerships among power-

ful people, which could be used to widen a dispute. The narrator of
Porphyry's life well understood their role. They drew even non-
Christians into church disputes.[21]

In Milan, Bishop Ambrose's doctrine brought him into conflict
with the emperor himself (a little boy, Valentinian II) and his
mother—hence "the church itself ringed about with soldiers bearing arms," in Augustine's summary. Thereafter, many tense moments.[22] Augustine is likewise our source (along with other materials) for the struggles inside the church in North Africa, in which
bishops and priests had their eyes torn out, as he relates, and "one
bishop had his hands and tongue cut off."[23] At the roots of such
atrocities lie not only the strength of passion on both sides but the
invocation of civil force. Mustered under one of Constantine's
"most savage laws, against the party of [Bishop] Donatus," by 317
it had filled the well outside the chief Donatist church in Carthage
with the bodies of the slain, long afterward to be discovered by excavation. The tale of armed violence in North Africa far into the
fifth century has been told by W. H. C. Frend and others.[24]

Last, in A.D. 383 at Bordeaux, Urbica was stoned to death for her
beliefs, and the bishop she followed, Priscillian, was charged as a
heretic by a synod there assembled in the next year. He appealed to
the western emperor, whom other bishops in turn inflamed against
him. He was accordingly tried, found guilty, and executed by the
praetorian prefect, along with others of his views.[25]

My object in this brief glance at Arianism, Meletianism, Donatism, and Priscillianism is, I hope, clear: it is not to deal with them
on their own terms, but rather to convey some sense of the habits
of action that prevailed wherever people discovered religious views
among their neighbors that they could not or would not tolerate.
Only as illustrative of those habits, and not as especially pressing in
itself, can the campaign against paganism be understood. Against
that larger background of purely internal Christian bitternesses just
sketched, we find the hot point, so to speak, in Alexandria; much
less common and much less lethal rivalries in other eastern parts; se-
vere collisions in North Africa; others in northern Italy; little elsewhere; and recourse by the disputants to the courts, the emperor,
and his soldiers, requesting them to intervene. All this is also exactly what we find in the less published story of pagan–Christian
relations.

Two points may be added to what has been said earlier in this chapter and elsewhere regarding the active persecution of non-Christians: first, there began to be laws; and second, there began to be leaders. The latter were bishops of increasingly broad and well-defined authority. The energetic preaching of those at Turin, Brescia, Verona, Ravenna, Como, and of course Milan, is reported to us or can be read today in their sermons. I suppose we have this cluster of North Italian evidence by the chance of manuscript tradition, not because that region produced an especially large number of very active historical figures. From other regions we happen to know only of Caesarius of Arles and Priscillian in northern Spain; but we may count Martin, bishop of Tours (A.D. 372–97), who certainly preached and certainly destroyed temples. Nothing from his pen has survived.[26]

Earlier there were bishop-martyrs. Before setting off to attack the enemies' shrines, no doubt they assembled and inspired their flock around them (see above, p. 65); later, at the turn of the century, Augustine addressed his congregation in Carthage with ringing invocations to smash all tangible symbols of paganism they could lay their hands on; "for," he tells them, "that all superstition of pagans and heathens should be annihilated is what God wants, God commands, God proclaims!"—words uttered "to wild applause," as one modern biographer puts it, and very possibly the cause of religious riots, with sixty dead, in a city to the south. So another biographer supposes, very reasonably.[27] For mobs must be worked up, the impulse spreads, and region and times alike were inflammable.

Laws mattered less. They should be thought of as licenses to take action, like a hunting or barber's license today. Compulsion was unlikely and soon spent, except where the most particular effort was given to it from high authorities. A person, or more probably a group or interest, obtained support from the emperor; he issued his edicts; the original petitioners then spurred or bribed or nagged a provincial official into enforcing it until he got tired or was deflected. There were no police, state prosecutors, detectives, or the like to initiate coercion. Accordingly, a law reflects somebody's pressing need at a certain time. It does not show what was thereafter common practice in the empire.

Emperors themselves, unchallenged autocrats for centuries, interfered on their own initiative whenever they saw something that needed their attention. Constantine, the first in the Christian line, as soon as he began to think of himself as a Christian, thrust his pre-

dictably peremptory patronage into the center of Christian problems—first in Carthage and then in Alexandria. In the course of
speaking out on the disputes there associated with the names Donatus and Arius, he also spoke out on non-Christians, as we have
seen. They were a bad lot. He would have liked to obliterate them,
no doubt. But, lacking the means for that, and only toward the end
of his reign, he had to be content with robbing their temples. That
in itself, when one thinks about it, was of course a highly provoca-
tive and risky piece of sacrilege. The cries of outrage, however, are
heard only long after the event.

By established tradition, he restrained religious practices that
might diminish divine favor or disturb the state. With this, we first
begin to sense anti-pagan legislation, through which religious liberty was to be reduced, at the last, to nothing. Needless to say,
hexing the imperial house was illegal. Divination except at the usual
shrines was suspect. If it touched on political questions, it was a
capital crime (and Constantine, for added emphasis, specified death
by burning as the penalty). Nocturnal rites were held suspect (A.D.
353—the Eleusinian mysteries tolerated by afterthought). Constantius (A.D. 337–61) was extremely concerned about the whole
matter and wrote a string of decrees; so did Valens, over the years
364–71. The latter shows what was on his mind: the reading of the
future through inspection of animal entrails. As appears abundantly
in the history of his reign, he was quite paranoid about his subjects'
finding out the "who" and the "how" of his replacement. His
brother ruling in the west had to intervene with contradictory legislation: "I judge that *haruspicina* [reading animal entrails] has no connection with cases of magic, and I do not consider this *religio* [reli-
gious belief] or any other that was allowed by our elders, to be a
kind of crime. . . . We do not condemn divination but We do forbid it to be practiced harmfully."[28]

The concern expressed here explains another seeming contradiction when, in A.D. 341, Constantius banned sacrifices. He had to
explain what he meant a year or so later: temples were, after all, not
to be destroyed. They were to continue serving as the sites of public entertainment and spectacles. Then, a little later, he ordered
them closed; and, a generation after that, a successor reopened at
least one of them by special legislation.[29]

Besides the trouble emperors always had enforcing their will—a
fact on the periphery of my subject but already mentioned more

than once—they were of two minds about locking the doors of all sacred precincts in all their realm. Their problem must be seen in the mind's eye. At Damascus the sanctuary of Hadad enclosed an area as big as two football fields which served as the city's chief bazaar. This is only an exaggerated illustration of a common fact: temples were centers of commerce. Their porticoes were also commonly used as classrooms by grammar-school teachers and professional rhetors and lecturers; and in Rome the physicians customarily met daily for professional discussions in the shadow of Pax—the closest thing there was to a medical school. Sometimes there were local senate meetings in the porches, banquets of workers' fraternal associations, and so forth.[30] The most used, and ordinarily the most handsome and central, facilities in the empire's cities really could not be declared off-limits. Reality was acknowledged in the careful wording of later laws specifying "loitering with intent" (as our laws say, meaning intent to commit a crime)—that is, no walking about or frequenting temples *for worship*.[31]

In A.D. 356, worship of images was also declared a capital crime. The law was promulgated at Milan. Perhaps it was obeyed for a while; but we know that the city prefect in Rome at the time was not only a pagan but an energetic and public one who dedicated a temple to Apollo in 357 and was by then, or in any case a little later, chief priest both of Vesta and Sol.[32] I need not here repeat all the testimony already cited on the vitality of paganism in mid-century, on the renovation of shrines, and so forth, which continued with barely noticeable diminution for decades. The 356 law was generally ignored. Further, it seems to have been interpreted explicitly as applying only to animal sacrifices, and even those continued to be publicly offered (though remarked on) till the very end of the fourth century.[33]

In the 380s, however, non-Christian cults came under rather suddenly increased attack of a physical sort after a long period of less than mortal danger. It so happened that the church's energies were little occupied in internal strife; responsiveness of congregations to episcopal leadership was well established; and appeal to mobs and armies by that leadership, in the throes of religious dispute, was seen as a more than tolerable option.

Attack began in the eastern provinces with one of the emperor Theodosius' chief officials. He is described by the non-Christian Libanius as a man thoroughly submissive to his wife, as she in turn

was submissive to the monks she had around her. This concatena-
tion—just how we are not told but can easily imagine—led to the
razing of a vast and famous temple on the empire's frontier, perhaps at Edessa, around 385. The date points to the praetorian prefect Cynegius as the official concerned, for the years of his term of
office are known, 384–88. He made a trip to Egypt at the end of it,
remembered as notable for the shutting up of shrines and knocking
down of idols.[34] Theodosius had issued to him, or he had somehow obtained, a particularly harsh edict against anyone making
burnt offerings. A person like the prefect, armed with such legislation, would naturally welcome and vigorously pursue charges of
forbidden sacrifices brought by monks; and, Libanius laments, they
used their license to rampage around the cities (of Syria, evidently)
and particularly the countryside, in vandalizing mobs. They resemble the Egyptian monks a generation later, whose leader, when his
victims brought suit for the return of their holy images, boasted, "I
peacefully removed your gods . . . there is no such thing as 'rob-
bery' for those who truly possess Christ."[35]

At some date between Libanius and these latter figures, Syria saw
Bishop Marcellus of Apamea in operation. He felt he could get no
further with the non-Christians by peaceful exhortation and so used
the license of the law to call in the army against both the chief city
of his see and the villages roundabout. While the demolition crew
was at work on a vast Zeus-shrine in the suburbs one day, and he
was watching from the sidelines, the locals noticed him, grabbed
him, carried him off, and burnt him alive. Later the provincial
council forbade his sons to seek vengeance, saying they should
rather consider him blessed in the opportunity of his martyrdom.
There is something quite unsubdued about the council's reaction, a
reminder that to the very end non-Christian defiance could not be
discounted.[36]

When Theodoret points to Marcellus as "first among the bishops
to use the law as a weapon, and to destroy temples," he doesn't say
what law he had in mind. In fact, there was none we know of before 398. On the other hand, it is clear from Libanius that Christians were in a mood to employ even a 385 law against sacrifices,
and alleged violation of it as an excuse to overthrow or burn down
shrines and altars. When a still more emphatic and sweeping re-
statement of it reached the east in June of 391, it must have offered
an irresistible temptation. Marcellus' campaign, then, and his death
probably belong to that year.[37]

In Alexandria, A.D. 391 produced events rather more violent and, in historical perspective, most important. The familiar elements were at work. The bishop there wanted the temple of Dionysus for a church. He asked Theodosius to assign it to him, and he got it. He used that success as a claim on all the city's temples, took control of them and rifled the vaults of some to learn their secrets. Then, whatever would best arouse contempt and mockery he paraded through the main square. Non-Christians reacted by taking over the Serapeum en masse. They were said to have Christian captives with them, whom they tortured and crucified. After a stand-off of some little time, the bishop called in the provincial troop commander with his soldiers to conduct a sort of siege, while reports to the emperor solicited his intervention. It came in the form of a letter declaring the Christian casualties in the rioting to be martyrs in need of no avenging; but the temple itself was forfeit and, along with all the others, was condemned to destruction.[38] As to non-Christians, their lives were safe, but the emperor's antagonism was clear from his opening words, accusing "the idle superstition of the heathen." Monks were called in from the desert to help in the task of demolition; they next moved on to the sacred buildings at Canopus (where they themselves afterward settled among the ruins); and the impulse to destroy spread rapidly over all of Egypt.[39]

No doubt because Egypt was so wonderfully rich and for centuries had been exporting from Alexandria the fruits of her good fortune, borne in Alexandrian ships by Alexandrian sailors especially to Rome and Constantinople but also to every other harbor in the Mediterranean, for these reasons, her greatest treasure, the Serapeum, was more widely talked about than that of any other center, and so, in proportion, the power and glory of Serapis. Now for the world to hear that Serapis had gone, that he was nothing, that he had been driven from his home by the Christians, exerted a powerful effect. There were conversions almost on the spot.[40]

And, indeed, why not? Theological demonstration by exorcism—behold a God that is a *real* god, not a more daimon!—had here been provided on a scale unprecedented, the greatest conceivable scale. What followed could be no more than minor police operations. So, concludes an eastern emperor a little later (A.D. 398), "If there are temples in the country areas, they shall be destroyed without disturbance or commotion. When they are overthrown and obliterated, the material foundations for all superstition will

have been done away with." Urban shrines were to receive different treatment: they were to be emptied out and the shells of
the buildings given over to ecclesiastical or public use (A.D. 399),
or broken up to provide materials toward utilitarian construction
projects.[41]

And the bishop of Constantinople, "learning that Phoenicia was
still infatuated with the rites of its daimones, assembled monks inflamed with divine zeal and, arming them with imperial laws, sent
them against the sanctuaries of idols," there to provoke resistance
and bloodshed on both sides. This was one of the many postclimac-
tic incidents that belong to the fifth and subsequent centuries.[42] It
would be better, however, not to venture beyond my boundaries of
time; rather, to turn to the western provinces.

The law of June 391, issued by Theodosius from the North Italian city of Aquileia on his way east, was one of a pair, in fact a close
copy of the other of February. The February law was issued from
Milan and represented the will of its bishop, Ambrose; for Theodosius—recently excommunicated by Ambrose, penitent, and very
much under his influence[43]—was no natural zealot. Ambrose, on
the other hand, was very much a Christian. His restless and imperi-
ous ambition for the church's growth, come what might for the
non-Christians, is suggested by his preaching (see above, pp. 55
and 64), and some of the quality of the man is suggested, too, in
the exchange with his sovereign over Callinicum. At issue was the
outburst of that city's bishop and monks against the local Jews. The
emperor proposed to punish the offenders, Christians though they
were. Ambrose would have none of that. "Perhaps that bishop did
grow a little inflamed over the conflagration," he says with an airy
play on words (referring to the burning of a synagogue); "but
should not the rigor of the law yield to piety?". Theodosius for his
part grudgingly conceded that, after all, the monks probably ought
to be forgiven because they were always into crimes of one sort or
another.[44] From the two minds thus revealed, non-Christians
could expect little concern over their "rights."

Indeed, what were they entitled to? The question, even at this
late date, is not wholly rhetorical. "The rights of temples, that no
one should deprive you of them, you litigate daily"—this we find
in the Verona courts a couple of decades earlier; and a couple of decades later, in a Court with a capital C, before the emperor himself,
non-Christians were appealing against "the laws sent to Africa . . .

for the destruction of idols and correction of heretics."[45] Such mentions, bare and puzzling though they are, show one more field on which the contestants met to settle their religious claims.

But force and violence in this period could break through law at any moment. Archeological demonstration of this fact is abundantly scattered across the northern provinces, for which written sources hardly survive: broken buildings, burnt-out buildings, hastily buried icons and sacred vessels.[46] To the south, there is testimony in the fact (A.D. 399) that "Gaudentius and Jovius, Counts of the emperor Honorius, on March 16 overthrew the temples and broke the images of the false gods" in Carthage. "From that time to the present" (writes Augustine, a quarter-century later) "who does not see how much the worship of the name of Christ has increased?"[47] Experience in Carthage thus matched that of Alexandria: smashing the physical fabric of all competing cults could produce solid results, though not absolutely final ones. Smashing spread out from Carthage to other towns, and still there remained some people not convinced or converted. They only became fewer in number and more remote as time went on.[48]

From Rome in 407 issued a decree to the west, "If any images stand even now in the temples and shrines . . . , they shall be torn from their foundations. . . . The buildings themselves of the temples which are situated in cities or towns shall be vindicated to public use. Altars shall be destroyed in all places." Nothing could be more explicit. It was no longer enough to favor the church, no longer enough to forbid the murkier practices of pagan cults; now anything and everything to do with them must be annihilated. It had been a long war. "We recognize," the emperors continue, "that this regulation has been very often decreed by repeated sanctions."[49] But by A.D. 407 it could be fairly claimed that non-Christians were outlaws at last, and (it followed) that a state religion had at last emerged.[50]

XI

Summary

Anyone at all curious about what is being explored here must regret the lack of decent sources of information. Yet the quite limited sources to which we do have access are enough to convey the complexity and changefulness of our subject, and therefore to make simple assertions untrue—not wholly untrue, but mere half-truths, quarter-truths, or truths of still more watery dilution: "The army was officially Christian after 312" or "The church triumphed because of . . ." any one of ten elements or factors. Such statements are unacceptable, not because any of us wants complexity in and for itself, but because, by their excessive clarification, they filter out too much fact.

Unfiltered and unsorted, however, our surviving information remains entirely obscure. If it is all to be held in the mind and understood, its most significant elements must be identified—I mean significant in historical impact, according to the sense defined in an earlier chapter.

Nothing counts for more than the year 312, which brought Constantine's conversion, or 313, with the Edict of Milan. The toleration of the latter simply made manifest the meaning of the former date.

Prior to that, the clusters of Christians inside the cities had been obliged over many generations to conduct themselves very discreetly in their relations with their unpersuaded neighbors. They did not advertise themselves in writing. This fact is worth thinking about. Anyone who wants to acquaint himself with the religious life of the empire, whatever literary sources he may also find useful, must really begin and end with inscriptions. He is, of course, not too ill-served by that medium. They are numerous (in Latin alone, on all subjects and of all types, a quarter of a million), they arise from ubiquitous habits of display; they particularly record moments and events in people's lives of religious significance (prayers, deaths, and thanksgiving); yet from the Christian population they exist in only tiny numbers. Then, for reasons not relevant here, the habit of inscriptions is more or less given up for a half-century. When it returned, partially, Christians were prominent among inscriptions. What happened? Merely, A.D. 312/313—that is, the prominence of Christians postdates and is explained by the grant of toleration.

Therein are two points to be observed. First, our sense of the church's size and significance depends on sources of information that reach us in deceptive trickles or deceptive floods. Second, relations between the clusters of Christians and their neighbors determined how much "presence" the former might have, how much "noise" they might make—in short, how openly they might indulge their evangelical impulse.

Viewed from the outside, those clusters differed from other cult groups that we know of in keeping very much to themselves, at least prior to 312. Their neighbors looked on them with suspicion. They were ready to believe the worst of them, indeed freely to invent it. Occasionally they expressed in mob terms (shouting in the theater, most likely) those feelings that must also have been expressed by individuals in less harsh ways. So Christians kept quiet. Whether they did so because of the ill-will around them, or rather aroused it by their exclusive behavior, is unclear. No doubt both explanations are partly right. We sense how they got on with non-Christians in second-century Lyon and Smyrna and Carthage, through passages of famous martyr-acts and from Tertullian's recalling of the shouts, "Christians to the lions!"

The Christians, for their part, held jobs as aldermen or the like, as soldiers, laborers, entertainers (I mean the professional athlete mentioned above or dancers or jockeys in Rome), but most commonly as workers in urban employments not worth mentioning at all. They are not heard of in the countryside. A few (Origen, Cyprian, Lactantius) were teachers and thus gained some little fame. All stirred about in the world because they had a living to make.[1] That was as individuals. As a community, however, meeting for the purposes that defined them, they had drawn a line around themselves, a line guarded against their enemies by a curse. They refused their sons and daughters in marriage to nonmembers. If one half of a couple joined them, the other half had to be talked around, too, or detested.[2] Detestable also, in their descriptions, were many activities which routinely went on in a town and which made for fellowship and good feeling. Suspicion and latent hostility that surrounded congregations were thus returned in good measure by the Christians themselves.

A sort of invisible mine field, ready to produce scowls and pointed derision aimed in both directions at important parts of a person's culture, and occasionally exploding in violence (always anti-Christian, in the period before 312), thus divided church and town. To cross it required a conscious decision.

From the outside, that decision was occasionally made by people of leisure, education, and some special interest in cults and philosophies. They tried Saint Cyprian's work and found it little to their taste. They tried Scripture with the same result—more often than not, I would judge from the defensiveness about the style of Scripture on the part of various church writers, and from the obvious unacceptability of New Testament Greek, according to the usual literary conventions of the time. If Christians wanted to have their Apologies widely circulated, as seems certain, there is no sign they succeeded. In sum, initiative and movement on the part of the educated observer toward the church, like the latter's success in reaching out to such an audience, amounted to very little.

The mass of ordinary people had apparently no greater inclination to cross the barriers of prejudice and find out more about their Christian fellow townsmen. By their own standards there was certainly much in Christian groups that they would have valued—that is, much that they valued and enjoyed in their own non-Christian cult-groups, artisan associations, and retirement and obsequies insurance societies (as they may be termed) common among the lowest classes. It is actually hard to imagine just how the comparison might have appeared to someone in the second or third century. As was quite natural, the non-Christian groups held out promise of loving and considerate behavior by one member toward another, regular meetings under the unseen presidency of a divine being, a little financial help for the weaker members, and many diverse psychological benefits that come from belonging to a close community.[3] Ubiquitous as associations were in the empire's cities, however, too little is known about their internal affairs to say whether many of them offered all or most of these rewards for membership:

the whole list is assembled from bits and pieces of information about scattered individual examples. On the other side of the comparison, we know even less—a lot less—about individual churches.[4] Those of the half-century before my period of study can be seen far more clearly. No doubt they changed as time went on. How much and in what directions cannot really be determined. We therefore lack the necessary evidence to say whether an outsider would have been drawn across the barrier by what he might learn of behavior inside a Christian community.

It is an idle question, not only because the materials for an answer are inadequate, but because the curiosity of contemporaries could not penetrate beyond Christians' own exclusiveness *except through conversion.* First must come belief; only thereafter admission to the group; then, perhaps, further spiritual, psychological, or social rewards. They are never mentioned as inducements to conversion anyway.

Before Constantine, the barrier had to be passed from inside out. That much seems to emerge from what facts we have at our disposal. But the motivation needed to make the passage must have been considerable. As everyone knows, a tradition of advocacy of faith and of drawing other people to the veneration of God was recognized in Judaism and taken over by and fortified in Christianity. The impulse to reach out from the inside was a part of belief itself. In post-Pauline times, however, until official toleration made it safe, open-air preaching is not reliably attested. Even Paul and his fellow preachers had found it, or rather their words had made it, a dangerous business. No one, of course, objected to their publicly discussing religion or exalting their own deity. A lot of that sort of discussion went on among non-Christians, generally in sacred precincts (but since temple grounds were used for all sorts of purposes besides the narrowly cultic—even for the advertising of alien gods—they may be fairly counted as public). What was rather bound to cause trouble was the express denial that the gods existed and that their images and services should be respected. Such talk was "no-god-ly," atheistic. After enough experience of the reaction it produced, Christians gave it up. Within the period studied here, as far as Constantine and a good deal beyond too, they deployed their evangelic energies in different ways.

Those of sufficient intellectual training, themselves believing and speaking to unbelievers of the same cast of mind, are described as

succeeding in their missionary role through the attraction of the
logic in their words. In that effort they were competing with Greek
philosophical schools on their own ground. (And here we should
just note that, among religions of other times and places, logical co-
herence will not often be found as one of the characteristics given
weight; so its existence separate from cult and with its separate tradition in antiquity is therefore quite natural.) It was, however,
common for students in the Greek-speaking half of the empire to
wind up their education with some exposure to the quarrels of Sto-
ics, Peripatetics, Epicureans, and so forth. The convention spread
into the Latin-speaking provinces. It specially attracted youths of an
academic bent; and they sometimes found the experience as necessary as it was troubling to their spiritual development. Their more
intense, complicated thought-world is reflected in long stretches of
Christian propaganda tracts of the second, third, and earlier fourth
centuries—the natural consequence of Christianity's entering new
circles of the dominant culture around it, circles with their own
ways and expectations. As non-Christians discussed the operations
of oracles in their treatises, or the degree of god's concern with this
world, so must Christians; as the latter, like Saint Hilary, tried out
the answers of one philosophical system after another, so had Menippus in Lucian's essay. Purely in terms of numbers, no doubt the
contribution made by such types to the church's growth was insignificant. Yes, but on the other hand it was important that the new
teachings should not be found ill-equipped in intellectual terms, or
incomplete, or vulnerable to tests commonly used in the evaluation
of any school of philosophy. Christianity's elite could make people
take the new creed seriously, not dismiss it through perceptions
perhaps superficial but none the less likely.

Access to higher circles and the effects following from that are
seen more naturally in the period after Constantine. I return to this
matter a page or so further on. Here it is enough to give as illustration only one scene. It is from Philippi, where Paul meets and
speaks with a businesswoman, Lydia, "who was a worshiper of
God, was listening, and the Lord opened her heart to respond to
what Paul said. She was baptized, and her household with her."[5] I
take this to be a true if brief description of what anyone could have
observed at the moment or on other similar occasions both in Paul's
wanderings and in the church's later growth. But of course the
household cannot be polled nor the innermost thoughts of the
daughter of the doorkeeper discovered. I do not believe the girl was

really converted (I invent her just for purposes of explanation). My doubts arise from knowing how few among those who listened to Paul anywhere really did believe, even according to the most partisan accounts, and the consequent small chance that the entire circle of relatives, slaves, free workers lodged on the premises, dependents and their families—perhaps a couple of dozen human beings—would all share Lydia's unusual change of heart on the same day. From which it follows that, by my definition, some were not really converted at all—that, in the whole early church, more than a trivial portion at any given moment can have been Christian only in name, though among them no doubt belief often developed in time, as a result of a person's going through the motions.[6] Why should one do even that? Surely to gain social and material benefits. These need not be spelt out to anyone willing to imagine living day to day in the shoes of the doorkeeper's daughter.

In a person like that, what did produce a genuine conviction that God really existed and his will should be obeyed? This, it will be recalled, is the working definition (not always working!) that I have tried to use. Now to resume discussion of evangelism, which reached across the barriers between non-Christian and Christian: if the exchange between the two was not on that high theoretical level just mentioned, and need not deal with the terms and quarrels of philosophical schools, then by what means could the Christian message be authoritatively driven home?

Here a distinction must be made between proof and content. The latter as it was attested in currency among nonbelievers, or at the moment when first placed before them and subsequently accepted by them, was not complicated—nor could it be, in the circumstances. In some respects it was indeed familiar to its non-Christian audience, perhaps already believed: that there is a single supernatural being greater than all others; that he bestows benefits on those who pay homage to him, bringing blessings on their household, as Celsus puts it;[7] and that the world will one day end in total destruction. Further, and strange, were the views that immortality in a higher world awaits us all, not only a few heroic souls; that there the chosen will continue to enjoy blessings, while unbelievers will suffer endless tortures; and that the whole mass of unbelievers and the realm they serve, with its own supreme being, are at war with the good, and must be continually fought and ultimately conquered.

As presented, these teachings contained alarming news. In occa-

sional glimpses, people's emotional response is indicated. They
were naturally frightened. The teachings, however, might be false.
They had heard other such ideas. All sorts and varieties of millenar-
ian horrifics were in circulation. Certain further points sounded
very improbable. Why believe them? But at that juncture Christian
modes of demonstration were brought to bear. They are clearly,
frequently, and prominently described by church writers; offered
for denial to the most skeptical contemporary readers; and suggested, though in a depreciating and antagonistic way, by the observer Celsus, writing at some time in the last quarter of the second
century. He sums them all up as "trickery." Christians themselves
pointed, rather, to supernatural cures and the expulsion of supernatural beings from diseased persons or from their dwellings in altars
and statues, dramatically performed before clouds of witnesses.

When careful assessment is made of passages in the ancient written evidence that clearly indicate motive—a train of thoughts or sequence of feelings, or the two together—leading a person to conversion, they show (so far as I can discover): first, the operation of a
desire for blessings, least attested; second, and much more often attested, a fear of physical pain—*timor* as Augustine puts it later, *timor*
belonging invariably to conversion; third, and most frequent, credence in miracles.[8] Miracles further served as a proof, not only of
divine authority behind Christian teachings, but as a proof of God's
unique claim to his title, whereas other supernatural beings deserved only to be called daimones.

In taking our measure of Christian wonders, on which Christians
so continually insist, what needs emphasis is not that they were reported and believed, since, after all, the wonders wrought by all
other divine powers were equally reported and believed. We need
not struggle, either—as we did near the close of chapter III—with
the question Did they really occur? Because of our encumbered
imaginations, that could only be a prejudiced sort of struggle anyway (because we ordinarily dismiss non-Christian miracles out of
hand). Nor do we need to stress the fact that the most talked-about
Christian miracles were routinized, in the hands of special officers
of the congregation (there were also special persons trained and paid
for at oracular shrines, to produce and interpret oracular gibberish
and riddles). No, the unique force of Christian wonder-working
that does indeed need emphasis lies in the fact that *it destroyed belief
as well as creating it*—that is, if you credited it, you had then to

credit the view that went with it, denying the character of god to all other divine powers whatsoever.

Let us suppose (if the illustration does not seem too artificial) a hundred pagans confronted with competing miracles wrought by the holy men or holy means of some pagan deity and of the Christian deity; and let us suppose the miracles to have been wonderful in the same degree, and to have produced the same number of converts—fifty each. Yet in the end only the pagan ranks will have been diminished. Fifty pagans have simply added one more name to the pantheon they venerate; but the remaining fifty now deny that pantheon entire. It was this result, destruction, that non-Christians of the time perceived as uniquely Christian; and it was this result which in turn gave so grave a meaning, from the pagan point of view as well as the Christian, to the successive waves of persecution. They were so many waves of desperation.

Wonderful acts, those that restored mental or physical health, of course also constituted one of the "blessings" that awaited converts. To accept such a blessing, however, without loyally maintaining allegiance to the source was dangerous. It brought *timor* into operation once again. Of other thoughts and feelings at work there is no mention in the literary record. Love, remorse, joy, gratitude, spiritual ease, personal fulfillment, the peace of faith, psychological gratifications of any sort—such rewards could come later, with further service to the divine. But there is, in any case, no evidence and therefore no sound reason to think that richer emotional or spiritual experiences could be had in churches than in temples. If anything, surviving texts seem to indicate the opposite.[9] Christian writers themselves, while ignoring such factors in conversion, or very nearly, choose rather to portray the learned and sophisticated as having been won over by sheer force of logic, and the unlearned, by a sort of stupefaction or terror before the greatness of God's power. Of course, this is not what we would expect if we reasoned backward from more recent missionary successes to the ancient; but it is very much what we might expect if, as nearly as we could, we thought ourselves into the forums, the streets and halls and houses of the empire, and as born members of that world listened to the Christian message.

Prior to the Peace of the Church in 313, the great mass of new members entered under the impetus of this message, won over both by its proofs and its content. It was a great mass indeed: on the order of half a million in each generation from the end of the first century up to the proclaiming of toleration (the increase was unevenly distributed, and the figure is meant only to suggest the dimensions of growth). No other new cult anywhere nearly approached the same success. It can only be called extraordinary—just how extraordinary depends in part on whether one thinks the Christian credo *as it was actually known to potential converts* must have seemed much more pressing than the credo of any non-Christian cult. Certainly it was presented in sharply yes-or-no, black-and-white, friend-or-foe terms; and those were unique. In part, however, the plain fact of evangelical effort in itself set Christianity apart and must be counted in any estimate of what happened. Belief in no other god but Yahweh entailed an obligation to speak in his praise and win over other worshipers to his service. That tradition, carried forward from Judaism, was also unique. Urgency, evangelism, and the demand that the believer deny the title of god to all but one, made up the force that alternative beliefs could not match.

Underlying these three characteristics taken together was an evident readiness for battle. Nothing like that belonged to other cults. It found expression in Saint Paul's words, already quoted, where he exhorts his readers to "take up the shield of faith, wherewith ye shall be able to quench all the fiery darts of the Evil One," and so on. The same spirit animated a view of wickedness in the world that saw, all round, demons and their terrestial agents ever at work against good Christians, in the service of Him-Who-Hates-the-Good (*misokalos,* common epithet for the Devil). Apologists spoke in these terms; so did Origen's fellow Christians (his report likewise was quoted earlier). But I have noted, too, how Christians, at least by the first half of the second century, had established a reputation for themselves as blasphemers, a reputation which they could have avoided without betraying their beliefs (as Bishop Dionysius showed, for example, in a noncombative passage that I cite in chapter II). Instead, they preferred to confront their neighbors with the unwelcome truth: "gods" were only daimones.

Beyond that, Athenagoras and Tertullian and Justin and other spokesmen who aimed at a large audience derided those daimones and said everything they could think of to make them seem repellent and ludicrous; from which it is surely a safe inference that Christians in general thought it a part of piety to open their neighbors' eyes—or, as their neighbors might have said, to insult the sacred, vilify the holy, and behave perfectly frightfully. (It is a very good exercise, at least from a historian's point of view, to imagine oneself a devout pagan while reading various Christian writings.) Athenagoras' abuse of the gods in the second century is thus of a piece with the call to the fourth-century emperors (by Firmicus Maternus, cited earlier) that they raze and destroy all heathen error; or you could say that the "atheists" that suffered under the persecutions were natural parents to the vandals and vigilantes that later embarrassed Theodosius and outraged Libanius—natural parents to these later throngs and differing from them in only one particular: they as yet had no access to civil powers.

After New Testament times and before Constantine, very little open advertising of Christianity is attested. Celsus mentions some exorcizing and healing in public, but he reminds his readers, too, of the dangers entailed in open preaching. Likelihood and chance descriptions from other sources direct us, rather, to private houses as the chief locus of conversion. Even there we should probably not expect to find any very active or official mission. Missionaries are just not mentioned. Moreover, in the glimpse given us of Syria (it may be) around the mid-third century, the Pseudo-Clementine Epistles to Virgins (2.6) describe how teachers did and should circulate around their district, from one Christian house to another; but, if they should be benighted in some place where there were no Christians at all, they should keep themselves to themselves, strictly separate, strictly well-behaved, "and shun evil in all respects, lest we give away what is holy to the dogs or cast pearls before swine. . . . Where pagans are assembled we do not sing psalms nor read scripture lest we appear like musical entertainers." So even people who thought of themselves as teachers would not care to spread the Word, however natural the opportunity.

In one private house a sick man, thought by his family to be in extremis, was converted through an exorcist. Later he was to become bishop of Rome. In that sort of discreet setting it is easy to imagine much spreading of familiarity with Christianity, if not precisely evangelical conversations. I sketched such a scene in an earlier chapter. Not only exorcists but the already converted holding no church office at all could have been at work. We cannot take the next obvious step toward the quantifying of such activities, so as to say whether they were the chief means or only an insignificant factor in winning new recruits. Or rather, we can only say what appears likely but unproven due to plain shortage of cases. It is some sort of comfort to find that recruits to pagan cults in roughly the same numbers and over the same centuries are just as rarely reported. The sparseness of the Christian record therefore seems less troubling.

As a reminder of much that has been said earlier on the subject, here is how Saint Athanasius in the 350s, writing the Life of Saint Anthony, depicted the old man demonstrating the superiority of Christianity. He had been visited and challenged by "persons counted as wise among pagans" (§74). In answer to them, he undertook to offer proof (§80) that "believing, *pistis*, in Christ is the only true religiousness," derived not by "seeking logical conclusions through reasoning" but rather through that believing in itself. "We convince," he says, "because people first trust in what they can actually see, and then in reasoned argument."

Well said!—defining in a few words a distinction (I have called it "proof and content") and a sequence already met with in dozens of scenes. But Anthony adds, as his biographer imagines, "'Look now: here are some folk suffering from daimones' (for there were present some who were troubled by demons and had come to him; so he brought them forward, and went on). 'Either cleanse these men by your logic-chopping or by any other skill or magic you wish, and calling on your idols, or otherwise, if you can't, lay down your quarrel with us and witness the power of Christ's cross.' And with these words he called on Christ, sealed the sufferers with the sign of the cross twice and a third time, and straightway the men stood forth all healed."

This moment sums up and sharply delineates a great deal that has been discussed in the preceding pages: emphasis on miraculous demonstration, head-on challenge of non-Christians to a test of power, head-on confrontation with supernatural beings inferior to God, and contemptuous dismissal of merely rational, especially Greek philosophical, paths toward true knowledge of the divine. The learned and intellectual indeed existed, though always few in number. But the church that counted lay, rather, among the simple folk illuminated through ascetic experience. A century later, the abbot Shenute, as we have seen, is still continuing in these traditions. He outfaces and humiliates, he tramples down and smashes, foul heathenism. He scorns the whining litigants against him: true religion is above the law. And Saint Martin at the other end of the empire is doing just the same things, with just the same vigor, fame, and success.

The canons of a Spanish council, even before 312, give us our first sure glimpse of idol-smashing. Men who had done it were receiving something too close to worship, said the assembled bishops. Christian communities very naturally heroized their members who waged active war on the demonic world and all its servants. Three such, the blessed Alexander, Martyrius, and Sisinnius, had penetrated into the backlands of northern Italy toward the end of the century and mingled with the natives in the midst of the high point of their religious year, going in procession around their holy places. The three attacked the natives' errors in speeches to their very faces. For this they had received a terrible beating from the enraged crowds. That same sequence of attack and reaction we have also seen in Syria, Numidia, and elsewhere. "Let us chastise the misguided!" cries the bishop of Turin, recalling the blessed Alexander and his companions, and exhorting his congregation to ever more energetic missionizing.[10]

But the saints and bishops alike in these episodes belong to the post-312 world. Therefore they carry forward earlier impulses into greatly altered settings. They can act in the open and go on the offensive. No need now to hang about the corners of the marketplace or, more likely, their neighbors' kitchens. Where once they had driven devils only from poor souls possessed, now they can march into the holiest shrines and, with spectacular effect before large crowds, expel the devils from their very homes. Accounts of their triumphs can circulate freely, too. Whereas formerly church leaders had remained in ignorance of much that happened in some other province, their post-Constantinian successors could write up their heroes in full-dress literary form, as Athanasius did, and see the work translated into some other current language and sent all round the empire, till it ended (via Germany!) in Saint Augustine's home in Milan. Every form of publicity, in Syriac and Coptic as well as Latin and Greek, and of course in symbolic and artistic form, could be bent now to the service of the ascendant church.

Bishops now actually dined with Constantine himself; they used Constantius' palace as their headquarters.[11] They were seen riding along provincial highways in state conveyances, bent on their high affairs, as guests of the government. All the world could behold what fantastic changes had come about in the repute and position of ecclesiastical officials. What they said now had an authority acknowledged by the emperors themselves; it hardly needed miracles to rest on. There were correspondingly fewer tales of miracles, then, and they circulated most often in remote areas.

Yet the successes of Christian conversion were multiplied many-fold. The extraordinary rate of growth became still more rapid—growth, that is, measured by the only means available to us. They include number and size of basilicas, number and distribution of bishoprics, and size of following or congregation reasonably estimated from these data, matched by correspondingly fewer and less well-cared-for pagan temples, fewer priesthoods, and less attendance at festival days. What can have accounted for such dramatic developments?

In this second period of the church's rise to predominance, there are some, though fewer, direct testimonies to motive. They are of the same sort as before, but there are now material benefits also to be won through joining the church. Are these to be ignored? To give them serious consideration seems like an indecent attack on the church of the martyrs, indeed on the whole city of God. But that is theology. Everything else makes me think that converts, in their moral nature, temperament, motivation, and every other characteristic, differed not a whit from the neighbors they left behind them. So, then, if we can credit the emperor Julian's calculation that adherents to his cause could be won over in part through money, then we must suppose that Constantine's calculations were of the same order—and his gifts, of course, over ten times as long a reign, were vastly greater. Or if the emperor Maximin Daia thought that whole communities could be swayed to "the better view," as he would have said (in this case, the pagan), through promotion to higher civic status, then why should not Constantine hope to appeal to the port town of Maiouma in the same way? There is no sign or likelihood that the church after Constantine, more than any other cult, attracted a kind of person who felt himself above material benefits. The very temptations to our partisanship that exist here serve to remind us of the need to treat both sides, or all sides, of the religious contest with equal respect.

Emperors or ecclesiastical officials controlling the distribution of material benefits waved them in front of non-Christians obviously in the hope of changing their allegiance, or they handed out money and food (and advertised the fact) at the instant of change, or threatened to take money or food away from the already converted if they would not abide in their allegiance. From all of which actions the conclusion seems certain: people were joining the church partly to get rich, or at least less poor. That was a motive assumed by contemporaries. It hardly needed to be explained; nor was it considered anything especially to boast about. Accordingly, explicit testimonies of the sort, "I call myself a Christian because I can't afford not to," are quite lacking. But the thought must have been there.

That it was a major element in a mixture of motives, I am inclined to suppose, in order to explain the remarkably generous inducements offered and the equally remarkable acceleration in church growth. There is no reason to think that life was any easier for the urban masses once they were Christianized than it had been before cult groups, retirement and obsequies insurance societies, civic banquets, and the surplus offerings at temples were all suppressed. The disappearance of these institutions, however, left pressing needs unfilled. Thereupon the local bishop stepped forward, to the great benefit of his stature in the community.

He was now a landowner, too: in Italy, overnight, on a very large scale indeed, thanks to Constantine; elsewhere, on a scale we cannot yet measure. Thousands of field hands and shepherds and so forth came under the direction of ecclesiastical bailiffs and slave drivers. So did their counterparts on private estates and in grand city houses, as their masters were attracted to the church by the prospect of more rapid promotion in the civil service and a more cordial welcome as a dinner guest or son-in-law. Among the many persons, daughters of doorkeepers and the like, who were dependent on such great men, prudence would teach conformity to their choice of worship.

Where there were recurrent charges of bribery to become a priest, still more to gain higher ecclesiastical office, and a large-scale pattern of bought bishoprics reported in Asia Minor (it was the tax exemptions that proved so irresistible), it is fair to assume that material interests must have played some part, though a smaller one, in the thoughts of ordinary honest converts.[12] The proportion between material and spiritual motives, naturally quite indeterminable, would only matter if sincerity of allegiance were reflected in conduct. That will never be true. Bishops from Eusebius to Augustine thus report on new members who went through the motions and talked like Christians on some occasions but not all, and therefore were changed in their behavior, though incompletely. Meanwhile, such converts strengthened the church by their very numbers, just as they had formerly given to non-Christian cults more money, weight, and presence in the community, with just as little felt religion. Partial converts—call them simply unreligious people—do not lack historical significance.

Sincerity in non-Christian cults was never an issue. Neither your fellow-worshipers cared nor your god. What counted (not, of course, what yielded spiritual rewards) was payment, *do ut des*: payment for ritual, with hymns, incense, and the like in exchange for divine goodwill that might turn into good fortune. "We beseech you to be mindful of us," runs an African inscription, "and thus you will get" (here, a word erased, or corrected) "a banquet: Grannius of Mammarius and Elpideforus who built these four places with their own hands and money"—the "places" (*cubicula*) being no doubt gazebos for groups of diners.[13] The custom of making a present of a meal to the deity invoked and joining in the meal oneself, was very widely diffused throughout the empire and accounts for the dining-couches, arbors, and similar facilities attested everywhere in temple precincts, in Africa as in Syria or Italy.

But the particular text here quoted begins, "Holy and blessed martyrs." These are the saints who suffered in the persecutions, whether at the hands of pagans or other Christians. The inscription and the cult, then, are not pagan themselves but, like many a glimpse we have of the veneration of saints, strongly colored by pagan tradition, which could not be suppressed. On other inscriptions, undoubtedly Christian but Italian not African, appear dedications "to the gods and spirits of the departed," showing the survival of a pagan picture of the afterlife; and, in Egypt, Christians likewise held views on that subject essentially unchanged from their remotest past, and therefore of course not Christian. We happen to know from Origen that the prevailing views on sin that he encountered had also remained pagan.[14] He may be speaking of third-century Christian communities in Egypt or in Syria. In chapter IX, illustrations were given to show the confusion of conduct, at the point of contact between the older cults and the new one, in burial practice, symbolism, even in worship itself. All of these facts about the real as opposed to the prescribed beliefs within the church, and without any adventuring into heresies, need still to be studied. The effort might be rewarded with results as surprising as those that met ecclesiastical visitations in Germany toward the turn of the seventeenth century (see above, chap. I). But quite enough is clear for a conclusion. What had been a point difficult to cross before A.D. 312 was so no longer; yet people who did cross were reluctant to leave behind all their old ways. So they made such adaptations as were really necessary and kept what they could. In this process changes were slow but important.

Another inscription in Italy of A.D. 367 honors the distinguished Minucius Aetherius. He had been chosen patron to one of the capital's larger workmen's associations, which commissions a statue of him to be set up "in front of god's temple" according to a resolution taken "with the favor of the divine majesty."[15] A generation had passed since the senate congratulated Constantine on triumphing over his enemies "through the divine presence," *instinctu divinitatis.* Ambiguity of phrasing persists in the most public documents, since the non-Christians had no interest in pressing differences to the point of war and were themselves too strong to be challenged. Aetherius, in proof of this balance of power, had held office, a curatorship or the like, in Rome itself. That explains his being sought out as patron. Within the senate, the balance rather tipped toward the non-Christians. In particular, the family of Quintus Aurelius Symmachus and its connections formed by marriage held a wonderful list of great appointments over half a century. They represented the absolute summit of the empire's pagan Establishment, defending peace and ambiguity so long as they were able.

Symmachus did nothing better known or more eloquently recorded than to deliver to the emperor in A.D. 384 an address requesting the restoration of religious privileges to the pagan world he represented. They had been lost under the emperor's brother and predecessor a few years earlier, and were now sought from what was thought to be a better-disposed government. "Afford to your divine brother," Symmachus urged, "the correction of a policy imposed on him from without, smoothe over an act that he did not realize had given pain to the senate—for their envoys, it is generally agreed, were refused access to him so that a public judgement might not reach him."[16] Urgent and adroit request! What had been an unfortunate mistake from the start could now be set right, no trouble to anyone. The balance of power, mutual respect, toleration of any and all ways of approach to "the divine mind" (careful terminology), "that great secret," could and must be now preserved. The appeal, however, failed when Ambrose intervened.

Symmachus' reference to the rings of informants and courtiers that surround an emperor and bring to bear competing pressures on him (which he cannot fully understand) to grant or to withhold his consent to things is not mistaken. The next year, in the east, Libanius refers to actions engineered behind the emperor's back which had produced anti-pagan legislation. Bishop Porphyry's biographer imagines similar palace intrigues that led to the despatch of army units to Gaza, there to destroy the high god's temple.[17] In secular affairs, such pressures and intrigues are often referred to.

They enter the picture now, to disturb relations between Christians and non-Christians, because Christians could sense that they would get no further without armed force—the plea is entered specifically for the bishops Marcellus and Porphyry, by the historical accounts—while they themselves had no such force at their disposal. Yet they also began to sense their own influence. As Saint John Chrysostom says of any bishop who chooses to enter the palace, "No one is honored before him." Given these various considerations, we naturally expect to find high churchmen bringing their weight to bear on the emperor to help them out with his laws and troops; and that is just what we do see, in Symmachus' day and later. It marks the third and final period in the history of church growth that is being traced in these pages.

In the first period up to 312/3, the church could boast of a high level of commitment among its members. Though some were Christians only in name, and though persecutions shook out great numbers of apostates, as was only natural, nevertheless there were many extraordinary demonstrations of belief. In the fourth century, and indeed sometimes a generation or two earlier, Christians looked back on their predecessors with wonder and pride. As worldly advantages accrued to the church, however, people joined for nonreligious or mixed reasons—people for whom religion of any stripe was not at the center of life or for whom the rewards of ritual and membership in conflicting traditions made even that conflict preferable to a sharp choice. They left behind them non-Christians for whom religion was important and change impossible, or who could simply not be reached by the ordinary missionary methods. It was this remainder, constituting a majority of the empire's total population, that we now see the Christian leadership confronting.

Armed force in a civilized society must be approved by law, like citizens' arrests or other forms of self-help; or it must belong to the state itself. In this last period, it was brought to bear in both forms on both non-Christian worshipers and their places of worship. At the forefront were mobs. Theirs had been a major role in the church's internal wars; but they had not been turned against non-Christians before, nor imperial troops either, because of political considerations. Laws and armies, after all, mean politics; they mean decisions taken with many purposes and constituencies in mind. Government officers of low or middling rank up to the emperors themselves had to weigh how much they stood to lose by imposing their views on one particular subject too hard. They can be seen backing away, moving forward, and settling on decisive action only when they think they can win.[18] The inability of non-Christians to prevail in any competition with their persecutors is not clear until the opening years of the fifth century.

By then, the very short and decisive third period was almost over. Preceded by Constantine's pillaging of temples, by occasional recorded outbursts of destruction in the eastern and (archeologically attested) in the northern provinces, a phase of recognizably sharper physical attacks can be sensed only after 380. The mission was to be finished. Heads of households and owners of big estates were exhorted from the pulpit to get on with the job. They were to use every means of persuasion: flattery and battery alike. Laws were aimed at the facilities of non-Christian worship, to reduce their access for religious purposes. And, more than a step ahead of any law, now summoned forth from monasteries and basilicas by their leaders and watched benevolently or avenged by army units, the zealots for conversion took to the streets or crisscrossed the countryside, destroying no doubt more of the architectural and artistic treasure of their world than any passing barbarians thereafter. Through their triumphant forays, one thing they were able to make manifest and undeniable—undeniable in non-Christians' own terms of thought: that the gods were never more than mere demons, they availed nothing in the defense even of their own homes.

Silencing, burning, and destruction were all forms of theological demonstration; and when the lesson was over, monks and bishops, generals and emperors, had driven the enemy from our field of vision. What we can no longer see, we cannot report. Here, then, my book ends. But some invisible reality remained to be discovered by episcopal visitations, a thousand years and more after these events.

Abbreviations

I employ the conventional abbreviations of the ancient sources as they are listed in the Liddell–Scott *Greek Lexicon* or, occasionally, forms less cryptically shortened. Modern authorities are cited by name and publication date alone, full references to which can be found in the Bibliography.

ANRW	*Aufstieg und Niedergang der römischen Welt*, eds. H. Temporini et al. (Berlin)
CCSL	*Corpus Christianorum, Series Latina* (Belgium)
CSEL	*Corpus Scriptorum Ecclesiasticorum Latinorum* (Vienna)
GCS	*Die Griechischen Christlichen Schriftsteller der ersten Jahrhunderte* (Berlin)
PL	*Patrologiae cursus completus, series Latina*, ed. J. B. Migne (Paris)
PLRE	*The Prosopography of the Later Roman Empire*, eds. A. H. M. Jones et al. (Cambridge 1971)
PG	*Patrologiae cursus completus, series Graeca*, ed. J. B. Migne (Paris)
RAC	*Reallexikon für Antike und Christentum*, ed. F. Dölger (Stuttgart)
RE	*Real-Encyclopädie der classischen Altertumswissenschaft* (Stuttgart)
RIC	*The Roman Imperial Coinage* (London)

Notes

CHAPTER I

1 Theodoret, *Hist. relig.* 26 (*PG* 82.1476Af.)—"Saracens," 1477A, scripturally called Ismalites.

2 Djebel Druse = Jebel Druze = Hawran = Auranitis, in south Syria. For what follows, see Harding (1969) 21 and Harding (1969a) 7; Ghadban (1971) 82; Winnett and Harding (1978) 7f.; and the link to the name Saracen justified from *RE* s.v. Saraka (Moritz 1920) col. 2389. See further, below, chap. VII n. 2.

3 Winnett and Harding (1978) no. 2022, etc. ("security," with 77 texts in the collection—Index s.v. *slm*), and 1781, etc. ("vengeance"). The war-goddess Ruday is especially often invoked; and there is a specially large number of prayers mentioning enemies and booty (Index s.v. *sn* and *gnmt*). The 1957 corpus collected by Winnett alone shows similar concentrations of prayer.

4 Mk 5:27–30; 6:56p; Lk 5:13, 5:40, and 6:19.

5 Aug., *Civ dei* 5.26, after the Battle of the Frigidus *christianos hac occasione fieri voluit,* evidently only on the surface; cf. *Ep.* 227, where conversion is in Augustine's eyes complete only upon the reluctant convert's recitation of the creed; or *Ep.* 93.17, where *civitas mea . . . ad unitatem catholicam* (from Donatism) *timore legum conversa est.* See further, below, chaps. VI and X passim.

6 Hefele (1907–52) 1.1.242, the Council of Elvira can. 39; 2.1.36, the Council of Cple. can. 7, those willing are "made Christians on the first day and catechumens on the second."

7 Callinicus, *Vita S. Hypatii* 40.31, εὐθὺς ὡς συνετάξον τῷ θεῷ, ποιήσον καὶ γενοῦ χριστιανός.

8 Acts of John 41–42 = Bonnet (1972) 2, 1, pp. 170–171 = Hennecke and Schneemelcher (1963–1964) 2.237, comparing ἐπιστρέφων again in §23 and 33 = Bonnet (1972) 2, 1, pp. 163 and 168. The text (ibid. 190) finds an early attestation in Euseb., *H.E.* 3.25.6. For discussion of the Greek term, see Aubin (1963) passim, not very much to my purpose, but noting (74) the possibility of both "good"—i.e. radical—conversions and "bad" ones, in Saint Paul; also Heikkinen (1967) 314f., on uses of μετανοεῖν, repeated with little change in *Midstream* 8 (1969) 92–114.

9 M. Smith (1978) 205, on Mk 9:23 and Mt 15:28 and 17:20p.

10 Beschaouch (1975) 112, *pro comperta fide et pro servata salute,* the term *salus*, like πίστις, in various non-Christian inscriptions being commonly mistranslated

123

as "salvation," with doctrinal overtones. Compare Nock (1933a) 185, "The result of a miracle is πίστις—that is to say, those present or some of them take up an attitude of submissive reliance in the new δύναμις and its representatives." And he offers examples out of paganism, e.g. the speech of a devotee of Protesilaus that produces "religious conviction"—"like the effect of an Apostolic sermon," as Nock rightly says. He goes on to mention many other instances, Christian and non-Christian, of what he calls "conversion" (186, 187, 188) resulting from demonstrations of supernatural power.

11 Nock (1933) 14, here abandoning the more ordinary and obvious meaning of the word. (See above, n. 10.) Nock (1933) is the work best known, at least to anglophone readers, but more quoted than Bardy (1949) even in French works, I think, and a match in currency nowadays for the third competitor, Harnack (1908). Insistence on a person's "belonging body and soul" in order to qualify as a member of the church also inclined Burckhardt, and other historians less famous, to the view that Constantine or some other figure could not have been a convert because he did un-Christian things. I need not discuss this view, surely.

12 Strauss (1979) 271 and 303; cf. also 270, in one village "they knew nothing of Christianity," as one visitor reports; "everywhere people had recourse to sorcery" and "townspeople were as incompetent . . . in catechism recitation as villagers, and just as impervious to pleas and threats" (271); no one attended church, etc. (272, 274; cf. 275, 277, and 302–305)—all dealing with conditions reported between the 1580s and 1630s. Cf. Grimmelshausen (1965) 5f., stating that the hero is totally ignorant of Christianity, as is typical of "peasant lads from the Spessart who did not know God" (this, in the 1630s in the southwest).

13 The definition is essentially the same chosen for the period before Constantine, in MacMullen (1981) 206 and (1983) 184, and virtually the same as Nock's (above, n. 10). Any definition is, of course, just a word, not a thing: a means of talking about some subject without being misunderstood.

14 The abundant historiography post-312 is overwhelmingly ecclesiastical for centuries, so long as it is Christians that are writing it (correspondingly wider, nonsectarian interests are to be found overwhelmingly in the hands of non-Christians: Ammianus, Eunapius, Zosimus, and others). When the first account of the growth of Christianity was attempted in modern times, by Harnack, in this venerable tradition, he drew overwhelmingly on Christian sources, ignoring the non-Christian, as I have pointed out before, in MacMullen (1981) 206.

15 The fate of pagan works by Porphyry, Celsus, Hierocles, and others is well known; also, that of evidently a very great body of religious literature judged unorthodox—even acts of church councils such as Arles, Béziers, and Rimini. See Hefele (1907–52) 1, 2, p. 945, and Gaudemet (1977) 81 and 85 (these were Arian, in the 350s). For book-burning, see below, chap. X n. 49.

16 Notes 11 and 14 above and 20 below; but I trust that my differences from, as well as my respect for, these three writers will emerge more clearly as I go on.

17 Decapmaeker (1961) 52–54 and Lanternari (1963) 12, both of whom point out the origin of features of Kimbangu's visions in his ancestral conceptions and customs of thought.

18 Ibid. 26, "The attribution of magical powers to religious healing is a feature of nearly every new messianic cult rising among people subject to foreign rule" (examples given, 46f.). Whence it follows that we can frame a law? As Rambo (1982) 151 has said, "Among [students in the human sciences] there is a tendency to utilize theoretical frameworks which become so influential that the details of concrete historical situations and persons are ignored." That tendency most sharply touches my subject, conversion, through the argument that living communities similar to the early Christian are found to offer certain psychological rewards; *therefore* it was those rewards that attracted converts to the church in the first place. It is, of course, possible to build up a picture of what might have been found in Christian groups. Meeks (1983) has done this superbly. But the evidence does not avail to show that (or how) the picture differed from what could be found in non-Christian alternatives—see MacMullen (1981) 124f. for some hint of the difficulties—nor does evidence exist at all to show the alleged train of cause and effect (the "therefore," above). I return to the methodological problems below, in chap. XI.

19 Festugière (1959) 404, italics added.

20 For example, Bardy (1949) 157 declares, "Désire de la vérité, désir de la délivrance et du salut, désir de la sainteté, ce sont là les grands motifs de la conversion chrétienne au cours des premiers siècles"—a statement unsupported and in my view entirely mistaken, but arising, surely, from his sense of what man wants out of religion, in all cultures without distinction. Or Festugière (1959) 234 arguing that Libanius "en matière de religion est au fond indifférent. Cette indifférence religieuse parait d'ailleurs un phénomène ordinaire de ce temps"—simply because Libanius doesn't talk about religion much in his correspondence!

21 Kluckhohn (1942) 53; see further chap. X below.

22 MacMullen (1981) 99–108.

23 Tran Tam Tinh (1964) 177, answered by Juv. 6.531f.

24 Min. Fel. 22.8, ridiculing pagans "who go about naked in mid-winter," or Clem. Alex., *Protrept.* 10 (*GCS* 12 p. 67), ridiculing pagan "worshippers . . . a disgrace in their filthy hair, their dirty tattered clothing, who never heard of a bath or trimmed their nails," and so on.

25 Fox's diary quoted in James (1958) 25, James himself offering as comment, "no one can pretend for a moment that in point of spiritual sagacity and capacity, Fox's mind was unsound." For the ancient parallel, see Ael. Arist., *Or.* 48 (*Hieros Logos* 2) §7 p. 396 Keil and §80 p. 412; Versnel (1981) 167; and Bonner quoted in Dodds (1965) 43. The religious significance of Aelius Aristides' sufferings in mid-winter emerge from the reaction of the crowd of witnesses, who salute his survival of an icy bath with the shout, "Great is Asclepius!" (i.e. this is a great miracle), *Or.* 48.21 p. 399 Keil. On ridicule of a third highly religious person, the prophet Harris, see below, chap. III, n. 23.

CHAPTER II

1 Lucian, *The Dream* 2f., and Saint Paul in Acts 20:34, who earned enough as an awning-maker (for booths in the marketplace) to supply the wherewithal for three persons to live on. Cf. σκηνεῖται = *mercatores circumforanei* in *IGR* 4.190 (making *tents*—for hikers? bedouins?—never seemed likely).

2 On studying how to weep in public, see MacMullen (1980) 255; on inducing the appearance of ecstasy for stage effect, Menander Rhet. p. 160, along with the text quoted. A. Malherbe, in Meeks (1983) 241, draws attention to the passage, which Meeks discusses, giving weight also to Plut., *Moral.* 611D–612B. There, Plutarch offers these consolations on the death of a child: it feels no more pain (611C); its soul is indestructible, according to "traditional teachings" and Dionysiac rites; better (612A), according to "traditional and ancient customs," the soul returns to a "finer and more divine fate and country." I have tried to evaluate this in MacMullen (1981) 170, and the subject of immortality beliefs in general, in ibid. 54f. with notes, and in MacMullen (1983) 182. A second passage that Meeks adduces—from Sen., *Ad Marc. de consolat.* 23.1—resembles the Plutarchan (and Stoic doctrine), but adds (25.1) that heroes of the past, the Blessed (*felices*) Scipio and Cato, wait to receive the deceased in the manner promised in the Menander passage.

3 It is instructive to see ourselves reflected in the mirror of the past—and then to see that reflection corrected. Notice, for example, P. Paris, in Robert (1960) 417n.; also Ramsay (1897) 386 and his discussion of that inscription; also Bardy (1949) 188—all of whom find belief in immortality in a certain pagan inscription; but then Robert (1960) 423f. shows the text to be Christian after all. Or again, consider the "Benenata" inscription—Christian not pagan, as was clear to Carcopino and Charles-Picard (1965) 115–117. Or the very procrustean treatment of Gallic pagan inscriptions, forcing them to demonstrate belief in immortality, in Doignon (1971) 40f.—they rather show the reverse. Sahin (1975) 295 offers a convenient illustration of standard views in inscriptions: a 1st-century text reading, "Tombs are men's final dwelling and walls . . . and offerings of tears are the only abiding possession of the dead—a city of silence." For other similar clichés, see Robert (1960) 425–427; and for indications of how quite unanalyzable vogues played with clichés, and how different ones came and went in different regions, see Demougeot (1963) 25–26 and Kajanto (1974) 59–64. Interesting material. Compare below, chap. IX nn. 16–21, on the use of evidently meaningless clichés among both Christians and non-Christians.

4 The coexistence of monotheism and polytheism has often been recognized: by Harnack (1908) 2.140, among the Syrian population; by Bardy (1949) 175, more generally; by Chadwick, quoted in MacMullen (1983) 189 n. 19. See further, MacMullen (1981) 83–89 and Tertullian, quoted in MacMullen (1983) 189 and n. 18. Versnel (1981a) 12 has interesting points to make about a sort of henotheism found in Asia Minor, there first "*outside the circles of philosophers*" (his italics), citing, e.g., Aelius Aristides' *Hieros Logos* 2.18; but I think the phenomenon is more widely attested.

5 Bishop Dionysius calls attention to his words in court records of the 250s, where he continues, "For us, it is the one god creator of all things" (Euseb., *H.E.* 7.11.8). Compare Dionysius' contemporary, Alex. Rhet., in L. Spengel, *Rhet. graeci* 3 pp. 4f. = Walz. 9 pp. 337f., or, later, Symm., *Rel.* 3.8, in a famous summary: "Each of us has his own ways, his own religious customs. Divine purpose has assigned various cults to various cities as their guardians," etc.; the same thought is in Liban., *Or.* 30.33; and, on guardian deities of cities or peoples, see MacMullen (1981) 142 n. 17.

6 See Porph., *De abst.* 2.40: demons cause quakes, droughts, plagues, etc.; or Philostratus and other sources in MacMullen (1983) 188 n. 4—the pagan views here being those which also prevailed among Christians that Origen knew (*De principiis* 3.2.1, *PG* 11.305); for he concludes from the temptation of Jesus by Satan, etc.: "Sacred scripture teaches us throughout that there are certain invisible enemies contending against us . . . from which the uninstructed [*simpliciores*, i.e. the majority] who believe in the Lord Christ suppose that all sins whatsoever that men commit are done from the impulse of those hostile powers upon the minds of sinners." The same view is found elsewhere, e.g. in Tert., *Apol.* 22.4—daemones arouse wicked passions in men; or similarly in Just., I *Apol.* 57f.—re the persecutors. For the same agreement in views, pagan and Christian, at a later date, see Liban., *Or.* 19.7,29–31, and 34, cf. *Or.* 1.252, comparing Joh. Chrysos., *Homil.* 15 and 21 (*PG* 49.154 and 215, the Devil is to blame), on the riot of A.D. 387; Liban., *Or.* 62.18, a πονηρὸς δαίμων induces the neglect of eloquence. The pagan view is also seen in Plut., *Moral.* 168C, where he imagines that evils are caused by "strokes laid on by God, or attacks by a *daimon"*; and Carr (1981) 169, "δαίμων is never used in the LXX in any sense other than the maleficent," citing here Orig., *C. Cels.* 5.5. For demons invoked for evil work, see sources cited in MacMullen (1981) 185. By contrast, Porphyry writes, "God could not become wicked nor sin, for he is good in essence"—frg. 94 cited by Bardy (1949) 187, cf. other material in MacMullen (1981) 74–79. Only "superstition," δεισιδαιμονία, could ascribe evil to the gods, Plut., *Moral.* 165B, 167A and D.

7 MacMullen (1974) 113f.

8 Quoted in Meiggs (1960) 231 n. 3, comparing Ovid, *Fasti* 5.672, *te (Mercurium), quicumque suos profitetur vendere merces, ture dato, tribuas ut sibi lucra, roget;* and further examples of such open statements in MacMullen (1981) 52f., of the type (*CIL* 5.6596), *Mercurio lucrorum potenti et conservatori . . . ex voto* (a. 196?). Cf. Plautus, *Persa* 470, *quoi homini di propitii sunt, aliquid obiciunt lucri.*

9 Liban., *Or.* 30.33, providing a gloss on Julian's notoriously lavish hecatombs in preparation for the invasion of Persia, and echoed in even later parallels involving the salvation of Rome: "No one [in A.D. 394] was persuaded by [Theodosius'] summons [to be converted]. No one chose to give up an ancestral heritage transmitted from the days when the city was first founded and, instead, to prefer, to that, convictions that were irrational, ἄλογον. For by safeguarding the former they had dwelt in the city unravaged for almost 1,200 years, and they could not know the outcome, if they exchanged the one for the other"—Zos. 4.59.2, cf. 5.41.1f. with Soz., *H.E.* 9.6.3 (a. 408, pagan rituals against Alaric).

10 Soz., *H.E.* 1.8 (*PG* 67.876C), "Constantius announced in a public letter to his subjects in the west that they should observe the Christians' religion and carefully offer cult to the divinity"—evidently a quotation, since Sozomen goes on, "Expressing his gratitude," etc., and (876D) "he covered a great number of other subjects whereby he hoped to bring over his realm to religion." Cf. also the Apostles preaching to pagans in Lystra, Acts 14:17, or Constantine's open letter to the people of Palestine, in Euseb., *Vita Const.* 2.24, earlier; and perhaps even more clear and explicit, Justin, *Dial.* 8.2—happiness is the convert's lot,

καὶ τελείῳ γενομένῳ εὐδαιμονεῖν, i.e., in this life—along with instances
when adherence is promised by the non-Christian provided he gets what he
wants, in Callinicus, *Vita S. Hypatii* 40.27–29, in the *Vita Pachomii* 5 p. 6
Athanassakis = Festugière (1965) 161, in various episodes of Marc. Diac.,
Vita Porphyrii (below, chap. X), or as implied in the non-Christian's bargaining
with Saint Apollinaris, Lazius (1532) 140.

11 Orig., *C. Cels.* 1.68—he calls them "scoundrels."

12 Christians are called "impious and atheist, for throwing up their ancestral
gods," by Porphyry, in Euseb., *Praep. ev.* 1.2.2, and by various accusers at
other times, cf. some sources in MacMullen (1981) 176, including evidence of
danger to overt atheists (and add the incident at Rome in 308/9, Zos. 2.13.1).
Note, too, in the Arycanda inscription of A.D. 312, *CIL* 3.13132, the attack on
ἡ τῶν ἀθέων ἀπεχθής ἐπιτηδεύσις, and the accusation still in Julian's attack, *Misopogon* 357D. But Christians (like the pagan Lucian toward
Glycon, in his essay *Alexander* 45 and 55) were known to be hostile to the received faiths, perhaps by Domitian's reign (Dio 67.14.2, ἔγκλημα
ἀθεότητος, against a Christian?), certainly by mid-2d century. (By Just., I
Apol. 5f. and Athenag., *Leg.* 1 and 3, the charge is already customary.) The
martyr-acts confirm this: of Polycarp (§3 and 9), of Lyons (Euseb., *Hist. eccl.*
5.1.9), of Apollonius Sacceas (§4), and in charges of "impiety" *vel sim.* in other
accounts. Cf. Ste. Croix (1963) 24, with note 126, in an admirable article.

13 My statement greatly oversimplifies, to evade a long debate. See *Dig.* 48.13.4.2
(Marcian), *mandata, ut praesides sacrilegios latrones plagiarios conquirant*, which de-
fines sacrilege by the company it keeps; but, on the other hand, see 48.4.1
(Ulpian), *proximum sacrilegio crimen est, quod maiestatis dicitur. Maiestatis autem
crimen illud est . . .* (§1) *quo seditio tumultusve adversus rem publicam fiat*; and connected, Tert., *Apol.* 10.1, *deos, inquitis, non colitis, et pro imperatoribus sacrificia
non penditis . . . Itaque sacrilegii et maiestatis rei convenimur.* Sufficient to have indicated the question of the law underlying persecution. *CIL* 8.14683 = *ILS*
6824 (a. 185) lays down rules within the *curia Iovis* of Simitthus, *si quis flamini
male dixerit*, he shall pay a fine; but this protects civic dignity, not sanctity.

14 D. Fishwick kindly alerts me to Herz (1975) passim, for the western provinces.
The Lex Col. Genetivae Iuliae 64 (*quae sacra fieri publice placeat*), 65 (public
monies *ad ea sacra quae in ea colonia aliove loco colonorum nomine fient*), and 69
(contracts let for the supply of whatever the *sacra* require), in *FIRA*² 1.180 and
182, sheds light on general usages. For eastern provinces, the clearest calendar
is the Egyptian, cf. Sauneron (1962) 2; but others are easily inferred, e.g. at
Stratonicea.

15 The subject is obscure, at least in detail. There are helpful indications for the
west in the Lex (above) §128 = *FIRA*² 1.195, *magistri* to be appointed to su-
pervise cult acts and places, and in *CIL* 10.3698 (a. 289), where a Cybele priest
is chosen by the decurions of Cumae; also in Cic., 2 *Verr.* 126 (Syracuse, a *lex
de religione* on priestly elections) and 128 (Cephaloedium, election of a *sacerdos
maximus*). From the eastern provincial evidence, which I do not control, see
e.g. Malalas 12 p. 288, under Commodus in Antioch, women who win in
competitions of hymn-recitation are then named priestesses; also, endless epi-
graphic mention of what may be called "municipal" priesthoods.

16 *Ep.* 9.108 and 146–148, re an adulterous Vestal to be punished "with due re-
gard for the state" (*Ep.* 147)—cf. *Ep.* 1.46.2, *benignitas enim superioris, nisi cultu
teneatur, amittitur*—just like Constantine's mode of reasoning, see below, chap.
V at n. 40, and the fact, reported in Aug., *Retractiones* 2.69 (*CSEL* 36.181),
that, afterward, many non-Christians blamed the Christian God for the sack of
Rome.

17 A good test of the shapelessness of "state" religion lies in the coins declaring
one or another god to be the emperor's *comes*: Serapis, for Valerian and
Gallienus, in Zaccaria (1976–1977) 195f.; Hercules of Deutz, for Postumus,
along with other Herculeses, *RIC* 5, 2 (1933) 331 and 358; Sol, for third- and
fourth-century emperors, MacMullen (1981) 187; and the trailing off of these
condescending courtesies from high authority to local gods, to gain popularity,
in local issues like the Zeus-Ammon-plus-Third-Legion coins of Cyrenaica, in
Kindler (1975) 144f.

CHAPTER III

1 MacMullen (1981) 175 nn. 42f. (Plotinus called by the vaguer term δαίμων; the
priestess discussed in Robert's work cit.; and add Tac., *Ann.* 6.18.5 and *IG* 12,
2, 163b, Theophanes, worshiped as "the god Zeus Eleutherios Philopatris" in
Mytilene from the 30s A.D., and Epiphanes, worshiped in Cephallenia with a
temple etc., in Clem., *Stromat.* 3.2.2, *PG* 8.1106A.) We should perhaps exclude
Lucian, *Peregrinus* 11, who reports that that holy man was "venerated as a
god." See Wilken (1980) 111.

2 MacMullen (1983) 178 and n. 10, with Euseb., *H.E.* 7.30.10f., the bishop
hymned in church and venerated as a divine being, ἄγγελος . . . ἐξ
οὐρανοῦ, in the 260s and 270s.

3 *Acta Acacii* 1.9f. p. 58 Knopf-Krüger.

4 "Demons" appears as a term for Olympians, in epic or classical contexts and,
from literary considerations, sometimes in writers of our period, e.g. Liban.,
Or. 61.2. Also, in a morally neutral sense, as (minor) divine beings, in Plato
and in discussions that draw on the Platonic, e.g. Plutarch, *Moral.* 360Df. and
944C. But a broad range of texts from our period (see examples below) depend
for their meaning on a common acceptance of *daimon* in the sense I give.

5 For the Jews' ideas, citing 1 Hen. 19:1 and Dt. 32:17 (LXX), see Klijn (1962)
261; further, noting that "the Hebrew word 'gods' is translated 'angels' by the
Septuagint in Psalms 8.6," etc., M. Smith (1978) 201; also see MacMullen
(1983) 189 n. 23. For the non-Christian sense of divine ranks, see Orig., *C. Cels.*
8.15 and 7.68 (*GCS* 2.232 and 217); also *IG* 7.413 = *SIG*³ 747, where the
question of tax exemption for sacred precincts arises, and the young Cicero and
a consul, etc. hear the case and determine that the owner of the grounds, Am-
phiaraus, really was/is a "god."

6 1 Cor. 8:5; Gal. 4:8; Euseb., *Praep. ev.* 2.4.4; Athanas., *Vita S. Antonii* 37, writing in A.D. 357 (δαίμονες . . . ψευδόνομοι θεοί); Grégoire (1922) 34
no. 104, a. 435. It is rare for the pagan gods to be called *dii* or θεοί by a
Christian: Ambrosiaster, *Quaest. vet. et novi Testament.* 114.22 (*CSEL*

50.313—but also "correctly," *daemonia*), dated 366/384, or Dionysius in Euseb., *H.E.* 7.11.8. See also the next note.

7 Some exemplary passages in MacMullen (1983) 189 n.23, or (later) Cypr., *De idol. vanitate* passim (a work praised by Jerome and representative, even if perhaps not genuine). In disputing the power lodging in icons (as non-Christians believed), a Christian might say—so Celsus imagines—"See, even while I'm standing by this statue of Zeus (or Apollo, or whatever deity), I insult it and hit it and it doesn't pay me back." "He does not realize," Origen continues, describing such a Christian challenger, "that in divine law it is set forth how 'You shall not abuse the gods.'" But he immediately corrects the Septuagint: τῶν νομιζομένων θεῶν, and in the next lines Celsus calls Jesus τὸν σὸν δαίμονα (*C. Cels.* 8.38f., *GCS* 2 p. 253, Origen's ref. being to Exod. 22:28).

8 Orig., *C. Cels.* 8.11 (trans. Chadwick). The battle-passages are Ephes. 2:2 and esp. 6:12, which seem to me Pauline, *pace* Carr (1981) 108f. But the date Carr proposes little affects my argument; and he is certainly right in stressing (p. 174) that "the pagan world to which Paul went lacked any sense of mighty, hostile forces that stood over against man as he struggled for survival." Cf. MacMullen (1983) 176 and, for possible clues to a causal interpretation, the emphasis on and discussion of aggression in early Christian doctrines in Theissen (1977) 93f.

9 The standard pagan view in, e.g., Plut., *Moral.* 170E. Cf. Bardy (1949) 17, "Les dieux païens ne sont pas, comme Jahweh dans le judaïsme, des dieux jaloux"; or Aubin (1963) 195: "La question des châtiments envoyés par Dieu et celle des ses menaces mettent bien en lumière ce qui sépare chrétiens et païens à propos de l'action divine sur l'ἐπστροφή (conversion) de l'homme. Les païens estiment que tout cela est indigne de Dieu et de l'homme sage: un être parfait ne s'irrite pas." Or Cameron (1965) 26, "the Christian doctrine of a god of wrath was held to be monstrous by the educated pagan," citing Cicero and Julian to good effect. Perhaps Julian is clearest in *Contra Galil.* 155Cf., protesting that the Christian view is blasphemous (διαβολή) and against all sense (πῶς εὔλογον?).

10 Livy 45.23.19 (views attributed to Greek speakers); Liban., *Or.* 19.12 and 20.11f. But there are exceptional points in paganism which embrace the idea of divine punishment: above, chap. II n. 6 (Plutarch) and MacMullen (1981) 32. Feldman (1950) 203f. certainly forces the meaning of σεβομένοι toward "fearing" rather than "respecting."

11 MacMullen (1983) 190 n. 41.

12 *Acta Pauli* (*et Theclae*) 17 p. 246 Lipsius, at Iconium, comparing *Acta Andreae* 12, *Acta Pionii* 4.24, *Martyrdom of Polycarp* in Euseb., *H.E.* 4.15.24, and the *Passion of Phileas* p. 332 Musurillo; preaching of the Wrath, e.g. in Clem., *Protrept.* 2.22 (Plutarch); and, for Celsus' understanding of Christianity, see Origen, *C. Cels.* 8.48 (trans. Chadwick). The contrary message of "Peace on earth" (Lk 2:14) cannot be much stressed. It is a peace reserved for the already converted (the text is often mistranslated).

13 E.g. Ambrose (*Ep.* 18.30), supposing Mithras female; but most telling is the general impression the Apologists give of describing their opponents from books, not life. Pagan ignorance of Christianity is often noticed, e.g. by Freu-

denberger (1974) 134: "Erstaunlicherweise scheint sich diese Unkenntnis auf seiten hoher römischer Beamter bis in die valerianische Verfolgung" (with refs.).

14 On pagans not reading the NT, see Cameron (1965) 17, citing also Harnack and Norden; on reading the Apologists, see MacMullen (1983) 177 and n. 6, citing Nock; or see Bardy (1949) 278 or Brunt (1979) 506, or the views of Aland (1961) 32, who is even firmer on the exclusiveness of audience for Apologetic, but supposes that the texts provided ammunition for spoken contacts. Such indirect usefulness is exactly what Augustine and his friend Marcellinus in Carthage have in mind, in *Ep.* 136. But everything was wide open then, and so perhaps the situation sheds no light on earlier times, before the Persecutions were over. There is some hostile reading, as often noted, by Celsus, Porphyry, and eventually Julian; but note how some reading only became hostile through experiment, in the statement of Lactantius, *Div. inst.* 5.1.26 (*CSEL* 19.403f.) that Cyprian's style was not considered good, "and as a result his views were listened to only by Christians, *fideles*, while the learned of this world, if his writings became known to them, were accustomed to laugh at them." Frend (1974) 33 adduces some of the usual passages showing the disdainful reception often given scripture, on literary grounds. As to illiteracy, I depend on the very cogent discussion of Harris (1983), esp. 92 and 94f. (note 5 to 10 percent literacy in Russia in 1850).

15 That these various points had been made known is shown, I hope adequately, in MacMullen (1983) 178–183. Add only, on Jesus in the theology being presented, the brief and curious paragraph in Athenag., *Leg.* 10, with really no explanation of Jesus' role; his entire absence in Minucius Felix (striking at 29.6) and in Theophilus, *Ad Autol.* (striking at 1.12, 2.9, and 2.22); and his total unimportance for the one recent convert whose theology we can actually form some idea of, namely, Constantine. See Kraft (1955) 60 and passim and Frend (1952) 153.

16 MacMullen (1981) 96, citing explicit statements by various persons of the elite. We could add, from Lucian, *Alex.* 30 and passim, the consular Rutilianus, clearly persuaded by Alexander's miracles, or Aelius Aristides; or (if novelistic elaboration is stripped away) Lucius and his fellow-witnesses of a miracle in Apul., *Met.* 11.13, of whom "those of greater religiosity rendered honor to the most manifest efficacy, *potentia*, of such a great Power," while in due course (§20) Lucius is persuaded by a second miracle (a dream) to devote himself to the goddess for life. But perhaps there is proof enough in the broad statement of a hostile witness, that pagan gods win worshipers by their miracles, *quibusdam signis et miraculis et oraculis fidem divinitatis operatur*, Tert., *Apol.* 21.31.

17 For illustration, see Jones (1962) 85, who supposes that Constantine saw in the sky "a rare, but well attested, form of the 'halo phenomenon' . . . caused by the fall, not of rain, but of ice crystals across the rays of the sun . . . scientifically observed"; or, even more desperate, Twisleton (1873), who confronts the miracle of martyrs' inspired speech even after their tongues have been cut out. He notes, with Gibbon, how "the stubborn mind of an infidel is guarded by secret, incurable suspicion" (p. 5); but he rejects that in favor of real, live cases proving such speech possible (e.g. pp. 110 and 187, many cases in Persia, one

from Portugal, all absolutely extraordinary). Regarding Jesus' miracle, M. Smith (1978) 10 adds, as a careful understatement, "These facts have been neglected as unedifying by liberal exegesis." The function of miracles in Jesus' mission is very thoroughly discussed, in ibid. 11 (and Mk 3:10f.), 12 (and Mt 4:23f. or 14:23f., esp. 33–34), 13 (Jn 1:48f., etc.); also, p. 55, citing Just., *Dial.* 69.7, that even Jesus' enemies attributed the conversions to miracles (but miracles wrought not as the Son of God).

18 On the Apostles' healing powers, see below, chap. IV n. 1; on their manifestations, cf. Euseb., *H.E.* 3.24.3.

19 *CIG* 5980 = *IG* 14.966 = *SIG*² 807, a miracle in Rome, where "the powers were living then," in a previous reign; Euseb., *Praep. ev.* 5.1 (179df.), where Porphyry is speaking; and, on the Christian side, among others, Orig., *In Hierem.,* Homil. 4.3 (*GCS* 3.25), or Ambrosiaster, *Quaest. vet. et novi Testament.* 114.22 (*CSEL* 50.313), *tempus non est (nunc) faciendarum virtutum* (= ἀρεταί), *initio autem fieri oportuit, ut semen fidei per hanc crementum facerit; tamen etiam modo daemonia nominata cruce Christi terrentur,* etc.

20 On Jesus' and Apollonius' enemies, calling them γόητες, see M. Smith (1978) 84–93 and passim—the subject has a large bibliography behind Smith—and, more recently, Poupon (1981) 79f. or Remus (1982) 134f.

21 Veyne (1983) 11, 65f. (Galen), 107 (Pausanias), and passim.

22 M. Smith (1978) 9, 106f., 113, and passim, offers the best approach I have read to this manner of interpretation. He notes also (p. 190) a rare example where one can see the story of wonderful acts in process of quantifiable amplification. But my own focus is on conversion, arising from what people thought; so, if *they* believed the things they saw to be miraculous, that is enough for me.

23 Haliburton (1971) 3; also, on Harris' exorcisms (47 and 66), his being taken for "a great fetish" or "a harmless maniac" in the words of the French District Supervisor in 1913 (49; 55 and 66), his raising of the dead (77), healing (67 and 191), burning idols (80 and passim), and inducing rain.

24 Baynes (1931) 7.

CHAPTER IV

1 2 Cor. 12:12 and 1 Cor. 2:4; and casts out devils, Acts 16:18, etc. For the prominence of miracles in Peter's and Paul's preaching as it was portrayed in the 2nd cent., see MacMullen (1983) 185–187 and esp. M. Smith (1980) 249, noting Paul's "repeated claim that his converts had been won by his success in working miracles and invoking the spirit, *not* by his skill as a preacher" (Smith's emphasis, with many refs.). I do not, at this and other junctures, make use of Ps.-Clementine *Recognitiones,* relevant though the material there appears, because the work seems to me too unreliable. Besides obviously invented features, note the date: A.D. 360/380 (?) and based on a source of ca. 230 (?), as B. Rehm suggests in *RAC* 3 (1957) s.v. Clemens Romanus p. 198.

2 Lucian, *Peregrinus* 11f. On Origen, *C. Cels.* 7.9 (trans. Chadwick) see Chadwick (1965) 402f. and n. 6. He may be right in seeing these figures as missionaries parodied. For the context of seer- and wizard-types, see MacMullen (1966) chap. IV, adding the interesting sketch in Polemo, *De physiognomonia* 1 pp. 160 and 162 Foerster (A.D. 130s). I quote the description below, p. 38.

3 *Acts of John* 38–45, Bonnet (1972) 2, 1, pp. 170–173, trans. Hennecke and Schneemelcher (1963–64) 2.237. Notice ἐπεστρέψαμεν ὄρωντες σοῦ τὰ θαυμάσια, cf. Bonnet (1972) 2,1,163 and 168 (ἐπιστρέφω): so "conversion" is instantaneous. In ibid. 190, the text finds an early attestation in Eusebius and probably goes back to an origin in 2d-century Asia or Syria, possibly Encratite. "Gnostic" has also been suggested. But Kaestli (1981) 55f. not only rejects that but sides with others in the view that "les frontières entre orthodoxie et hérésie sont encore floues dans le christianisme du IIᵉ siècle," i.e. it is quite anachronistic to exclude material from assessment because of much later canons. See further, on the *Acta Pauli*, ibid. 50–55 and sources in MacMullen (1983) 186; or, making free use of the early 3d-century (?) *Acta Petri*, Bardy (1949) 259 or Green (1970) 237, to the extent of quoting long stretches of *ipsissima verba* without reserve. But I would not go that far.

4 Blinds: MacMullen (1983) 185, as told by or of Paul and Peter; conversion out of terror of Judgment, ibid.; and danger, from the prophet himself, Jesus (Mk 11:12f. and 20f.), Peter (Acts 13:10f.), Paul (1 Cor. 5:3f. and 1 Tim. 1:20), Gregory Thaumaturgus (in the Syrian version §4), and various later figures in ascetic hagiography, below, chap. VII n.3.

5 Veyne (1983) 103, on the importance of having other believers around one; on the importance of hearsay evidence of miracles, needed to give weight to other teachings, see MacMullen (1983) 186.

6 Brown (1980) 107; compare Kretschmar (1974) 103, "Die hier vorausgesetzte Dämonologie scheint für uns befremdlich, wenn nicht sogar peinlich." For the quotations that follow, see MacMullen (1981) 50, adding, as a fourth, Cypr., *De idol. vanitate* (*Quod idola dii non sint*) 7 (*PL* 3.595Bf.—a work praised by Jerome, therefore of high standing, even though its genuineness has been challenged), and a fifth, Athanas., *De incarnat.* 48.3. I give many further refs., ibid. 168 n. 4. The crucial importance of the test is plain in Iren., *Contra haer.* 1.13.4 (*PC* 7.585): what gives an order that others obey is μεῖζόν τε καὶ κυριώτερον—and the same logic in *Acta Petri* 23 p. 71 Lipsius.

7 M. Smith (1978) 113, ἐξουσία, cf. Mk 6:13; and "exorcism seems to have been . . . unusually prominent in Jewish tradition" (114). That is confirmed by the rather small scattering of pagan references that can be found in *RAC* s.v. Exorzismus (K. Thraede 1969) 52, with a few more in MacMullen (1981) 168 n. 3; the number of exorcists in the Roman church ca. A.D. 500 is to be compared with the 90 lectors, and their prominence is plain in many inscriptions—add Palestra (1961) 36, a. 377, in Milan—and in Latin sources (less in eastern ones, Thraede cols. 73f.). Tert., *De prescr.* 41, mentions with irritation even female exorcists (they are heretics).

8 For the confrontation of Peter with Simon, see the *Acta Petri* 8–29 (Lipsius-Bonnet 1 pp. 54–78); for Eusebius on exorcists, see the *Martyrs of Palestine* 1.1 in the translation of Lawlor and Oulton (1927) 1.332. On the Wonderworker in the Greek version, see Greg. Nyss., *Vita S. Greg. Thaumat.*, PG 46.916A; cf. exorcisms in the Syrian version, chap. 11, or (Euseb., *H.E.* 7.15.17) the permanent exiling of the local deity from its habitation by Christian prayer, in Caesarea (Palestine).

9 The future bishop of Rome, Novatian, became a Christian through calling (or his family's calling) on the local church's exorcists when he was gravely ill—so

says his successor, in Euseb., *H.E.* 6.43.14; further material on conversion through exorcism in Tert., *Apol.* 23; in Soz., *H.E.* 5.15 (*PG* 67.1260B), perhaps after Christianity became tolerated in the east; and in Euseb., *H.E.* 5.7.4 = Iren., *Haer.* 2.32.4. For examples post-312, see below, chap. VII.

10 Suhl (1980) 499.

11 Tert., *Apol.* 4.6.

12 Hieronymus, *Vita Hilarionis* 8.8f., the date approximately A.D. 315, reckoning from a birth in 291, cf. Bastiaensen and Smit (1975) 292. See also below, chap. VIII n. 3.

13 Basil, *Ep.* 164—less famous than Tertullian's *mot* on *sanguis-semen*. The role of martyrs, however, must be considered against their small numbers, "hundreds rather than thousands," says Frend (1965) 413, and, to the same effect, Grant (1977) 5; further, heresies produced martyrs, but (except perhaps for the Montanist, in the conventional picture) were not helped thereby. The evidence has not, I think, been assembled, but cf. *Acta Pionii* 11.2 (Montanist) and 21.5 (Marcionite); Euseb., *H.E.* 5.16.21 (Marcionite and Montanist) and *Mart. Pal.* 10.3 (Marcionite bishop); and Mitchell (1982) 102 (Montanist) and 110 (Saccophori).

14 Lucian describing as "driveling idiocy" the auto-da-fé of *Peregrinus* (§2); the judge, in ridicule, bids martyrs to find their own ropes and cliffs (Tert., *Ad Scap.* 5) or accuses them of acting senselessly (ἀλόγως, *Acts of Phileas* line 173); and non-Christians express "amazement" at Christians coming forward to be martyrs, Euseb., *Mart. Pal.* 3.3. Similarly, Epictetus (4.7.6) attributes only to unreasoning regimen the Christians' indifference to wives, children, and the danger of death itself.

15 *Passio S. Perpetuae* 9.1 and 16.4. The causal connection, to be sure, is not quite explicit. Euseb., *H.E.* 6.5.7, tells of conversions in jail, in Alexandria, but from a miracle: visions = dreams of a martyr reported to fellow prisoners by one of those in custody (ἱστοροῦνται in the narrative may imply doubt). Cf. Arnobius similarly converted, *ad credulitatem somniis compelleretur*, Hier., *Chron.* a.340 (A.D. 327).

16 Just., *2 Apol.* 12; confusion in modern interpretations, pointed out by Skarsaune (1976) 54. Nock (1933) 255, for example, speaks of the passage as marking the author's "conversion."

17 Skarsaune (1976) 53f. (Goodenough, Hyldahl, and others doubt genuineness).

18 Tat., *Ad Graec.* 29 (*PG* 6.868A), the date ca. 180s. Or, for the same quality of logic and discipline of thought leading to religious conviction, read the whole of Minucius Felix's *Octavius*.

19 Lucian, *Menippus* 3–7; Nock (1933) 107.

20 Bardy (1949) 63, on Porph., *Vita Plot.* 3; p. 127, on the physician-pharmacist Thessalus; p. 130, on the wanderings of Clement, in *Stromat.* 1.1.10 (but it sounds as if Clement were converted before coming under the spell of his Sicilian teacher); Hieron., *Vita Hilarionis* 2.1f., converted evidently in his midteens, cf. 6.1; and Cyprian argued into belief by a certain Caecilianus, who *eum ad agnitionem verae divinitatis a saeculari errore correxerat*, in Pontius, *Vita et passio Cypriani* 4. The sum appears (with much exaggeration) in the picture of the 2d and 3d centuries, in J. C. Smith (1979) 217: "conversion from one philosophy

to another, from one religion to another, and from one sect to another became an almost frenzied activity"(!).

21 Orig., *C. Cels.* 1.9f. (trans. Chadwick). Notice that, for Origen, "conversion" (ἐπιστρέφειν) might lie in reading (though not only there), as Aubin (1963) 144 points out, citing *In Jer. homil.* 4.6, etc. Origen distinguishes (ibid. 154) between such privileged initiation as he himself or his like might gain, and the level of understanding of the masses.

22 Just., *Dial.* 8.2, δέος τι ἔχουσι; cf. Tatian, who ends his account in a reference to the Last Judgment; and, earlier, compare the woman whose view of conversion, when she turned to her husband's salvation, centered only on "punishment in the eternal flames [for those] who do not live modestly and according to right reason," cited in MacMullen (1983) 185.

23 *Dialogue with Theopompus* translated from the Syrian by Ryssel (1880) 73–99, beginning abruptly, "As I was about to start, one day, for the place where I usually abode, a man called Theopompus asked me if God was immune to suffering *(leidensunfähig)*." Gregory gives a quick no and hurries off to his "friends, where they usually gathered," where Theopompus catches up with him; "for [his] thoughts are continually in mind and leave [him] no rest." A good case of *homo religiosus*! Perhaps Gregory is imagining the scene to be a catechetical group. So Knorr (1966) 76f. supposes. On Gregory perhaps writing under Origen's eye, see Ryssel (1880) 124. Date, then: ca. A.D. 239.

24 The earliest sign of this gap being seen consciously, outside of NT texts, must be Papias frg. 3 = Euseb., *H.E.* 3.39, which depreciates glib speakers that go over well with οἱ πολλοί; the last, within my period of study, may be Jerome in various passages, e.g. *Tract. in ps.* 91.11 (*CCSL* 78.139), *loquor simplicius propter simpliciores fratres qui non possunt intellegere sublimius*, or, on Cyprian, *In Ionam* 3.6 (*PL* 25.1142Cf.), well discussed by Duval (1972) 552–554. In the interval between these termini, sources show abundantly the problem of class prejudice, e.g. Min. Fel. 2.4 and 3.1 (*haec inperitiae vulgaris caecitas*) and passages cited in MacMullen (1983) 144 n. 33, from Tert., Athenag., and esp. Euseb.

25 The danger of monocular perception of the ancient church is well signaled by Aland (1961) 33.

26 There are several such pockets of prevalence to be found in the east. See Harnack (1908) 2.116, 145 (Edessa), 189f., and 217. But the best known is in and around one of the small coastal towns of Pontus in ca. A.D. 110 (note Plin., *Ep.* 10.96.9, even *vici et agri* are touched by Christianity). Sherwin-White (1966) 693f. adds, "It is noteworthy that Pliny had trouble with Christians only in Pontus—the common reference of the affair to Bithynia is misleading" (and the error may go back to Harnack's treatment, 2.186f.). As to my A.D. 300 estimate, I arrive at it by supposing an empire of 60 millions and Christians close to a tenth within the eastern provinces (which were more populous). A proportion of 5 percent or a little more, in the entire empire, is the one most often conjectured, see Molland (1974) 54, or Soden (1974) 35, "Christianity can have approached a half of the population, around A.D. 300, only in the areas of its greatest penetration in certain cities (and ancient Christianity was and remained essentially an urban religion)"; or see Grant (1977) 8, and the very sane discus-

sion, 5–9. An estimate twice as large, or only half as large, I think would be almost demonstrably wrong (by arguments not worth the pages they would take); and nothing closer seems possible to me from the second volume of Harnack, nor anything significant missing therefrom. Of course, every item in Harnack's dossier needs interpretation. Notice, for illustration, how he reasons (2.190 n. 2) that, throughout Asia Minor, individual churches must have been small (here he persuades me, but the question is tricky). Or again, note (2.286) how North Africa bishoprics in A.D. 300 numbered under 250 but, in A.D. 400, between 500 and 700 (so, at the earlier date, Christianity had touched only a minority of the region's small towns).

27 To the reason I offer, Bardy (1949) 272 would add two others: "Nous ne pouvons insister longuement sur le rôle joué par les écoles chrétiennes dans le conversion du monde, d'abord parce qu'il est certain que ce rôle a été minime," and further, there is almost no evidence.

28 Orig., *C. Cels.* 3.8 (*GCS* 1 p. 209), a passage much discussed, along with the whole question of how many martyrs there really were (see above, n. 13). For historical purposes, what counts most is their impact, and how they were perceived. Note must be taken, too, of really odd statements by Melito (he knows of persecutions only under Nero and Domitian, in Euseb., *H.E.* 4.26.9), by Tertullian, *Apol.* 5.5 (no persecutions under Trajan or Marcus Aurelius!), and in the *Passio SS. Montani et Lucii* 21.3 (no martyrdoms in Carthage prior to Cyprian), all of which show how church writers might have been ignorant of other regions or times.

29 Orig., *C. Cels.* 8.69 (trans. Chadwick); Min. Fel. 8.4; and other more specific indications in MacMullen (1983) 191 n. 46. I mention here, however, several texts which scholars cite, but which should be set aside. First, Eusebius is of little help, saying (*Demonstr. ev.* 6.20.297a–b) that "the word of the Gospel teaching has waxed stronger among the Egyptians than among any other men," and (298a) that there was much teaching done. Vague, and having in mind the Alexandrian schools? Campenhausen (1953) 217 supposes that Clement's teaching in Alexandria was open to pagans, i.e. not in the catechetical school, but that assertion has not displaced the older view, see e.g. Frend (1974) 36. And Frend (1965) 413 and Molland (1974) 60, by only partial citation of Cypr., *Ad Demetr.* 13, make it appear that Cyprian knew of Christians preaching in public places; but it is actually a case of their reiterating their faith even under torture, during the Decian persecutions. Finally, it is recognized that the church developed no conscious, formal, or institutionalized missionary effort or personnel. See, for example, Soden (1974) 28, Frend (1974) 32, or Molland (1974) 66.

30 Meeks (1983) 103, citing 1 Cor. 16:22; but (p. 106) he notes 1 Cor. 14:23, which supposes outsiders may happen on meetings in progress and not be instantly expelled. Celsus, on the other hand, says that Christians "go about their doings and teaching in secret," *C. Cels.* 1.3 (*GCS* 1 p. 57).

31 Tert., *Ad uxorem* 2 passim, e.g. 2.3; Cypr., *Testimonia* 3.62 (*PL* 4.483) and *De lapsis* 6; Council of Elvira (a. 305) can. 15, Hefele (1907–52) 1, 1, p. 231; Council of Arles (a. 314) can. 11 (modifying the absolute prohibition of mixed marriages); Council of Hippo (a. 393) can. 16, specifying only clerics in the ban; full and horrified excoriation of mixed marriages in Zeno Veron., *Tract.*

2.7.8.14–17; Ambrose's dire warnings, *De Abraham.* 1.9.84, *Expos. ev. Luc.* 8.2f., and *Expos. ps.* 118.48.1; cf. his *De offic.* 2.136, implied (*idolorum contagiis*). A few passages acknowledge reality, i.e. proper conduct for a Christian toward a non-Christian spouse, in 1 Peter 3:1, and Pauline passages cited by Harnack (1908) 1.69 and 81, and Clem. Alex., *Stromat.* 4.19.123, cited by Bardy (1949) 225; but notice various warnings against interested "conversions" only to obtain a wife, which imply the existence of rules or customs against mixed marriages, e.g. Aug., *Sermo* 47.18 (*CCSL* 41.589) or Ambrose, *Expos. ps.* 1.c.

32 "Scandalous tricks," τὰ ἐπιρρητότα, Orig., *C. Cels.* 3.52 (*GCS* 1.248), "trickery" as Chadwick says, like the γοητεῖα practised by Christians, ibid. 1.6 and 1.9. For the whole passage (Chadwick's trans.), see 3.44, 53, and 55 (*GCS* 1.239f., 248, and 250f.). Compare the instant contempt with which a cultivated man dismissed two early Christians' doctrine when he found out they worked with their hands (a wonderful vignette, almost too perfect to trust, but not doubted by good scholars: Euseb., *H.E.* 3.20.1–4).

33 Clem. Alex., *Paedagogus* 3.4.28f. (*PG* 8.596A). The idea that women were especially given to silly religious ideas and experiences is as old as Plato, *Laws* 909D. See some interesting views on the subject in Straten (1976) 17; also, the charge against Jesus that he especially surrounded himself with, and misled, women, cited in Harnack (1908) 1.65. In our period, see also ibid. 2.139 (numerical majority of women among Christians) and Tert., *De praescr.* 41, where women presume to offer instruction, even to exorcize and promise cures; later, in writers like Liban., *Or.* 16.47; Hieron., *Ep.* 50.3 (*CSEL* 4, 1 p. 390); Sulp. Sev., *Hist. sacra* 2.46 (*PL* 20.155); and Soz., *H.E.* 7.10.4—all of whom discredit views held only by "contemptible girls" (or similar phrases).

34 The adjoining rooms are T, V, and Z, published in exceptionally perplexing fashion by Vermaseren and Van Essen (1965). They assign T to Mithraists (p. 114), the rest to Christians. They also try to reconstruct the history of relations between the two groups from the history of building alterations. Their interpretations do not persuade me at all. The communicating door, if it allowed disturbances, could have been easily closed (door o/o, formed by afterthought, p. 73), rather than being screened off only partially by afterthought walls of unknown purpose; or the west door of T could have been walled up by the Mithraists. Similarly with entrance P (p. 83, etc. —"see groundplan," but in fact it cannot be located on *any* of the many plans or reconstructions): walling it up was easy, screening walls served no clear defensive purpose. My criticisms, however, stretch out too long. The site retains its interest and significance.

35 See below, chap. IX n. 21.

36 Tert., *Apol.* 42.2f.

37 Harnack (1908) 1.35, *Shepherd of Hermas, Mand.* 10.1; date, mid-3d century. On the inscription, of rare interest, see Robert (1960) 423f., comparing other theatrical performers in Diehl (1925–67) 1.115 nos. 577f. On Christians in magistracies and in non-Christian priesthoods, see Council of Elvira can. 2–4 and 55f. The best illustration of what must have been the usual relations between Christians and their neighbors appears in the dossier of reports lying under the Donatist controversies (below, chap. X n. 3).

38 MacMullen (1981) 36–42, esp. 40, where I offer substantiation for saying

"there existed—it is no great exaggeration to say it of all but the fairly rich—no formal social life in the world of the Apologists that was entirely secular."

39 Ibid. 49f., cf. M. Smith (1978) 107, "cures are also a major concern of magic. They stand first among the miracles for which *The Book of Secrets* (1.1) gives instructions."

CHAPTER V

1 MacMullen (1969) chaps. IV–V gives a longer account. I need not, for my purposes here, justify every point in this rapid synopsis of much troublesome material.

2 For parallels, see e.g. chap. II n. 9, above, and below, chap. X

3 Palmer (1981) 378–380; for the relations of emperors to favored deities, see the sources cited in MacMullen (1981) 186f.; but the subject is a very large one. I need only distinguish between imperial *preference* in cult (Augustus' for Apollo, for instance) and imperial *courtesy*, which might very likely be intended to win friends (Postumus and Hercules Deusonensis, for instance; see above, chap. II n. 7).

4 The coins sometimes puzzle historians; but it is not very plausible that they appeared contradictorily simply because the mint-people did not know or care to find out what the emperor wanted. So Barnes (1981) 48 and 309 n. 47 seems to believe. Would an engraver in Mongolia today produce, and postal offices distribute for a year, postage stamps depicting the Crucifixion? For later usages, see below, n. 23.

5 A classic statement recalled by Brown (1972) 63 and, in 1977 in the *TLS*, once again in Brown (1982) 97.

6 For Constantine's army in 312 being virtually all non-Christian, see, e.g., Jones (1963) 33. Probability amounts to a certainty, but direct evidence is scant. Soldiers, in the past, were sought in the countryside by preference; and *rus* was pagan, so reasons Mazzarino (1951) 248, with a reference to Piganiol that actually affords no help, and to *paganus* = non-Christian = *rusticus*; but cf. Mohrmann (1952) 118f., with a better derivation, *paganus* = outsider or noninitiate. And *CT* 7.20.2 gives us Constantine's soldiers shouting, "The gods [plural] guard you!" But there is something suspicious in the dating of the law. It is not of the given A.D. 320, apparently; so Barnes (1981) 309 n. 42 moves it back to 307, which suits his argument, and Gabba (1978) 46 and others move it up to A.D. 326. *Non liquet* (and see below, n. 10). Gabba (p. 45) also adduces Zos. 2.95.5—too late and too partisan a source, in my view—and Libanius' testimony. The latter says (*Or.* 30.6) only that Constantine's troops "attacked the gods though earlier worshipping them," seeming to say they were no longer pagans; but this happened, says Libanius, when he was still a boy, i.e., ca. 330 (see n. ad loc., Loeb ed.)—so, unreliable.

7 Euseb., *Vita Const.* 4.18. Chance items on recruitment prove nothing: that Pachomius was non-Christian (*Vita Pachomii* 5 p. 6), or Saint Martin's father non-Christian and he himself Christian and drafted in A.D. 331, cf. Sulp. Sev.,

Vita Martini 2 (father evidently under Constantius Chlorus) and Fontaine (1961) 205.

8 Barnes (1981) 48—though it must be said in fairness, and as the reason for my calling attention to the statement, that a great many almost similar ones can be found in modern works on the period. For more on the matter, earlier, see above, chap. II n. 16.

9 Lact., *De mort. persecut.* 46.6; 48, with slight differences in Euseb., *H.E.* 10.5.4; ibid. 10.7.1; idem, *Vita Const.* 4.19f.; *Paneg. vet.* 9(12). 2.4f. and 3.3; and *CIL* 6.1139, *instinctu divinitatis*, etc.

10 The passages cited are by that army specialist (non-Christian, but cool), Ammianus 24.1.1, *deum usitato clamore testati*; 24.3.6, *deo meque . . . ductante*; 15.8.10, 16.12.18, and 17.13.33, *contio omnis . . . deum ex usu testata non posse Constantium vinci*. Cf. similar phrases proclaimed at or by army assemblies, 16.12.12, *pace dei sit dictum* (Julian) and *caelestis dei favore . . . freti*, or *salutaris quidam genius praesens*, ibid.; 21.13.14, *favor numinis summi praesens* (Constantius); and 24.1.12, Ammianus himself regularly uses such monotheistic ambiguities (16.12.52; 17.7.3; 17.13.28; 25.7.5; 29.5.40; 31.10.18; 31.16.4), but his wording, above, indicates expressly that they were also army routine. More on this below, chap. IX n. 16.

11 Theodoret., *H.E.* 4.1.4 (*PG* 82.1124 = *GCS* 19.211), built upon Rufinus 11.1, all of which Seeck (1911) 4.366 dismisses as "certainly a fiction." I am inclined to agree, but the judgment is peremptory.

12 Amm. 26.7.17, *testati more militiae Iovem invictum Procopium fore.*

13 Soldiers at dinner, Greg. Naz., *Or.* 4.84 (*Against Julian* I, *PG* 35.609C); pagan practices: Amm. 22.12.6 (a. 363 in Antioch); said to be pagan, by Liban., *Or.* 18.166f.; Julian, *Ep.* 26.415C p. 54 Bidez, a. 361.; and Soz., *H.E.* 5.17.8f. (*PG* 67.1268Bf.).

14 Liban., *Or.* 18.168, Julian "persuaded the man that took up a spear to take up a libation and incense as well . . . , and, if reason did not avail, gold and silver combined to persuade."

15 See Amm. 21.2.4 (a. 360), Julian "in order to elicit the favor of everyone, without let from anyone, pretended devotion to Christianity"; also, below, n. 23, where a pagan emperor still resorts to the Chi-Rho on his coinage.

16 Toleration is what is argued for by Gabba (1978) 47, in the subsequent discussion joined by Straub and myself, p. 52; "peaceful coexistence."

17 "Pious pagan," Secundius Salutius, cf. *PLRE* I p. 816.

18 Amm. 25.5.12 (Arintheus at least *died* a Christian; Victor was Christian after Julian; all members of both parties except Dagalaifus went on under Valens, with notable continuity).

19 Haehling (1978) 511; exposition of his percentages of known names out of the known total of incumbents (505: 89 percent under Constantine, 100 percent under Julian, etc.) and their religion (507: 32 percent under Constantine, 100 percent under Julian, etc.). The whole study appears to me excellently done. Ups and downs in his tables show nothing decisive till after A.D. 400, supplying one of my reasons for choosing that date as terminus.

20 Ibid. 537; compare Jovian's new appointments (548): all but one a Christian,

and the exception a *magister militum*. Or Gratian's twenty-two appointees (569f.), of which only five are pagans, and one of them a *magister militum*. The last pagan occupant of any of the thirteen posts is a *magister militum* whose tenancy takes us right up to the middle of the fifth century (242).

21 Above, n. 19; Oros. 7.28.18, *omnes christianos e palatio suo iussit expelli* (with Euseb., *Vita Const.* 1.52 and 54), but cf. Haehling (1978) 45, on the *notarius* Marianus.

22 See *PLRE* 1.476 and 478–479, correcting *RE* s.v. Ceionius 1859f. (Seeck 1899) and Schoenebeck (1939) 76.

23 Kellner (1968) 88, a coin of 327/8 of Cple. (but rare: p. 90); from A.D. 334 on, in Arles, Siscia, Antioch (91–93), perhaps (so Kellner thinks) more a mint mark than a proper legend, yet by then "well-known military victory- and honor-insignia," dating from the Milvian Bridge. On the three sons' coins, see ibid. 86 and 98–105; on Magnentius' coins, ibid. 58f. and 79f. and Ziegler (1970) 53–57. The Christogram also appears on the shields of Constantius' Guard, depicted on a well-known silver dish, in Kent and Painter (1977) 25 no. 11 and on the shields and *labara* of soldiers shown on a 4th-century presentation cup in Fremersdorf (1952) 1.68f. and 71f. For Magnentius' religion, see Philostorgius p. 52 Bidez, καὶ τοὺς οὖν αὐτῷ ἅτε τῇ τῶν δαιμόνων θεραπείᾳ προσανακειμένους, discussed by Geffcken (1978) 193 n. 61 and Piganiol (1972) 95; also Ziegler (1970) 62–64, on several sources, concluding that the Christianity in the coins is propaganda to make the regime (74) acceptable among Christians.

24 Barnes (1981) 191 winds up considerable discussion with the conclusion that "a pagan emperor" (in A.D. 324) "could no longer govern without the acquiescence and good will of his Christian subjects," and means by this "political advantage" to be found thereby in both Constantine's and Licinius' own domains. In support of this view, he simply cites (368, ref. to n. 5) his "chapters III, IV." But in fact I can find in those chapters no substantiation. My argument, rather, leads me to the opposite view, well summed up though reached along other paths by Chadwick (1978) 9: "the church was nothing like numerous or influential enough to be a source of political power. In 300, it remained a small minority group, especially in the west." For completeness' sake, I here mention also the notion of politics and religion mixing to form a party, in P. Ryl. 624—see now Moscadi (1970) 108f.—and, earlier, in Decius' reign; see *Orac. Sibyll.* 13.85f., Euseb., *H.E.* 6.39.1, and Zon. 3 p. 132 Dindorf. Against the perception in these texts, however, that Decius persecuted Christians in order to pain the pro-Christian emperor Philip, we must set the pagan sources which present Decius and Philip as friends and mutually loyal.

25 Veyne (1978) 206f. and, on a grand scale, in his work *Le Pain et le cirque* (1976).

26 The Olympieion in Athens, Paus. 1.18.6 and other sources; Dio 76.16.3 and Birley (1972) 218 on the enormous Hercules (?) temple; Palmer (1981) 378f. on Elagabalus; and Zos. 1.61 on Aurelian's Sun-Temple in Palmyra. On a far smaller scale, imperial patronage such as Augustus showed to the Artemis shrine, assigning it certain local taxes, is similar (*SEG* 4.516B).

27 Waltzing (1895–1900) 2.202f., 479f., and 485f. on shrines built by guilds; for

shrines paid for by cities, see *CIL* 2.3557; 8.21665; 13.5562; and other material in MacMullen (1981) 105 and n. 46.

28 MacMullen (1981) 108f.; on Ostia, Meiggs (1960) 327f. and Hermansen (1981) 61–71.

29 There is a good example in his resort to entrail-divination in *CT* 16.10.1 (320): *retento more veteris observantiae, quid portendat, ab haruspicibus requiratur,* etc. On the disputed question, how well informed and orthodox was Constantine's Christianity, see one view in MacMullen (1969) 109f. I would now diminish the role of formal instruction he might have had before A.D. 315, in the light of Lippold (1981) 14f.

30 The sites are all familiar, I think, except Cirta (in *Ep. Constantini CSEL* 26.215, Optatus), and Savaria, cf. Kadar (1969) 180.

31 Gaudemet (1959) 311f.

32 Theodoret., *H.E.* 1.10 and 4.4 (*PG* 82.937B and 1129A = 1.11.2f. in the 2d ed. *GCS* of 1954).

33 Euseb., *H.E.* 10.6.1f. and 6f.; *CT* 16.2.1.2–7; *Chron. pascale* a. 325 (*Chron. min.* 1 p. 232): and Gaudemet (1947) 27–32.

34 Brown (1982) 98, instancing Euseb., *Vita Const.* 3.58, which describes how he "bestowed abundant provision for the necessities of the poor." Add, that his agents offered money in A.D. 320 to those (Donatists) who would accept his faith, in Carthage, *Sermo de passione SS. Donati et Advocati* (*PL* 8.754A).

35 Soz., *H.E.* 2.5 (*PG* 67.945Bf.); on seizing of temple treasure, cf. Hieron., *Chron.* a. 331; Liban., *Or.* 30.6 and 37; Theophanes, *Chron.* a. 322 (*PG* 108.117), adding that the temples "were annihilated" (not true); brief mentions in Julian, *Or.* 7.228B, and Liban., *Or.* 62.8; and a general tableau with strong colors in Barnes (1981) 247.

36 I hope to present the evidence more fully at another time. It is quite striking. For the moment, a sampling can be found in *CJ* 9.11.1 and 13.35(36).9 and *CT* 2.30.1, 7.1.1, 9.15.1, 9.16.1, 9.18.1, 9.22.1, and 9.24.1, from which it appears how influential Constantine was in setting the level of judicial savagery.

37 Euseb., *Vita Const.* 4.25 (no doubt with the text of the decree before his eyes).

38 Emphatic; and for the most likely meaning of the texts on mantic ritual—Zos. 2.29, *CT* 16.10.2, and Euseb., *Vita Const.* 2.45—see Schoenebeck (1939) 67 and Drake (1982) 464f.; and on more banning of magic, below, chap. X n. 28.

39 Drake, loc. cit., or Dörries (1954) 52, explicit about the "Toleranzerklärung," or (54) the "Toleranzgesetz," in describing Const., *Vita Const.* 2.56.

40 Constantine's address to the bishops in 314, *Appendix* III *Optati* ed. Ziwsa p. 206.

41 Above, n. 37 and below, chap. XI n. 18; and note such examples, too, as can be read in a publicly advertised letter against one Christian party to a dispute in North Africa: *ii, qui a diabolo possessi sunt . . . , qui malo impiae mentis infecti sunt,* and so on, *Appendix* X *Optati* p. 214 Ziwsa; or again, in Euseb., *Vita Const.* 2.56 (*GCS* 1 p. 64), "As to persons holding themselves aloof from us [i.e. non-converts], let them, if they want, keep their temples of lies. We have the glorious dwelling of Thy truth. . . ." Accommodation to the reality of pagan strength, here reluctant, perhaps appears also in the sequence of his laws

of 319/20 on *haruspicina, CT* 9.16.2 (319) and 1 (320), as Piganiol (1932) 127 surmises.

CHAPTER VI

1 *Acta Petri* 8 p. 55 Lipsius, showing incidentally how such a man as the Marcellus of the tale could provide leadership: when he turned to follow a heresiarch, so did the congregation. Similarly, there is the rich Lucilla in Carthage, her house the church headquarters, in Monceaux (1901–23) 4.16f.
2 Aug., *Ep.* 125f., A.D. 411.
3 On the runaway election of Ambrose, see, among several sources, Paulin., *Vita S. Ambros.* 6–9 (*PL* 14.29f.); compare that great official Nectarius, not yet baptized when chosen for the Cple. bishopric (Soz., *H.E.* 5.8). On Synesius, see Bregman (1982) passim. On the worldly role of bishops, see the excellent account by Chadwick (1980), esp. p. 9, where "Augustine remarks to Jerome that wealthy candidates with low educational and spiritual qualifications are often preferred to poor men with higher qualifications (*Ep.* 167.18)." Also see further perspectives in MacMullen (1980) 27f. In eastern episcopal elections in the same decade or so, candidates were promoted (i.e. it was assumed they would be broadly favored) on the basis of their pedigree or money, γένος and πλοῦτος, or as fugitives from other, earlier feuds. Cf. Joh. Chrysos., *De sacerdotio* 3.15 (*PG* 48.652).
4 Some ecclesiastical building in Milan (S. Lorenzo) where "imperial building appears likely," in Krautheimer (1983) 88; on a great patron constructing a church, at Reims, see Pietri (1970) 444; on the stimulus to building by rich and vigorous bishops of the 4th century (Italy), see Chadwick (1980) 13. Aside, however, from Ovadiah's work (1970) passim, showing 4th-century Holy Land church-building and superseding Butler's work, I know of only one other collection of evidence, that of Harrison (1963). He discovers no identifiable church building in Cilicia before the 5th century. We should remember, however, secular building also—cf. the boast of portico, aqueduct, etc., constructed from church funds in his town by bishop Theodoret, *Ep.* 81 (*PG* 83.926C).
5 Soz., *H.E.* 1.8 (*PG* 67.876D); special testamentary privileges, ibid. 877A-B; cf., generally, 3.17.2f. (*PG* 67.1093B) and *CT* 1.3.1 (343) and 1.3.2 (357).
6 Examples of ad hoc imperial gifts (aside from several reported by Constantine) are: Theodoret., *H.E.* 4.16 (*PG* 82.1161), where Valens impulsively presents Basil with "some splendid rural properties for the poor whom he [Basil] had under his care"; and Marc. Diac., *Vita Porph.* 100, where a woman and her aunt, on conversion, are assigned a daily corn allowance in perpetuity out of the Gaza church funds.
7 *CT* 5.13.3 and 10.1.8 (a. 364); cf. Julian's suspension and Jovian's restoration of a grain allowance to churches, Theodoret., *H.E.* 4.4.1 (*PG* 82.1129 = *GCS* 19.216); Eugenius' restoration of state monies to sacrifices, which Theodosius stripped away, Chastagnol (1967) 54, thus reviving Gratian's harsh measures of 376/7, Chastagnol (1969) 143. For Gratian's removal of public subsidies of cult-costs, see further King (1961) 73 n. 3, and McGeachy (1942) 141 and n. 1; the

change struck at "the very foundations of Roman paganism" (142) and rendered it "no longer a source of income and prestige to the aristocracy, a sort of symbol of their dominant position in Roman society." Thereafter, note *CJ* 11.66.4 (382/4), confiscating all temple lands and gold and cutting off annual payments to priests; *CT* 6.3.1 (393), abolishing payments to the chief priest of Syria out of the senatorial tax; 16.10.4 (396), depriving all non-Christian priests of all privileges (financial? or of civic status?); and 16.10.19 (407), stripping temples of all rights to taxes payable to them in kind.

8 MacMullen (1981) 204 n. 50, as illustration of costs; ibid. 36–39 on very widely popular cult meals.

9 Liban., *Or.* 2.30; cf. 30.20 (a. 380/1) referring to the recent "expulsion of people who offered help to penury through their attentions to the elderly, men and women, and to orphans too"; also Julian, *Ep.* 84a.430C, Galatian priests support the poor, who serve them. Laumonier (1958) 397 describes how in one center "ainsi la majorité pauvre de la population est entretenue littéralement (car les fêtes sont nombreuses) par la minorité riche"; and see more examples in MacMullen (1981) 165 n. 43.

10 Philostr., *Vit. soph.* 549, Herodes' μεγαλοφροσύνη.

11 In Rome, the Jewish epitaph, the deceased φλοπένης, cf. Frey (1936–52) 1 no. 203. For Judaism, besides many emphatic texts (Leviticus, Deuteronomy, Job, Psalms, etc.), cf. the concern for gleaning, the corner of the field reserved for the poor (*peah*), and the poor-box, Graeven (1901) 161. There were offertory boxes at pagan shrines: Graeven (1901) 162–164 and 178, Edgar (1902) 140f., and MacMullen (1981) 164 n. 36. But these were for sacrifices, not for poor-relief.

12 Paulin., *Ep.* 13.15, cited in Brown (1980) 36; Greg. Nyss., *Pauper. amand.*; Ambros., *De Nabuthe*; and Callinicus, *Vita S. Hypatii* 6.45, 31.5f., and 34.2, on supplying of food and clothing in Thrace in the period around A.D. 400. I cannot find much other evidence for poor-relief in the 4th century, though thereafter it becomes quite abundant. Cf. Patlagean (1977) 188–196, or, in Egypt, Shenute's activities, or Rees (1950) 92.

13 *Ep.* 84 p. 144 Bidez (= *Ep.* 49 = *Ep.* 22 in the Loeb edition), regarding ἡ περὶ τοὺς ξένους φιλανθρωπία, which (145) must be matched with non-Christian hostels for the poor and sick, with free feed such as the state supplied to the churches. See also Soz., *H.E.* 5.15 (*PG* 67.1256B), Julian's relief system for widows.

14 Ambrose, *Ep.* 18.11.

15 Callu (1981) 236f. and Matthews (1975) 208f., relying largely on Zos. 4.59.3, where the senate's pagan envoy declares μὴ κατὰ θεσμὸν . . . πράττεσθαι τά τελούμενα μὴ δημοσίου τοῦ δαπανήματος ὄντος. The source is, after all, sixth century, and must invent the dialogue; but see the additional evidence and discussion in Mazzarino (1974) 379.

16 Ambrose, *Ep.* 3.29.150f., after Ticinum, bishop and *clerici* alike had half succumbed to an *imperiale rescriptum* and to the *magistri officiorum*—all very terrifying.

17 Athanas., *Hist. Arianorum* 54f. (*PG* 25.757C and 760A); for the removal of the dole, see §10 (705B) and 31 (728C) as well. In the outcome (760B) Heraclius,

plus the Prefect of Egypt and the Catholikos, stir up the mob of non-Christians to attack the church and stone the congregation inside, resulting in some deaths (all this being, of course, reported by a partisan, yet one subject to correction at the time). Note similar tactics on the part of the Arian emperor Constantius, who in A.D. 359, at the Council of Rimini, tried in effect to corrupt bishops by giving them *annonae et cellaria*, Sulp. Sev., *Hist. sacra* 2.41 (*PL* 20.152).

18 Ambrose, *Ep.* 20.5f. Her reasoning is the same as Pope Gregory's later: among the tenant farmers on church land in Sardinia, if any is still a *paganus, conversio* should be wrought by "burdening him with so heavy a rise in his rent that the penalty itself will drive him to righteousness, and quickly, too" (*Ep.* 4.26 = *PL* 77.695).

19 The emperor's attempt to win them to the Christians' πίστις, Zos. 4.59.1f.

20 Euseb., *Vita Const.* 4.54.2 and 3.66, cf. above, chap. V n. 33, and later, Libanius protesting against the "constraint" to convert (προσαναγκάζειν) being applied by Theodosius. It could produce, he says, only a change in "a matter of words," not in reality (*Or.* 30.28f., of the A.D. 380s, probably late 380s).

21 Liban. *Or.* 2.31 (a. 381).

22 For the well-known monetary rewards in high imperial posts and the prevailing ethic (if that is the right word) in those posts, see Jones (1964) 383f. and 1055–1057.

23 Soc., *H.E.* 2.5.

24 The best example I know is a certain Jovinus, see Pietri (1970) 443, 446, and 450; others similar, below, n. 28. For Constantine's preferences expressed in appointments, see Schoenebeck (1939) 74–76 and, on this and other reigns, Haehling (1978) passim, esp. 1f., 5, 273, and 557f.

25 Soz., *H.E.* 2.5 (*PG* 67.948B).

26 See passages above, chap. IV n. 31, on interfaith marriages; Ambrose, *Expos. ps.* 118.20.48f., *dum honorem affectat sub imperatoribus christianis simulata mente orationem deferre se fingit, inclinatur et solo sternitur qui genui mentis non flexerit;* Aug., *De cat. rud.* 16.24, *vitae praesentis aliquod commodum* is the motive, and (17.26) *ut aut promereantur homines a quibus temporalia commoda expectant, aut quia offendere nolunt quos timent;* similarly, *Sermo* 47.18 (*CC* 41.589), avoidance of some *pressura huius seculi* or gain of some *temporalis commoditas* or *ut maiorem amicum conciliet;* or to gain a lucrative city office (*exactor*), *Sermo Morin* 1 cited in Lepelley (1979–81) 2.42; and good pages in Daut (1971) 174–176 and 179 (passages from Zeno of Verona, bishop A.D. 361–371, and Gaudentius of Brixia, bishop A.D. 385–397) and Mesot (1958) 18. The subject blends into that of semi-Christians from indifference, not those motivated by worldly considerations. See below, chap. IX n. 28.

27 Aug., *Ep.* 89.7 (a. 406) on reformed Donatists, *ficti*, perhaps; but he explains that they may be truly reformed not only by *terror* but by teaching.

28 Haehling (1978) 28 on Julian's uncle, married to a Christian but leaving that faith under his nephew's rule; other distinguished converts by Julian, sincere or false depending on our different sources, cf. Felix 3 and Helpidius 4 in *PLRE*; also Vindaonius Magnus, apparently, see Haehling (1978) 119; and notice Eunap., *Vit. soph.* 501, in Lydia in Julian's day, where "everyone was hurrying to build temples, with all zeal and fervor." In the 390s Marcianus (later PVR a.

409–410) is an instance. There were many more: King (1961) 91 citing Prudentius, *Contra Symm.* 544f. and 578; Haehling (1978) 405 quoting the *Carmen contra paganos*; and Bloch (1963) 200 on this poem and the *Carmen adv. Flavianum*,
which names individual turncoats and indicates "a veritable stampede by osten-
sibly Christian office-seekers who succumbed to the proselytism of Flavianus."
For a careful translation and the context of the two poems plus a third, see
Croke and Harris (1982) 78–89.

29 Ambrose, *Ep.* 17.2, *etiam sub principibus christianis plerique sunt lapsi*, in search of
certain obscure *privilegia*; unexplained individuals like Seleucus or Aristaenetus,
evidently raised as Christians, see Haehling (1978) 29; *quidam Christiani* around
Tarraco in the 380s, so reports bishop Eumerius (*PL* 84.632); and *CJ* 1.7.2 (a.
383). But there were unforced apostates back in Pliny's day, *Ep.* 10.96.6.

30 Mesot (1958) 18, "to be a Christian was à la vogue," and "zum guten Ton"
(56); or Jones (1963) 36, "a more potent cause of conversion than calculations of
material gain was the fact that Christianity became respectable."

31 Having no competence in the subject, I rely on Anawati (1973), who emphasizes *in Syria* the tax policies, political sympathies, cultural similarities, and admiration for Islamic morals (20, 29, and 31); *in Egypt*, social advantages, political promotion, exemption from taxes, and admiration for doctrinal clarity
(ibid. 27 and 29f.), with Lapidus (1972) 255, Lapidus especially emphasizing
taxes, 256 and 258f.; and *in Anatolia*, Ménage (1979), who stresses the economic base needed by the churches (63f.), social pressure (66), and, in the
countryside, the sanctity of the dervishes, "for they can do what the orthodox
cleric cannot: interpret dreams, induce rain, cure diseases, and ensure fertility"
(59f.). All the forces seen to have been at work by these scholars are much the
same as those I discover in the post-Constantinian empire.

CHAPTER VII

1 It is wrong to quote Greg. Nyss., *Vita S. Greg. Thaumat.*, at all trustingly, as I
did in MacMullen (1983) 186 and as Harnack (1908) 1.206 does also—even
Ryssel (1880) 22 himself—all of us before seeing the Syriac in translation.
Ryssel (1894) supplied the deficiency, offering also excellent analysis. We have
a 6th-century MS (228) that draws on an original of the first quarter of the 4th
century (240). Granted, it contains some nonsense (e.g. §2, p. 241) in an account otherwise acceptable on grounds of simplicity and logic, and on grounds
of comparison with Rufinus' (Latin) and Gregory of Nyssa's (Greek) versions.
Telfer (1930) knows nothing of the Syriac but is useful on the other two versions; Abramowski (1976) 162 places the Greek version in its contemporary
context of controversy, along with the forged *Confession* of Gregory, p. 164,
and Riedinger (1981) 311; finally, Knorr (1966) reviews the value of the Syriac
version, whose neglect he rightly considers "erstaunlich" (80 n. 3), adding (81
n. 24) an extra good reason for rating that version highest, in comparison with
the others. In my text here, I cite by chapters in the work, as they appear in
Ryssel (1894) 241f. The bulk of the incidents belong to the A.D. 240s, others
(chronology seems unimportant) after the Decian persecutions. Early, for example, must be §5 p. 245 (also almost verbatim in Rufinus), "Wenn sonach ein

Jünger so viel stärker ist als du, um wie viel mehr erst sein Meister! Darum ist es meine Pflicht, dass ich hingehe, um dem zu dienen, der mehr ist als du!" Compare Simon Magus, made to say, to his own later undoing, "'He that has a master is not a god.' And when he said this, many said, 'You put it well'" (*Acta Petri* 23 p. 71 Lipsius). Or again, Athanas., *De incarnat.* 48.6, exorcized demons "flee Christ as their master."

2 Athanas., *Vita S. Anton.* 70 (*PG* 26.941Cf.—a generation *post eventum*, but our reporter was very close to the scene); and Sulp. Sev., *Vita Martini* 17.1f., the saint is capable even of producing levitation in his patients, §3.6. Similarly among the Goths, captive Christian priests by their exorcisms, healings, and ascetic conduct "astonished" the barbarians and thereby induced their conversion (so reports Soz., *H.E.* 2.6, if he can have known); or again, in mid-4th-century Palestine, where, when Hilarion at Elusa is begged by the Saracens to cure the possessed among them and at last to build a church wherever he wishes among them, as part of his bargain, he says he will come often on condition that they will worship God—i.e. be converted. But on the historicity of the text, see Mohrmann (1975) xliii: "la Vita Hilarionis . . . non è, e non vuole essere, un opera storica." The motivation in it would then reflect what Jerome, living thereabouts in the 380s, thought credible—still of value, and partly confirmed by Soz., *H.E.* 5.15 (*PG* 67.1260B), who tells us that, evidently under Constantius, Hilarion cleansed a possessed person of a devil, whereupon "they [the family] were converted to the religion of the Christians." For the miracle of healing that converts "the whole race of the Rugians," see *Vita S. Severini*, dated to the 460s by Thompson (1982) 117. For Hypatius' cures in Thrace in the early 5th century, see the *Vita* by Callinicus 22.8–10 and 21, and notice the bargain he strikes with a bureaucrat (40.31) whom he had miraculously assisted: "Now straightway do as you promised God, and become a Christian." Finally, note the cures producing belief wrought by Gregory Thaumaturgus in the Greek text, *PG* 46.957C—which at least reflects views of the time of composition regarding religious motivation.

3 *Historia monachorum* 8.26–29 and the translation by Festugière (1964) 4, 1, pp. 54f.—to be dated, I suppose, around the 370s, since the ascetic Apollo had lived through Julian's reign (ibid. §10 p. 50). "Apollo catechized them and united them to the church." For similar miracles of binding, see also Soc., *H.E.* 1.12 (*PG* 67.104C) or Greg. Turonensis, *De gloria confess.* 76 (bystanders are *conversi ad unitatem ecclesiae* straightway on discovering a greater power); or see Theodoret, *H.E.* 4.23 = *PG* 82.1188 = 4.26.7–9 in *GCS²*, where abuse of the saint leads to one's dying in boiling water; Marc. Diac., *Vita Porph.* 72, "many surrendered to the holy faith, some from fear . . . ," explained by §70, where a pagan officer dies horribly in a collapsing temple, and the Christians exult with hymns; Pallad., *Hist. Laus.* 17 p. 44 Butler, the ascetic Macarius' saying comes true, the man who robbed the poor-box gets elephantiasis, or idem, *Dial. de vita S. Joh.* 23 p. 37 Coleman-Norton, a "deserved" death for stealing church money; Saint Basil in various similar stories, cf. Greg. Naz., *Paneg.* 54f. (*PG* 36.654f.) and MacMullen (1980) 29; and Saint Ambrose's threats of God's judgment against a nun (but a heretic) who assaulted him and who was dead within a day, cf. Paulin., *Vita Ambros.*, 11. For the prior church tradition, see above, chap. IV n. 4.

4 Endelechius Severus, *De mortibus boum,* lines 117f., 121f., and 130f. (*PL* 19.797–798 and 800).

5 Above, chap. VI n. 28; Labriolle (1950) 352f.; Duval (1972) 563 n. 108; and, for the earlier date recently argued, Callu (1981) 243 and nn.

6 MacMullen (1966) 109; Mesot (1958) 89 on the part played by Ambrosian hymns in the struggles of 386 for the audience's loyalty; and the use made of hymns by Bishop Severus in Antioch to draw the idle from the public places into his church, in Kugener (1907) 244.

7 Labriolle (1950) 470, a counterblast to Julian's *Contra Galilaeos* by Cyril of Alexander, and (ibid. 478) a treatise by Theodoret on a *Remedy for Hellenic Ills,* cf. Theodoret., *Ep.* 113 (*PG* 83.1317C), mentioning his tract and also (1316D) his violent conflicts with pagans "in every city" of a broad region. But both literary works postdate our period of study.

8 Eunap. frg. 78 (*FHG* 4.49), in error on where Persa served as urban prefect—actually, Cple. in A.D. 400–402, cf. Chastagnol (1960) 81 n. 1 or *PLRE* 1 s.v. Clearchus 2. For Julian's iconographic propaganda, but in the old traditions of emperor worship, or even quite secular, see Greg. Naz., *Or. contra Julianum* 2.80 (*PG* 35.695).

9 Rufin., *H.E.* 2.29 (*PL* 21.55.6f. = *GCS* 9, 2, pp. 1034f.).

10 Like Augustine, *Conf.* 6.3.4, as pointed out by Mesot (1958) 57 n. 52—listeners and readers also.

11 Mesot (1958) 57, 59 (*De apolog. David* II 3.20, addressing *gentes,* or *De excess. Sat.* II 70, to *gentibus*), and 60 (Ambrose argues down or mocks sun-worship, myths, etc.). Notice esp. *In ps.* I 41 (*CSEL* 64.35), where Ambrose actually has some nice words for *gentiles*—would they only reform their beliefs! I have seen no comparable examination of Greek sermons, e.g. Chrysostom's.

12 Ambrose, *Ep.* 4.7 (*PL* 16.891), cited by Mesot (1958) 50.

13 Max. Taurin., *Sermo* 91.2, *iudicii diem incendia gehennae fervere,* etc., and Aug., *De cat. rud.* 5.9, no conversion from hope, only from fear: *rarissime quippe accidit, imo vero numquam, ut quisquam veniat volens fieri Christianus, qui non sit aliquo dei timore perculsus.*

14 Joh. Chrysos., *Homil.* I *in Jud.* 4 (*PG* 48.848); see also *In II Cor.* 9.3 or *In ep. ad Rom.* 19.2 (*PG* 60.585) for reminders of God's inexorable judgment, and esp. *In ep. ad Rom.* 5 (*PG* 60.633), "Let us bear ever in mind the Judgement of Terror, the river of fire," etc.

15 Max. Taurin., *Sermo* 91.2, *Sermo* 107 (*De idolis auferendis*) §1, and 106 extr. 1f. (*CCSL* 23 p. xxxiii, date ca. a. 400); cf. Ambrose, *Exameron* 3.55 (*CSEL* 32, 1 p. 98) and *De apolog. David* II 3.6 (*CSEL* 32, 2, p. 362), both refs. from Mesot (1958) 59 and 65.

16 Joh. Chrysos., *Homil. in Act.* 18.4 (*PG* 60.146), continuing, "Can you not offer examples and apply persuasion? Among your own people, bring persuasion by being open-handed and their ready defender, by your mildness, by flattery, by every means"; cf. Aug., *Ep.* 58.1 (a. 401) to Pammachius, congratulating him on how he has handled *colonos tuos,* "your tenants," through strong speeches inclining them to adopt "the view they thought had been adopted by a man of such eminence and quality as yourself." Compare *Enarr. in Ps. LIV* 13, arguing that the lowly follow the lead of the mighty; and further, on urban settings, see Salvian, *De gub. dei* 8.3.14 (Carthage in the 440s, evidently a second-hand re-

port). He complains of the *nobilissimi* in the city, seeming Christians but also open pagans, whose lead the people follow "because the great, rich houses shape the city's crowd. . . . Slaves are all like their masters—or worse."

17 For households as religious blocs: in paganism, see, e.g., the Dionysiac association in Italy, MacMullen (1981) 109, and worshipers of the Twins of Samothrace, ibid. 172 n. 19; among Christians, see above, n. 2 (in Palestine), or the *Acta Petri* 14, or esp. passages in Acts discussed by Theissen (1979) 86 and Meeks (1983) 75. Theissen (p. 75) takes for granted that, because of a convert's "elevated social status, it is thus explained how his conversion produced a great impression on others"; but the observation is not pursued to the point of asking whether a "true" conversion can result out of imitation of one's social betters.

18 Hippolytus, *Tradit. Apostol.*, in Bardy (1949) 202; Coquin (1966) 363, ascribing the editing of the text to the late 330s (and to Alexandria?), also pp. 301, 325, and 329. Notice the end of the tenth canon—no baptism even if the slave dies in sin—and §16 in Botte (1946) 44 on the conclusion (in Coptic), "If his master is pagan, teach him to do his master's will, so there may be no criticism." The procedures are representative of the 3d-century church in Rome (pp. 8f.). Later, see *CT* 16.5.52.4 on beatings (the text in n. 20, below) and the Council of Toledo III chap. 16 (a. 589).

19 See above, chap. V at nn. 14f., and chap. VI at nn. 25f.

20 Aug., *Ep.* 185.21: *multi prius tamquam mali servi et quodam modo inprobi fugitivi ad dominum suum temporalium flagellorum verbere revocantur*, and similar sentiments in *Ep.* 93.3 (a. 408), explaining that the deluded "have been beaten out of love," they are redirected from fear, *timendo* (§16), and a whole city may be converted thus, *timore legum imperialium conversa est* (§17, cf. 18); cf. *CT* 16.5.52.4 (a. 412), *servos etiam dominorum admonitio vel colonos verberum crebrior ictus a prava religione* (Donatism) *revocabit*; and, much later (late 6th cent.) Sardinian non-Christians are the concern of the letters of the pope to the secular and ecclesiastical powers, Greg. Magnus, *Ep.* 4.23 (*PL* 77.692), none—*nemo*—of the natives is Christian; 24 (the *dux* shall make conversion the condition of declaring peace), 25 (big landowners must exert themselves to convert tenants, on pain of their own damnation if they fail); but, 25.38, the natives purchase peace, *iudici praemium persolvunt*.

21 Pliny, *Ep.* 9.39.1–4; other illustrations of rural shrines etc. supplied by the landowners are in MacMullen (1981) 197 n. 63.

22 Council of Elvira can. 40: gifts now (A.D. 305) are now no longer remitted to the tenant, who must himself pay *aliquid ad idolum datum*.

23 *CT* 16.5.40 (a. 407), against Manichaeans and others; cf. 16.10.19.2 (a. 407), *domini* shall be compelled to destroy idols on lands they own.

24 Cf. *CT* 16.5 passim, from A.D. 326 to 435, e.g. §6 (a. 381) or §20 (a. 391).

CHAPTER VIII

1 Duval (1972) 554, on Hieron., *In Ionam* 3.6 (*PL* 23.1143Af.)—matched with the warning of Aland (1961) 32 about *die Gebildete*, to whom "we often attribute too much significance . . . because only this upper class is accessible through literature."

2 On the tension of the spiritual search and the psychological experience of attaining certainty, see Bardy (1949) 130f.; Nock (1933) 107–112; and Aubin (1963) 97f. (conversions to Gnostic systems). On suspicions of bookish men, see MacMullen (1972) 13, or Victorinus, *In Cic. Rhet.* 1.29 p. 325, *multi enim credunt, quod philosophi contra deos faciant*; ridicule of non-Christian *sapientia, per scholarum lupanaria, per trivia sectarum, dissipavit Dei Patris dementi disputatione substantiam*, in Petrus Chrysologus, *Sermo* 5 (*PL* 82.198B); a similar emphatic passage in Joh. Chrysos., *Homil.* 19 *de statuis* 1 (*PG* 49.189); and passages in MacMullen (1972) 13f.

3 MacMullen (1972) 14f., on ignorant philosophers, or Schede (1911) 103, on a nun φιλοσόφισσα. The new meaning of the word appears especially well in Euseb., *Mart. Pal.* 4.5, where a Christian is praised for dedication to ἔνθεος καὶ ἀληθής φιλοσοφία as opposed to sterile book-learning. Note, too, that Augustine may refer to his own enlightened times, *tempora erudita*, that reject the supernatural, but himself goes on to recount many miracles of recent report at work among the population in Milan and Hippo, *Civ. dei* 22.8.

4 Basil, *Ep.* 223 (a. 375), quoting 1 Cor. 2:6.

5 James (1958) 28f., the lectures at Edinburgh in 1901–02.

6 See Hieron., *Vita Hilarionis* 2.2f., or Zacharias Schol., *Vita Severi*, in Kugener (1907) 16, and some similar spiritual development under Origen at Caesarea, in Gregory Thaumaturgus, cf. Koetschau (1894) p. ix.

7 Aug., *Conf.* 8.2.3; and, for the date, Labriolle (1950) 34 and Hadot (1971) 28, Victorinus being then about seventy years old (ibid. 25). I do not know why Hadot (58) supposes that "le paganisme ne fut donc, pour Victorinus [before conversion] qu'un conformisme politico-social."

8 Doignon (1971) passim, esp. 80 (a *peregrinatio animae*, "itinéraire spirituel fictif"?); and I quote from p. 82. For Doignon's probing for Hilary's sources, see esp. 104, 107, 112–115, 434, and 518. For the same caution on the question—real or merely literary?—in earlier writers, see above, chap. IV at n. 17.

9 Notice phraseology like *festinabat autem animus* (§3), *studio flagrantissimo animus accendebatur*, or *animus sollicitus* (§4, comparing the state of his *religiosa mens*, §§6–7), cf. Doignon (1971) 521, "faith is born," as Hilary sees it, "in a crisis of the individual consciousness, apparently independent, at least in its origin, of belief in a Christian community."

10 Eunap., *Vit. soph.* 475, Julian being then in his twentieth year, cf. Bidez (1930) 72, and Julian, *Ep.* 51 (= no. 11 in Bidez's edition, p. 191), I was "on that road [i.e. Christianity] until my twentieth year." The importance of Maximus is also stressed by Soc., *H.E.* 3.1; but Julian went on in further study and initiation, see esp. Eunap., *Vit. soph.* 476, Soz., *H.E.* 5.2, and Greg. Naz., *Or.* 4.55. On his earlier wide reading, see his *Ep.* 23.378C. There are many modern descriptions of the whole process of his religious development, among which, see a good short one in Browning (1975) 44 and, most recent, Athanassiadi-Fowden (1981) chap. I, esp. pp. 26f.

11 Brown (1967) 39, on Augustine's "first religious conversion" to the "Wisdom" of Manichaeism (40), where he remained loyal for nine years (46), with other details on which I draw further, esp. pp. 45, 47f., and 101–105. Augustine at this time counted himself a pagan, *ego ad te veneram ex gentibus, Conf.* 7.9.5.

12 Brown (1967) 101.

13 Ibid. 111f.; Aug., *Contra epistulam* (Manichaei) *quam vocant fundament.* 1 (*CSEL* 25.193, a. 397, cf. his views on conversion, above, chap. VII n. 13).

14 Apul., *Met.* 8.30, *vir principalis et alias religiosus*; for the manifestation of the type in non-Christian cults, see *ILS* 1264, a well-known individual, or other examples in MacMullen (1981) 65; and on the Christian side, the most obvious illustrations are to be found in the Egyptian desert.

CHAPTER IX

1 On the *sortes Virgilianae* (later *apostolorum*), see, e.g., SHA *Vita Had.* 2.8. On the other device, see Plut., *Moral.* 356E, "the Egyptians believe that children possess prophetic powers and they listen to their sayings at play for purposes of divination, especially in sanctuaries, when they are saying things at random." Similarly, the mode of divination credited by Saint Anthony in church, to which Augustine refers in the garden-episode of his *Confessions*, 8.12.29, *audieram enim de Antonio*, etc. Courcelle (1951) 228 doubts that the scene as described was historical; but, if that goes too far, he is persuasive (221–223) in deriving its form and presentation from Xen. Ephes. and Apis-divination.

2 Ambrose, *Ep.* 58.6, on David's dancing (quoted immediately below); *De officiis* 1.43.213; Dölger (1934) 249; Caesarius Arelat., *Sermo* 13.4; and Dölger again, pp. 249f., on John Chrysostom and the Synod of Laodicea; p. 245 on Egyptian Christian practices of hand-clapping and dancing; p. 250 on St. Basil, *Homil.* 14 *In ebriosos* 1 (*PG* 31.445f.); p. 251, Aug., *Sermo* 311.5; and p. 255, Greg. Naz., *Ep.* 193, against pipe-playing. Andresen (1974) discusses the church's attitude toward dancing at length, e.g. pp. 345f. and 365f.

3 For the ubiquity of music and dancing in non-Christian cults of the empire, see MacMullen (1981) 20–25 and passim. In general, notice the insight of Price (1980) 41, that "modern scholars wrongly tend to divide what was a single Greek semantic field" (i.e. worship) "into two, and to distinguish between religious and secular aspects. The Greeks did not do this," nor any other non-Christian group, for that matter.

4 Geertz (1966) 28.

5 See above, chap. VII n. 6.

6 On pagan drinking, see MacMullen (1981) 39f., 47, and 57f., adding an Isiac's graffito which I translate, "I vow, if I get out with a whole skin, there will be a whole skinful of wine for the brothers," *votum feci, se recte exiero, qui sunt intra vini sextarios* (the promise of full publication, in *CRAI* 1945, 397 n. 3, apparently having never been fulfilled). On Christians' drinking, cf. Ambrose, *De Helia* 62; Aug., *Conf.* 6.2.2; Brown (1980) 26; and Duval (1982) 1.457.

7 Aug., *Ep.* 29.9, quoted by Brown (1980) 29 and 32 as "mass conversions"; but there is no reason to see them as coming over in any other way than the usual, *singulatim*.

8 *CJ* 1.11.41 = *CT* 16.10.17 (a. 399), temples shut but *festos conventus civium* etc. are excused in North Africa; cf. Liban., *Or.* 30.18, which says that the emperor Theodosius evidently, though banning sacrifices, meant still to permit "their [his subjects'] drinking together, with all sorts of incense and . . . singing hymns

among their loving-cups, *and their invocation of the gods*" (that last, obviously Libanius' personal and calculating gloss on the law, the date being A.D. 385, probably—see below, chap. X n. 34).

9 Aug. *Sermo* 46.8, referring to *festa ista quae celebrantur per universas civitates in laetitia convivantium, et publicis mensis,* etc. (public tables for civic banquets, just as in non-Christian days); *Morin Sermo* 1 (*Miscellanea Agostiniana* . . . 1, 1930) p. 592, deploring the coincidence of Christian and non-Christian holy days; *De cat. rud.* 25.48, careless celebration *per dies festos Christianorum* and *per dies solemnes paganorum*—these, for North Africa. For Italy, in Rome, see Alföldi (1937) 32, noting the *feriale ecclesiae Romanae* side by side with pagan festivals (in A.D. 354) and, there and "throughout the Empire," the continuation of the Isis-day, *navigium Isidis,* in the 5th and 6th centuries (ibid. 47). Cf. also Wissowa (1912) 101 (the Saturnalia of 387), 212 (Lupercalia in 5th cent.), 229 (Neptunalia), and 232 (Vulcanalia). An ivory relief of ca. 400 shows the opening of games with a libation, the relief being, I think, of Italian origin: Volbach (1976) no. 59. Bowder (1978) 150–157 gives a valuable discussion of the Roman 4th century calendar. In Antioch, cf. Liban., *Or.* 21.28, and Theodoret., *H.E.* 4.24.2f. p. 262 Parmentier, where the Zeus, Dionysus, and Demeter festivals continue under Valens; in Apamea, Liban., *Or.* 48.14, with the Loeb ed. n. ad loc.; and, in *Or.* 45.23 and other authors, the notorious but tremendously popular Maioumas still celebrated—for its later history, see Rey-Coquais (1977) 87. At Edessa, the chief temple opened for festival days though it was closed to sacrificers, *CT* 16.10.18 (a. 382). In Spain and France, the Celtic festival continued, "*Cervolum facere,*" cf. sources in Blazquez (1964) 119 n. 373; and the Council of Trullo can. 62 (a. 692), in Hefele (1907–52) 3.570, bans pagan festivals that still include dancing, transvestite mummery, invocations, and so on. But I have made no attempt to trace such survivals beyond my chosen period.

10 Zos. 4.3.2f. (a. 364), regarding *CT* 9.16.7. Eunapius was initiated at Eleusis at some later date, see his *Vit. soph.* 475. For a parallel compromise with pagan festivals, see *CT* 16.10.3 (a. 342, trans. Pharr), "since certain plays or spectacles of the circus or contests derive their origin from some of those temples (in the capital), such structures shall not be torn down, since from them is provided the regular performance of long-established amusements for the Roman people." So the people are to keep their pagan celebrations. *CT* 12.1.75 (Trier, a. 371) is interesting, in holding out rewards to anyone who ascends to the provincial chief priesthood, *sacerdotium provinciae,* cf. 12.1.12 (Cple., a. 386), limiting the office to those "who have not withdrawn from the cult of the temples"—so non-Christians had their uses!

11 Liban., *Or.* 21.21, and above, chap. I n. 19; *CT* 15.9.2 (a. 409), the Syriarch and Asiarch continue in office, evidently because of the popularity of the spectacles they were responsible for; Piganiol (1972) 339 on imperial images, their cult being a scandal to Jerome but banned at last only in A.D. 425, *CT* 15.4; Matthews (1975) 228f., quoting *Pan. vet.* 12(2).4.5, *deum dedit Hispania quem vidimus,* i.e. Theodosius; MacMullen (1981) 133 on ibid. §37.4; and Philostorgius, *H.E.* 2.17 p. 28 Bidez, τὴν Κωνσταντίνου εἰκόνα ἱλάσκεσθαι, κτλ.

12 Soz., *H.E.* 7.22.8 (a. 394) and other sources gathered in Matthews (1975) 246, adding Aug., *Civ. dei* 5.26. On John's busy prophesying, see Festugière (1964)

4, 1, p. 12, on the *Hist. monachorum* 1.11, cf. also p. 9 (*Hist. monachorum* 1.2), a *magister militum* likewise consults John about a coming campaign against Ethiopians in Syene; also Rees (1950) 86f., on consultation of God and saints by tickets of inquiry.

13 Ibid. 90 on "the healing gap," and responses such as Christian incubation, hospitals (91) and monks. On the latter there exist a great number of texts from the biographies of Egyptian ascetics, in Athanasius' *Life of Anthony*, Palladius, Rufinus, the *Apophthegmata patrum*, or the *Historia monachorum*. I need only recall, from the last-named (§61 p. 41 Festugière), how "the crowds of the sick came to him daily." See also Bell (1924) 108f. and 118 for an anchorite ca. 350 receiving requests for healing by mail, too; in Egypt in the 370s, healing by exorcism by the holy Barses, in Theodoret., *H.E.* 4.14 (*PG* 82.1153 = 4.16.1 = *GCS²* 19.238). Notice the early development of healing by saints, e.g. in Anatolia, the inscription of the 5th century "Saint Theodotus, come to the aid of the health" of the petitioner, in Mitchell (1982) 99. In the west, besides healing through various holy men already mentioned, and besides the woman miraculously healed by the mere touch of Ambrose's garment, in Paulin., *Vita S. Ambros.* 10 (*PL* 14.30), notice Caesarius of Arles's more general assertion (*Sermo* 13.3) that the sick need only get the priest to rub oil over their bodies. Most widely attested of all is the role of martyr-shrines, in such early catalogues as "Evodius," *De miraculis sancti Stephani* (*PL* 41.833f.), cf. Aug., *Civ. dei* 22.8 and below, chap. XI n. 13, on aid similarly asked of saints in Africa. At Milan, the remains of two saints were discovered and produced exorcisms and cured blindness, cf. Aug., *Conf.* 9.7.16, *Civ. dei* 22.8.2, and *Sermo* 286.4. Brown (1980) 75 lays emphasis on "the geyserlike force with which belief in miracles of healing at the tombs or in connection with the relics of the martyrs burst out throughout the Mediterranean world." But I do not accept Brown's explanation, which makes no mention of the vacuum in religious life created artificially by Christian persecution of non-Christians. Duval (1982) 2.516f. likewise remarks on the sudden great popularity of saint-veneration, but offers no explanation at all.

14 Caesarius Arelat., *Sermo* 13.3 and 14.4 (cure of one's family); Augustine in Daut (1971) 177.

15 On the practice of magic by Christians, see a few illustrations and testimonies in Basil, *Homil. in Ps. XLV* 2 (*PG* 29.413) and Caesarius Arelat., *Sermo* 12.4 and 13.3; the canons of church councils, like Ancyra can. 24, Laodicea can. 36, and later, in McKenna (1938) 112f.; Lengyel and Radan (1980) 169; Delatte and Derchain (1964) 283–287 and 330; Robinson (1953) 1721 and Praulx and O'Callaghan (1974) 83f. Notice also the openness of non-Christian apotropaic customs in the countryside, in *CT* 9.16.3 (317/9 or 321/4), Endelechius (above, chap. VII n. 4), and Pallad., *Opus. agriculturae* 1.35.3 (against blights, an odd ceremony) and 1.35.14. He was a pagan, cf. 1.1.2.

16 See above, chap. V n. 9, and compare the use of the phrase σὺν θεῷ in Rees (1950) 94; on ambiguity, or the use of the phrase *summa divinitas*, see Ziegler (1970) 46. For the use of the latter in Ammianus, routine, though not through indifference, see Camus (1967) chap. X.

17 Greg. Naz., *Or.* 4.55f. — *ben trovato*, but true to life; and MacMullen (1981) 133.

The deacon's non-Christian oath, referred to there, is only seemingly matched by Symmachus' invocation of the Christian God, *Rel.* 34.9, *testor custodem numinis vestri deum*, an example of high courtesy to the emperors addressed—or of high tolerance.

18 Hammerschmidt (1957) 236. He also examines other areas in which the church borrowed from non-Christian customs, imagery, arts, etc. See pp. 235f., 242f., and 248; also Parlasca (1981) 226f. The prevalence of overlap between Christian and non-Christian was recognized long ago, see Harnack (1908) 2.176; and the connection supposed to lie between symbolism in funerary art and actual religious beliefs (Dionysiac) has been often questioned. See authorities cited in MacMullen (1981) 170 n. 13, adding North (1980) 191.

19 Vago and Bona (1976) 186f. and 220; Lengyel and Radan (1980) 169; and Kadar (1969) 193f., including the emperor depicted as Jupiter Conservator (!). For similar mixtures of religious symbolism on caskets and sarcophagi from Rome, see Bowder (1978) 158 and 190.

20 *CII.* 15.6296, cf. 6550, the same mixture on lamps of another maker; also on glass vessels of Germany, Bowder (1978) 174; and mixed symbolism in mosaics in Fontaine (1972) 573 n. 8 and Février (1970) 178, with British examples in Bowder (1978) 158.

21 Charles-Picard (1965) 117, "DMS" on epitaphs until the 6th century, with examples from the Roman catacombs carefully discussed by Zilliacus (1963) 1, 2, 211–222; οὐδεὶς ἀθάνατος, εὐφραίνετε πάντοτε, and ἡδύς βίοτος on Christian epitaphs also of our period in Robert (1960) 426f.; cf. Rey-Coquais (1977) 167, nos. 27 and 38, surely Christian, and many others less surely so.

22 Cypr., *Ep.* 67.6, deplores Christians *apud profana sepulcra depositos*; mixed pagan-Christian catacombs of the 4th century at Rome, Bowder (1978) 182f. and 211f.; Fülep (1969) 169, mixing in a mid-4th century Pannonian ceremony; very full technical discussion by Vago and Bona (1976) 176–181 of 4th-century Rhine- and Danube-land burials, without the authors' arriving at decisive findings; and Young (1977) passim, to the same effect and on very much the same region. Even a very large corpus of data does not help, e.g. the 650 graves near Caen, extending over the 4th to 7th centuries, most with Charon's obols, with eatables by the body, etc., suggesting not a particle of change from pagan days, in Pilet (1980) 164f. To an ignorant reader like myself, it appears that no criteria for identification of Christian vs. non-Christian burials work at all well—e.g. the orientation (Young 16f.), position of arms (ibid. 26), or coin in the mouth (ibid. 70 and Pilet 165). In the eastern provinces I can instance, from casual reading, only inscriptions of a Beyrouth cemetery, Rey-Coquais (1977) 168 and passim. See further, above, at chap. IV n. 35, and below, n. 29.

23 On the gift of boyhood's locks to the gods, still in practice in our period, see Deschamps and Cousin (1887) 391f.; on the church's views about sex, see Joh. Chrysos., *De liberis educandis* 16 p. 98 Malingrey, Ἑλληνικῆς ἐστι δεισιδαιμονίας ἔρον, comparing Amm. 22.11.9, a Christian official in Alexandria who "cut off without excuse the long curls of the boys, thinking it was a fashion of pagan cult." For the setting in Antioch, see MacMullen (1982) 500f. Notice Liban., *Or.* 18.38, older men are blackmailed for seeking out the company of the

young too much (i.e. society doesn't approve), and 15.57, loss of citizen rights for male prostitution; so the old non-Christian views were losing their flexibility.

24 Veyne and "eds." in Ville (1981) 461 cite *CT* 15.12.1 (a. 325), where Constantine bans gladiatorial combat "very provisionally." Add Soc., *H.E.* 1.18, Constantine "abolished" gladiatorial contests, and the contradictory and more decisive evidence of *CIL* 11.5265, A.D. 333/337, adduced by Friedländer (1908–09) 80, the text translated in A. C. Johnson (1961) 241. *CT* 9.40.8 (a. 365) is likewise probative, saying that only Christians are not to be condemned to an arena-death; and many later testimonies exist, excellently discussed by Ville (1960) 299f. and 314f., showing that gladiatorial combats (not wild beast contests) only ended after the turn of the 4th to 5th centuries.

25 Judge (1980) 10: "When I once told A. H. M. Jones that I wanted to find out what difference it made to Rome to have been converted, he said he already knew the answer: None." I am not aware of anyone's having tested the view (which is, in my opinion, greatly mistaken); but chap. VI of Bowder (1978) suggests where one might begin.

26 Moreau (1960) 7, 26, and passim, and (1963) 115f., "rien de clandestin" (117).

27 On Italian pagans, see below, chap. X; to the east, earliest, note Himerius, in Geffcken (1978) 182; then Themistius, *Or.* 21, II p. 40 Schenkl; ibid. p. 48; *Or.* 20, II p. 14 Schenkl; *Or.* 24, II p. 100; *Or.* 25, II p. 115; *Or.* 9, I p. 192; and, especially striking, *Or.* 7, I pp. 135f. and *Or.* 11, I p. 217. In Libanius, advocacy of paganism is open (esp. *Or.* 30), and references to the gods (plural) are many and casual, e.g. *Or.* 45.11 (a. 386).

28 I have in mind here figures like Synesius (above, chap. VI n. 3) or Palladas, see Cameron (1965) 17, or Claudian, see Seeck (1901–21) 5.558f., Daut (1971) 187, and now Cameron (1970) chap. VIII, esp. p. 216 (the poet was apparently Christian).

29 Leschi (1941) 173, on Numidian 4th-century burials; Lietzmann (1908) 86n, ca. A.D. 405 in Syria; for the troops presumably Christian that engaged in temple-destruction in Apamea, see Theodoret., *H.E.* 5.21.1 (*PG* 82.1244A). The graves conventionally identified as *laeti* are widely spread and generally of a soldier folk (with families or not) in the western provinces; and the presence of animal bones along with the body strongly suggests unreclaimed paganism among them, e.g. Lémant (1974) 4 and 6, of date near A.D. 400; but cf. above, n. 22. In Egypt, note the non-Christian officer and troops in Alexandria in the 330s, Bell (1924) 59 line 28; in the 340s, MacMullen (1981) 133, a garrison commander, and Festugière (1965) 236 §138, a *dux*; in the 390s, icons and chapels *per cunctas Aegyptii urbes, per castellas, per vicos,* to be destroyed, Rufin., *H.E.* 2.28 (*GCS* 9, 2, p. 1034); and in ca. 405, in Shenute's country, Zoega (1810) 377, a *dux* of Antinoopolis, and a *comes* in Leipoldt (1902) 131. To the north, various barbarian commanders were pagan, e.g. Fravitta, cf. Eunap. frg. 60 (*FHG* 4.41) and more generally Haehling (1978) passim. Goths were only fake converts in order to get along with their hosts—so Eunap. frg. 55 (*FHG* 4.38) and Jordanes, *Getica* 25; some were really converted, see ibid. and Soc., *H.E.* 4.33, describing how a chief becomes Christian to please his employer Valens and urges his followers to do so, too. But

most remained pagan, as Pacatus and Zosimus indicate, cited by Gabba (1978) 49; other groups and individuals are identified by Scardigli (1967) 50f. from Aug., *Civ. dei* 5.23 and 18.52; and notice especially the general reference of Ambrose, *Ep.* 10.9, to someone *Gothica profanatus impietate*, not mere Arianism because of the further reference to *idololatriae sacerdotes . . . Gothorum*.

30 See Bloch (1963) 201 for the sources on the Battle of the Frigidus; and note that there was another pagan pretender still to come, the senator and great magistrate Attalus, cf. Philostorgius 12.3 and Zos. 6.7.5.

31 Wheeler and Wheeler (1932) 102.

32 Lewis (1966) 140f. The more significant sites are Silchester and Verulamium among urban shrines, and, among the rural, Chedworth, Cold Kitchen, Farley, Frillford no. 2, Pagan's Hill, Woodeaton, Coventina, and Carrawburgh— though this last, Richmond and Gilliam (1951) 42 think was inactive "long before" mid-century. See further, Lowther (1937) 35 on temple colonnades rebuilt ca. 400 in Verulamium; the great number of coins = visitors at Farley, in Goodchild (1938) 392; and the temple repairs in the late 4th century at Pagan's Hill, in Rahtz and Harris (1956–57) 22. For the presence of Christianity, see Frere (1967) 331f. and Birley (1979) 150–153.

33 Above, chap. VII n. 20; Greg. Magnus, *Ep.* 4.23, *pene omnes rustici*, where there were in fact no cities to speak of; for Spain, see Barlow (1950) 159, and indications in Martin of Braga's *De correct. rust.* 16 and 18, of Galicia in the 570s; Garcia y Bellido (1972) 490, on the (6th-cent.?) *Liber de similitudine carnis peccati = Anecdota Maredsolano*, Ser. 2, 1931, pp. 81f., which shows that this idolatrous population did not even speak Latin; McKenna (1938) 42 (erroneous inferences from scarcity of inscriptions) and 45–48 (Christianity apparently in the ascendant in the cities by A.D. 400); and Fontaine (1967) 130 n. 66, on cemeteries. On Gaul, cf. Sulp. Sev., *Vita Martini* 13, Tours and territory in the 370s virtually all pagan, cf. Schultze (1892) 2.104f.; most of the work of conversion accomplished during the 5th century and later, ibid. 107 and Griffe (1947–65) 3.113 and 260–298 passim. On Germany and Pannonia, I forbear to cite what evidence I have gathered for non-Christian cults in the 4th century because it yields no sense of ratios. On northern Italy, see Gaudentius' *Sermones* 4, 8, and 13, cited in Schultze (1892) 2.186, for Brixia, and Petrus Chrysologus, for Ravenna; S. Vigilius, *Ep.* 2.3 (*PL* 13.553—a. post 397, cf. p. 550), Anagnia wholly pagan; Zeno Veron., *Tract.* 1.25.6.10 (*CCSL* 22 [1971] 8* dated A.D. 360/380 by B. Löfstedt), where we see the Veronese countryside as thoroughly pagan; Max. Taurin., *Serm.* 105 (*CCSL* 23 p. xxiii, date ca. 400), the Trent region wholly pagan in the 390s; and above, on Como, etc., chap. VII nn. 11f. The scenes in Milan described by Ambrose, and the history of church-building there, indicate a large non-Christian population in his day, perhaps a majority. So, Mesot (1958) 124, "no small part was Christian"; further, 121f. Cattaneo (1974) 34, in calling the population mostly Christian, is less full and careful. For a southern city, see Symm., *Ep.* 1.3 (4) ed. Callu p. 67, where Beneventum is largely pagan in 375.

34 On the ratios in the senate, see Matthews (1975) 206, adding the remark of Aug., *Conf.* 8.2.3, that in 357 "almost all the nobility were pagan," and Alföldi (1937)

37 n. 50, who is quite certain that pagan senators outnumbered Christian in the 380s; further, Mazzarino (1974) 380, 391f., and 395. The decisive change post-dates A.D. 400. For households following the nobility's lead, see Duval (1972) 568 and above, chap. VII n. 17. For pagan inscriptions in Rome, see, e.g., *ILS* 1243, 1259, 1264, 3222, 4153, *CIL* 6.1675, and authorities cited above; for those in Ostia and Portus, see Stern (1953) 112, Bloch (1963) 200, and Chastagnol (1967) 47f. and (1969) 144; for the Isiac priestess in Ostia in 399, see idem (1967) 54, on *CIL* 6.512.

35 Moments of conversions post-312 in the northwest quadrant of the empire are, to my knowledge, seen only in the sources I cite above, showing exorcisms, healings, and miracles at work. See chap. VII n. 2 and IX n. 13; also, the intellec-tual path of Hilary, above, chap. VIII.

36 The *Ep. Severi* 14 (*PL* 41.829) cited by Brown (1980) 169f. n. 101, the converts being Jews fugitive from riots in A.D. 417 in Mahon; for the bargain of 394, cf. Aug., *Civ. dei* 5.26, *christianos hac occasione fieri voluit* (Theodosius).

37 Lepelley (1979–81) 1.355f. and 2.98f., 136, and 306f., and Salvian, *De gub. dei* 8.2.9–8.5.25 (interesting scenes of emotions and loyalties in the 440s in Car-thage). Lepelley interrupts his splendid account to question the depth or sincerity of non-Christian beliefs (1.333 and 360) but offers no evidence, against much on the contrary side. There was also violence at Mactar, where the Christians won, see Charles-Picard (1965) 104. There is more evidence of a vital non-Christian presence in other cities, Lepelley (1979–81) 1.132, 135, 349f., and 374; 2.148, 374 n. 9, and 377 n. 20, and 385; and Kotula (1982) 132f. cautiously indicates a parity between Christian and non-Christian, even well past A.D. 400, in the local civic leadership class. Cf. also above, chap. IX nn. 37f.

38 Lepelley (1979–81) 1.352: "l'attention trop exclusive portée par les historiens modernes aux sources ecclésiastiques a gravement faussé la vision de l'Afrique au Bas-Empire." Quite true, and fully demonstrated by his own book measured against many (excellent) studies of Donatism and Saint Augustine, the popular choices of focus.

39 Petit (1951) 303f., of A.D. 386; Soc., *H.E.* 5.16, and Soz., *H.E.* 7.15, on A.D. 391.

40 Themist., *Or.* 4, I p.70 Schenkl (a. 357), a pretty description of the ceremonies at Sais, differing enough from Hdt. 2.59.63 to indicate that he describes contempo-rary ritual; Olympiodorus frg. 37, last quarter of the 4th century, Isis-priests ac-tive in southern Egypt; Liban., *Or.* 30.35, regular sacrifices to the Nile still in A.D. 385; Amm. 22.11.7, the Serapeum (*Genii templum*) "crowded as usual," i.e. in Ammianus' own day; and Eunap., *Vit. soph.* 471, pilgrims to the shrine.

41 Oxyrhynchus' temples gradually close down, MacLennan (1935) 52f., and (in the *Hist. monachorum* 5.4) the city was totally Christian at the very end of the century; but (§8.24f.) the villages around Hermopolis were then still pagan, and Antinoopolis was wholly pagan, in Theodoret., *H.E.* 4.18.7 (*PG* 82.1157B = *GCS* 19.241, a. 377). An Isis temple near Alexandria much later was still a point of everyday resort, Kugener (1907) 18, the *Vita Severi* (early 6th cent.), and the Isis temple at Philae, one of the land's most famous, only became a church in the 6th century, while its half of the island had been pagan during the 5th, see Munier (1938) 44. Parlasca (1981) 225, drawing on a very good variety

of data, speaks of "the undoubtedly dominant role of paganism up to the end of state-permissible cults, i.e. up to the edict of Theodosius the Great toward the end of the fourth century," and that fits with a small sample of men's names around Hermopolis: under one-fifth Christian ca. 350, about a half in 388. Of these data in Bagnall (1982) I hope to publish my own interpretation elsewhere.

42 John Chrysostom speaks of 100,000 Christians in a city of 150,000–200,000, see Liebeschuetz (1972) 93f.; and Petit (1955) 200f. has good reason for seeing the masses as overwhelmingly Christian, while, within the "bourgeois" and upper class, not much more than a majority were Christian. In harmony with quite a different kind of evidence, however—nonliterary—Dauphin (1980) 117 concludes that "Antioch . . . was essentially pagan . . . as described . . . [by] Libanius . . . and further evoked . . . by St. John Chrysostom." The two chief sources are highly partisan, cf., e.g., Liban., *Or*. 19.25, where the masses in A.D. 387 call on (the emperor's) god; but Libanius wants to blame the Christians for the disturbances, cf. 20.3 and 22.5.

43 For villages around Antioch, cf. Liban., *Or*. 30.10 and 17 (but some Christians among peasants, §16); also *Or*. 47.19; Petit (1955) 200; active temples, in Soz., *H.E.* 5.15 (*PG* 67.1260A), and Theodoret., *H.E.* 5.21 (*PG* 82.1244 = *GCS*^{2} [1954] 5.21.17); Liban., *Or*. 48.14 and *Ep*. 663 and 668, Apamea in the 380s; Gaza overwhelmingly pagan, in Marc. Diac., *Vita Porph*. 17 and passim (the source is unreliable but in accord with other data); and Heliopolis is overwhelmingly pagan in 373, in Theodoret., *H.E.* 4.19 (*GCS*^{2} [1954] 4.22.22 and 26), cf. Soc., *H.E.* 5.10 (*PG* 67.1244A) and, for ca. 380, *SEG* 7.195; but the port of Maiouma is wholly Christian, Soz., *H.E.* 2.5.7f. (*GCS* p. 57), and in Bostra in 362 the Christians make up almost half of the population, says their bishop (Julian, *Ep*. 114. 437D, cf. Soz., *H.E.* 5.15). For general impressions among modern authorities, see Alt (1921) 55 on Palaestina Tertia; Harnack (1924) 2.654 and 659 on that region and Phoenicia; Liebeschuetz (1979) 17f., partly correcting Harnack; and Patlagean (1977) 312 on Syria overall, where "la christianisation n'est pas encore générale au 4ᵉ siècle."

44 Aug., *Ep*. 91 (*CSEL* 34, 2, 432) at Calama, cf. Lepelley (1979–81) 2.98 comparing (ibid. 1.350 and 2.136f., on *Ep*. 17.4) a similar noisy dancing crowd in Madauros forty years earlier; for the Antioch scene, see Pallad., *De vita S. Joh. Chrysos*. 54 p. 96 Coleman-Norton. Add a third scene (late 4th/early 5th cent.) in Autun, where "there was an idol of Berecinthia (= Cybele) . . . being borne about on a wagon, for the blessing of the fields and vineyards," the worshipers "singing and dancing in front of the idol," described in Greg. Turonensis, *De gloria confess*. 76, with the date in *Bibliotheca Sanctorum*^{2} (1968) s. v. Simplicio. But the text suspiciously resembles *Vita S. Symphoriani* 3 (in J. Zwicker, *Fontes hist. relig. celticae* II 163).

45 For the pagan sermonizing, see Aug., *Ep*. 91.5, indicating that at the time (ca. 408) *in templis populis congregatis recitari huiuscemodi* (i.e. allegorically) *salubres interpretationes . . . audivimus*, in various unnamed *civitates*. For the quotation on conversion, see Bulliet (1979) 36, which describes the effects felt by Islam through its own success in winning converts from Christianity and other faiths. Note also Geffcken (1978) 325, referring to a "vast mass of cultural forms passed from

paganism into Christianity . . . a huge stream of tradition." His final chapter, however, is the only treatment I have seen of this subject, obviously inviting much expansion and reflection.

CHAPTER X

1 Mesot (1958) 119f., on church growth in Milan; Marc. Diac., *Vita Porph*. 93.
2 Grégoire and Kugener (1930) vii–xlv very fairly review previous scholarship and the chief challenges to the integrity of the *Life*; but their discussion thereafter, like Grégoire's preparatory articles there cited, show more than a trace of poetic faith in arguing for the historicity of 'Mark' 's account, esp. regarding high affairs in Constantinople, John Chrysostom, and Eudoxia. "That willing suspension of disbelief for the moment, which constitutes poetic faith" (Coleridge) is, for example, little disturbed by Mark's saying he saw the empress within a few days, which must actually have been more than five months (pp. xxxf.); by the very heavy "re-editing" required to explain the debts to Theodoret's work published only in A.D. 444 (pp. xxxvf.—debts not just of style but of substance, cf. pp. xli and cviii); by the people in prominent positions but otherwise not known to us (pp. xxxviif.); and by items best explained through a 7th- or 8th-century composition (pp. xliii–xlv). Peeters (1941) 82 adds an item pointing to composition post-534, reinforces objections raised earlier (e.g. the unknown prominent persons, p. 84), and indicates others, principally linguistic, showing the primacy of a Syriac text (98 and elsewhere). His tone towards Grégoire is one of courteous irony (e.g. 78 and 84). Anyone who has watched the scholarly discountenancing of the *Historia Augusta* over recent decades will recognize certain touches in Mark's work, e.g. §88, the stenographic report that Mark has at hand as he writes, and his promise of fuller documentation elsewhere; and this and many like touches, *being in both Greek and Syriac texts*, carry the taint back to the source.
3 Grant (1977) 10 points to the very humble status of Gaza's bishop (therefore, of the congregation there) in 325. Further, beyond the mention of the "great number" of pagans (*Life of Porphyry* 99) in the army's last round-up, note (§97) that up to that very moment Porphyry had to hide from pagan violence, fleeing over (not *into*) house after house (§96f.). He does not know where he is sure of welcome. The city is presented to us as still largely, or mostly, unconverted even after all the miracles and the great building campaign.
4 Monceaux (1901–23) 3.95—"better known" potentially, but largely neglected. Jones (1962) 51f. translated a few pages, reprinted by Stevenson (1963) 287f.; but otherwise the material is rarely referred to. It is highly informative: pp. 185–204 of *CSEL* 26, appended to the works of Optatus, ed. Ziwsa. But accounts of the community in Aptungi in the period (ibid. 197–204) are almost equally enlightening, showing, for example (200f. Ziwsa), how the pagan and Christian officials at the local level are collusively friendly, as they are similarly in Asia Minor during the Great Persecutions, in Mitchell (1982) 109.
5 Theodoret, *H.E.* 3.3 (*PG* 82.1093): "through their afflictions they proclaimed the power of piety," εὐσεβείας ἡ δύναμις. The story is late and the au-

thor given to exultant tales of the sort, 4.16 (*PG* 82.1161–1164) or especially 3.9 (1101, lovingly told).

6 Council of Elvira can. 6, Hefele (1907–52) 1, 1, p. 256. There also is cited Prudentius' report of Saint Eulalia killed in the same manner. Augustine (*De consensu evang.* 1.16, *CSEL* 43 p. 22) speaks of "Christ's disciples" who advocate *eversio templorum et damnatio sacrificiorum et confractio simulacrorum* at a date before the *Christiana tempora* and before writers like Porphyry (ibid. 1.15); so he appears to mean the mid-third century (?). The urge to destroy paganism physically was not a post-Constantinian development.

7 Euseb., *Demonstr. ev.* 6.20.298b, brief and obscure (3d cent.), possibly the outburst of A.D. 249 referred to in *H.E.* 6.41.1?

8 Athanas., *Ep. encyclica ad episcopos* 3 (*PG* 25.228C) and *Apol. contra Arianos* 15 (*PG* 25.273A), a. 341; *Hist. Arianorum* 54 (*PG* 25.757C and 760Af.), a. 356. Compare the crowds of pagans at Ambrose's funeral, Paulin., *Vita Ambros.* 48 (*PL* 14.44), a. 395.

9 George "the Cappadocian monster," as Gregory Nazianzen calls him, hated by the orthodox, as Ricciotti (1960) 182 shows, or hated by all Christians, as Ammianus shows (22.11.10). See the account in Julian, *Ep.* 60 (10) pp. 69f. Bidez. With Julian's lenity (Amm. 22.11.11) compare Ambrose, below, n. 44. No doubt Julian would have agreed, but of course the mob at Callinicum had very much less excuse for their atrocities.

10 Eunapius reports (*Vit. soph.* 491) how a praetorian prefect in ca. 358 visits Athens and there "boldly" (note the implications of the term) "sacrifices and makes the rounds of all the shrines." On other incidents, see Soz., *H.E.* 5.4 at Neocaesarea; ibid. 5.10 and Greg. Naz., *Or.* 4 (2 *In Iulianum*).88f., regarding Mark in Arethusa. A law in *CT* 16.10.4 (dated 346, 352, 354, or 356, by arguments not important to me) indeed closed temples but did not call for their destruction; likewise 1.11.1 (354), cf. at Athens, its effect described in Liban., *Or.* 18.114.

11 Bare and vague mention of Constantine as "destroying" temples in Eunap., *Vit. soph.* 461; similarly of Constantius, in Liban., *Or.* 62.8, and Theophanes, *Chron.* a. 322 (*PG* 108.117)—explained if he merely caused disuse. For their deterioration, see Liban., *Or.* 18.23 and various passages in Julian's own writings, on the delapidation of sacred precincts in Asia Minor and Syria in the 360s; and at further sites, Bostra and Aegae, added by Fowden (1978) 61.

12 Firm. Matern., *De errore profan. relig.* 20.7; 24.8f.; 28.6; and 29.1. He wrote in A.D. 346. On similarly antagonistic rhetoric in Constantine's public statements, see above, chap. V nn. 37 and 41; and compare Eusebius' vocabulary, in the same decade, speaking to an assembly of bishops and exulting that Christians can now "spit on the faces of the lifeless idols, tread down the unholy rites of the demons," etc. (*H.E.* 10.4.16 and elsewhere).

13 Theodoret., *H.E.* 3.9 (*PG* 82.1101), dwelling emphatically on κόπρος, as other church historians—Lactantius and later ones—dwell on the disgusting features of Galerius' death, or of Arius'; or consider the wretched diseases that afflict bishops of the wrong views, in Pallad., *Dial. de vita S. Joh.* 58f. (104f. Coleman-Norton), a long vengeful passage ending, "For who shall heal a man that God is punishing?" Or read Gregory of Nazianzus' orations against Julian, overflowing with carefully elaborated hatred a long time after Julian's death. Basil, *Ep.* 204,

complains of the vulgar abuse he himself received from the congregation of
Neocaesarea (Mazaca). It is no worse than what the bishop of Rome heaps on an
opponent ("treacherous and malicious wild beast," and so forth), in Euseb.,
H.E. 6.43.6. Yet the bishop's own conduct, by someone who had doubtless seen
these words, is deemed "quiet in all respects and meek," etc.: see Cyprian, *Ep.*
55.8 (*CSEL* 3, 2, p. 629).

14 Tert., *Apol.* 39.7, often quoted; on care of the poor, see above, chap. V nn. 12f.
On conduct in time of plague, see Euseb., *H.E.* 7.22.7, at Alexandria in the 260s,
and (§10) the conduct of non-Christians contrasted; Pontius, *Vita S. Cypriani* 9f.
(*CSEL* 3, 1, p. xcix), at Carthage a few years earlier. Similar conduct appears in
Greg. Nyss., *Vita Greg. Thaumat.* (*PG* 46.957Cf.), depicting the same plague
years, though the source is not a good one. It is extraordinary that such actions
should be reported when the memory of the first general persecution must have
been still fresh in Christians' minds.

15 On the intemperate wrangling of Christians noted in 325 at Nicaea and Alexandria, see Theodoret., *H.E.* 1.7 (*PG* 82.921Bf.) and Euseb., *Vita Const.* 2.61 p.
66, 15f., "the sacred matters of divinely inspired teaching had to endure the most
shameful ridicule"; also the fisticuffs, in Harrison (1963) 119; and ten years later
there are shouting and attempts to kill an opponent in debate, see Theodoret.,
H.E. 1.28 (*PG* 82.988), at Tyre, where security guards had luckily been posted
against just that likelihood; in the 360s, Julian's attempts to reconcile the dispu-
tant bishops at Constantinople, "knowing," says Ammianus (22.5.4) "that most
Christians behave like wild beasts toward each other, beyond any that are man's
proper enemies"; and Liban., *Or.* 30.20, mentioning "how many have been
killed in their internal quarrels." Chadwick (1980) 8f. gives a clear picture of the
murderous ferocity that occasionally disturbed episcopal elections (the 137 dead
in A.D. 366 in Rome, Amm. 27.3.12f., are well known). John Chrysostom,
generalizing from the elections he had seen or heard about, describes the predominance of faction, confirming Augustine's experience in the west (*De
sacerdotio* 3.15, *PG* 48.652, and above, chap. VI n. 3). The roots of such characteristics can be traced back at least to the second half of the second century, in the
pages of Irenaeus' *Contra haereses* or in the comments of Celsus, in Origen, *C.
Cels.* 3.1 and esp. 5.63 (*GCS* 1 p. 203 and 2 p. 66).

16 *Acta martyrum Saturnini et al.* 17 (*PL* 8.700B and D). Compare the charge, publicly lodged against a bishop of Nicomedia by Constantine (who knew more
than we do), that the man had procured the death of other bishops whom he regarded as heretics by pointing them out to the authorities during the Great Persecutions. See Theodoret., *H.E.* 1.19 (*PG* 82.961) = 1.20 (*GCS* p. 66).

17 Epiphanius, *Panarion* 68.3.3 (*GCS* 3 p. 143), apparently in Alexandria—so Bell
(1924) 39; and the schism continued to grow, even with ordinations inside the
jails. See the text of Peter's letter, in the collection cited in ibid. (Routh's *Reliq-
uiae* IV p. 94, not accessible to me).

18 It would be safe to estimate Arian bishoprics under Constantius at half the number of the orthodox in the east (which also had many more Christians than the
west); for the number of Donatists prior to 348, see Frend (1952) 50–54 and
167–169, where they form a large majority of the North African Christians
(weak only in Proconsularis); for the Meletian bishops, an absolute majority in

Egypt in 325, see Martin (1974) 33. Novatianism also spread widely, its adherents being found everywhere in the empire and drawing attack by army forces that Constantius sent against them in northwestern Asia Minor. See Gregory (1975) 1–4. But I cannot estimate the numbers of this and other minor heresies. I work from a Christian total of twenty millions and aim only at a defensible guess.

19 Meletian papyri in Bell (1924) 56–63 help to balance, and in a way to confirm, the abundant descriptions by Athanasius. I draw a sampling of incidents from *Apologia contra Arianos* 15, 31, 33, 45 (*PG* 25.273A, 300C, 304A, 328C); *Apologia ad Constantium* 25 (*PG* 25.625C); *Apologia de fuga* 6 and 24 (*PG* 25.652B and 673D), on A.D. 358; *Ep. encyclica ad episcopos* 3–5 (*PG* 25.228C–233B), on A.D. 339; *Hist. Arianorum* 10, 18, 55, and 59 (*PG* 25.705A, 713B, and 760B), in A.D. 341–356 passim; Theodoret., *H.E.* 1.11, 2.4, and 4.19 (*PG* 82.1025 and 1177), in A.D. 356 and 373; and Oros., *Adv. paganos* 7.33.3. For the imperial edicts, see Opitz (1934–40) 3, 1, pp. 66–68.

20 For the strife in Nicomedia in 355 between pro- and anti-Arian forces, leaving "the church and all around it filled with blood and slaughter," cf. Soz., *H.E.* 4.21 (*PG* 67.1177A); for the punishment regarding Easter, see *CT* 16.5.9.2 (a. 382, from Cple.); cf. §1, the death penalty also for various kinds of heretics; for bishops torturing priests in secular courts, see *Sirmond.* 3 (a. 384) cited by Piganiol (1972) 275; for the burning down of monasteries by a bishop of a competing sect, see Theodoret., *H.E.* 4.10 (*PG* 82.1144), the Messalians or Euchitae; and Basil in A.D. 374, *Ep.* 164, on the Macedonian martyrs in the orthodox cause, see Courtonne (1973) 116. *CT* 16.5.3f. gives a conspectus of legislation, over the last quarter of the century and later, intended to make heretics pay in their corporate property or individual wealth or person, even to loss of life. But this leads me beyond my subject. With the last years of John Chrysostom's career, of course we enter scenes of much savagery. See Zos. 5.23.4 and Pallad., *Dial. de vita S. Joh.* 11–13 (pp. 12–17 Coleman-Norton), esp. 72 p. 129, where priests kill the cantor of the church by virtually flaying him alive.

21 For example, Haehling (1978) 205 and 565f. on Palladius, pagan colonel.

22 Aug., *Ep.* 44.7, and a similar phrase in Ambrose, *De spiritu sancto* 3.10.59 (*CSEL* 79.174); and on the struggle, much has been written, ancient and modern. Cf. Lenox-Conyngham (1982) 353f., with recent references on the conflict of A.D. 385/6.

23 Aug., *Ep.* 185.30. The atrocities he reports are naturally those committed by his opponents, the Donatists, e.g. in *Ep.* 51.3, 88.6, and 185.27; but cf. Frend (1952) 159f. on the *lex contra partem Donati severissima* and the Basilica Maiorum (?) in Cathage; the stoning of an opponent ordered by a bishop, *Gesta apud Zenophilum* pp. 189 and 191 Ziwsa; and Duval (1982) 2.487, on "hecatombs of Donatists."

24 Frend (1952) 179 (another body in a well); 180f., 188f., and passim; among many more recent contributions, see Février (1966), Lancel (1967), and Duval (1982).

25 The date is uncertain: A.D. 383 or more probably 384, in Sulp. Sev., *Hist. sacra* 2.46 (*PL* 20.155) and *Chron.* 2.49–51; Hydatius, *Chron.* 9, at Trier; Ambrose, *Ep.* 24.12, *episcopi ad necem petebant*, cited in Matthews (1975) 166f.; Chadwick (1976) 44f., 115–120, and passim; and a later history, e.g. in *CT* 16.5.40 (a. 407).

26 On most of these bishops' preaching, see above, chap. VII nn. 11f., and chap. IX

n. 33, adding Saint Vigilius, *Ep.* 2.3 (*PL* 13.553). He notes and deplores the un-converted character of the region near Aquileia (Anagnia) at the end of the 4th century. On Priscillian's preaching, see Schultze (1892) 2.136. On Saint Martin, see Sulp. Sev., *Vita Martini* 13, where the saint destroys a temple and then dis-arms the crowd of pagans by a miracle—whereupon, all are converted. On Theodoret, who must be referring to open-air preaching, see above, chap. VII n. 7.

27 On Aug., *Sermo* 24.6 (*CCSL* 41, pp. 324f.), for the date A.D. 401, and circum-stances, see C. Lambot ad loc.; Meer (1961) 39 and Brown (1972) 308, dating the sermon to A.D. 399.

28 *CT* 9.16.1 (a. 319; 320)—9.16.10 (a. 371), on magic, wizards, etc.; 16.10.53 (a. 353); above, chap. IX n. 10. Note also *CT* 16.10.9 (a. 385), which begins, *Ne quis mortalium ita faciendi sacrificii sumat audaciam, ut inspectione iecoris extorumque praesagio vanae spem promissionis accipiat*, etc. A contradiction in laws appears, however, between *CT* 9.16.8 (Valens in 370) and 9 (Valentinian in 371), quoted in the Pharr translation.

29 *CT* 16.10.2 (a. 341), banning sacrifices forbidden by a law of Constantine; 16.10.3 (a. 342), a change obtained by a pagan PPO, cf. *PLRE* I s.v Catullinus p. 298; and 16.10.8 (a. 382), addressed to an official in Osrhoene.

30 MacMullen (1981) 26; 146 n. 51, adding Philostr., *Vit. soph.* 618, and Liban., *Or.* 30.51, with Norman's note ad loc. in the Loeb ed.; Galen, *De libris propriis* 2.21, II p. 101 Mueller; and MacMullen (1981) 165f. n. 3. There is some evidence of temples desanctified and used for secular purposes: see Lepelley (1979–81) 1.349; the interesting dispute in Carthage (ibid. 2.42f.); and Charles-Picard (1965) 105. In Egypt, temples might be used as churches, above, chap. IX n. 41, and below, n. 39. But the references in Rees (1950) 93 seem to be not to the point.

31 *CT* 16.10.7 and 11 (a. 381 and 391), with the comments of Mommsen (1850) 70.

32 *CT* 16.10.6 and Stern (1953) 112. Charles-Picard (1965) 104 thinks temple-de-struction at Mactar and Cuicul may represent the result of the law. Even if true, "such measures seem to have been exceptional."

33 Above, chap. IX; Liban., *Or.* 30 (*Pro Templis*).8, 15, and 17f., sacrifices are all le-gal, not on altars, not burnt, not libations, in sum, all purely private and domes-tic, cf. King (1961) 71; and open sacrificing by a man of great influence (Amm. 19.10.4 a. 359 or Eunap., *Vit. soph.* 503) or, in 382/3, open boasting of piety, cf. *PLRE* s.v. Proculus 6 and *SEG* 7.195; or in cities off the beaten track like Gaza (Marc. Diac., *Vita Porph.* 63, Georgian text only) or Sufes (Aug., *Ep.* 50, bloody sacrifices to Hercules).

34 On ?Edessa?, see Liban., *Or.* 30.44f. I follow, in part, Petit (1951) 298f. on Cynegius' zeal and date (post a. 384), but I depart from the reading ὕπαρχος = *comes*, p. 301 (so also van Loy), instead of *praefectus*. On the Egyp-tian visit, see *Chron. min.* 1.244, *usque ad Egyptum penetravit et simulacra gentium evertit*, and Zos. 4.37.4, reporting how he burned the temples and banned all worship in Egypt; but also "everywhere in the east." The enabling law would have been *CT* 16.10.9 of May 385, obtained by intrigues in the Consistory, so Libanius implies, *Or.* 30.3 and 48f.

35 Liban., *Or.* 30.9f. Compare Zoega (1810) 377, Shenute "accused by the pagans of the towns Plevit and Sejmin before the *dux* of Antinoopolis (himself a pagan),

for having destroyed their temples and burnt their icons," with (p. 457) the defendant's defiant attack on the pagan deities and their foul acts in mythology; Barns (1964) 153, concluding, "Shenute's tone is one of brutal exultation; he is confident in the zeal of the Christian peasantry . . . ; the sympathy of a Christian Imperial court; and the influence of St. Cyril;" and the "Open Letter" that I quote, ibid. p. 156—a "tirade," says Leipoldt, *Sinuthii opera* III 79f. The priests' complaints included "the pigs and the cow which were slaughtered" ("shot while trying to escape," it would be said nowadays).

36 Slightly different accounts in Theodoret., *H.E.* 5.21.1 and 5f. (*GCS²* [1954], 5.21.7 = *PG* 82.1244), and Soz., *H.E.* 7.15.13f. (*GCS* 50 p. 322 = *PG* 67.1457A). Compare Aug., *Ep.* 50, in Lepelley (1979–81) 2.306, where the decurions of Sufes in 399 voted congratulations to their colleague, leader in the riot-deaths of sixty of the Christians who had destroyed an icon of the city's chief deity. Cf. Soz., loc. cit., noting that pagans organized (quite vain) armed defense of a number of cities in the southern Levant, Gaza included, in the years just before Marcellus' death.

37 For my purposes, the date of bishop Marcellus' activities is not important. By place in the narrative, Sozomen loc. cit. sets them in 391 or 392. O. Hiltbrunner, in *Der kleine Pauly* s.v. Marcellus col. 993 (1975), prefers 392; but *PLRE* I p. 236 prefers 384/388, citing older studies.

38 The date of the riots etc. seems reasonably certain: see, e.g., Matthews (1975) 237 n. 1 or Fowden (1978) 69. The most confused source is Socrates, but he agrees with Sozomen on the initial provocation (much emphasized, to heroize bishop Theophilus?). Rufinus preserves some phrases of Theodosius' letter, *H.E.* 11.22f.: *in exordio, vana gentilium superstitio culpabatur.* For aftereffects, see O'Leary (1938) 52.

39 Chitty (1966) 54f., on a passage in the *Apophthegmata patrum* and Eunap., *Vit. soph.* 472, where the role of the monks is described; Rufinus, *H.E.* 2.28 (*GCS* 9, 2, p. 1034 = *PL* 21.556f.).

40 *Admiratione rerum gestarum ad fidem convertabantur*, says Rufinus of a part of the Alexandrine population. For poems about the events by Palladas, see Cameron (1965) 21. For the effect of temple destruction in Syria in making converts, see Libanius, *Or.* 30.28, rightly noted by King (1961) 73 n. 3; also Marc. Diac., *Vita Porph.* 41 (Georgian text only), "For when they [the non-Christians] see them [the temples] treated with contempt, they will of their own accord quit their errors," so reasons the emperor. The line of thought is timeless and natural.

41 *CT* 16.10.16 (posted at Damascus) and 16.10.18; 15.1.36 (a. 397), the Count of the East is to assign to bridge and road construction, etc., material from demolished temples.

42 Theodoret., *H.E.* 5.29 (*GCS* 19 pp. 329f.); Joh. Chrysos., *Epp.* 123 and 126 (*PG* 52.677 and 685f.)—campaign supplies are being sent, monks are wounded.

43 Palanque (1933) 277 speaks of "l'influence d'Ambroise, ou tout au moins le développement de la politique inaugurée . . . à Milan et à Aquilée"; Gaudemet (1972) 598 says of the February law, "behind the emperor, we find the influence of Ambrose," the two laws being model and copy (601); Matthews (1975) 236 sketches the clash of 390, which "in effect excommunicated the emperor"; and King (1961) 78 takes the two laws as declarations of war on paganism.

44 Ambrose, *Ep.* 40.6, *sit alioquin iste episcopus ferventior in exustione* . . . , but (§11) *cedat oportet censura devotioni*; and (in 387) *Ep.* 41.27 (*PL* 16.1120), *monachi multa scelera faciunt*, an opinion more than seconded by the *magister militum* there present.

45 Zeno Veron., *Tract.* 1.25.6.10, *ius templorum ne quis vobis eripiat, cotidie litigatis*, date 360/380; Aug., *Ep.* 97.2 (a. 408), even Christians visiting *ad gloriosissimum comitatum* to get the laws canceled.

46 To MacMullen (1981) 205 n. 8, add Matthews (1975) 158, Lengyel and Radan (1980) 169, and Moreau (1963) 118–120; compare a similar sealed trove of religious objects in Africa, Charles-Picard (1965) 98–103.

47 *Civ. dei* 18.54 (*CSEL* 40 p. 361). Augustine says "thirty years ago," but he exaggerates the interval.

48 Lepelley (1979–81) 1.355f. and 2.42f., on references in Aug. and Quodvultdeus.

49 *CT* 16.10.19.1f. (a. 407 or 408), trans. Pharr; cf. the burning of the Sybilline books by Stilicho in the same years, Demougeot (1952) 91f., on Rutil. Namat., *De reditu suo* 2.52. Constantine had set the precedent, prescribing the burning of Arian tracts in 333, Opitz (1934–40) 3, 1, p. 67.

50 Bauman (1980) 203 considers and rejects "the subsumption of the Deity under the *lex maiestatis*" in late Roman legislation. For the concept of paganism as *Staatsreligion*, see Mommsen (1850) 71. He dates the end of it to Constantine's reign. That view still prevails—wrongly, as I hope I make clear, both here and in MacMullen (1981) 110f.

CHAPTER XI

1 Diehl (1924–67) and Zilliacus (1963) passim; see above, chap. IV n. 37.

2 On these various points, see above, chap. IV nn. 30f. For the "We-They" tradition in Pauline writings, which "invariably implies a negative perception of the outside society," see Meeks (1983) 94f.

3 On the "feel" of membership in non-Christian associations, see MacMullen (1974) 77–80; on comparison between them and churches, see Meeks (1983) 77–80, which stresses the first century and differences; also Wilken (1970) 13–20, stressing the 2d cent. and similarities. From the tiny number of recorded pagan views of Christian communities, perhaps two should be dropped as not genuine: those of Galen, cf. S. E. Johnson (1975) 92, and of Marcus Aurelius, cf. Brunt (1979) 484–498.

4 The best known is at Cirta—known, that is, to Monceaux and Donatism students (above, chap. X n. 4). About pre-Constantinian churches inside non-Christian cities, there is more *fact* to be found there and in Carthage and Aptungi than in all the rest of the evidence put together—which is not saying very much. On Pauline churches, see Judge (1980a) and Meeks (1983), both of whom offer access to a very large body of scholarly debate.

5 Acts 16.13–15 (trans. *NEB*). On the role of such an οἶκος (as here; or οἰκία), see Meeks (1983) 75f., who calls "the individual household . . . the basic unit in the establishment of Christianity in the city" (29).

6 Above, chap. IX n. 3, for a more scientific-sounding statement about the relation between belief and action (ritual action). For other indications of more (or less)

than spiritual reasons for belonging to a Christian community, see chap. VI n. 1, where Simon Magus lodges with the rich patron heading the congregation in Rome, just as Paul lodges with Lydia (Acts 16:15) and Gregory Thaumaturgus with the richest man in Neocaesarea (in the Life by Greg. Nyss., *PG* 46.921B); see also chap. VI n. 1 and chap. VII n. 17, above.

7 Orig., *C. Cels.* 3.55, Christians say that God renders τὸν οἶκον . . . εὐδαίμονα.

8 It may be useful to pinpoint some of the evidence adduced earlier. For benefits, εὐδαιμονία, see chap. II n. 10; for the operation of plain fear in conversion, see chap. IV nn. 2 and 22 and chap. VII nn. 3, 13, 20, and 27; for miracles, including exorcisms, as the cause of conversions, see chap. III n. 20, chap. IV nn. 9, 12, and 15, chap. VII nn. 2–3, and chap. X n. 26.

9 See Nock (1933) 155, who rightly finds in Lucius (of Apuleius' novel) "an outpouring of love and gratitude" toward Isis; similar feelings in Aelius Aristides, e.g. *Hieros Logos* 2.59 pp. 407f. Keil (awe), 2.23 pp. 399f. (joyful exaltation), 3 p. 395 or 11 p. 397 (gratitude), and esp. noteworthy §37 p. 402, "He [the deity] was my Savior, and has been so through giving me each day after each day, and he is now more than ever my Savior"; also other passages in MacMullen (1981) 38, 63f., and 177n. 11. All these testimonies are not easily to be matched in Christian literature; but see, perhaps most clearly, the *Odes of Solomon* 2, 7, 31, and 38, in Charlesworth (1963). I owe the reference to the kindness of W. A. Meeks. That other texts do not abound among church writings need not, however, prove Christianity a faith without feeling; for there simply was not much personal revelation of religious sentiments in the ordinary genres of ancient literature. The poverty of evidence proves nothing either way. On the other hand, there should be, but there is not, evidence to support the view that the non-Christian religions were mechanical, formal, and external only, though statements to that effect are easily found: see above, chap. I n. 20 (Festugière), chap. VIII n. 7 (Hadot), and chap. IX n. 37 (Lepelley); or, as a rather extreme example, Meer (1961) 44, who declares, "the whole of ancient cult was nothing but a vast growth upon what had for centuries been a stagnant pool . . . the dead flame"(!).

10 Max. Taurinensis (*CCSL* 23.414), *Sermo* 105.2: the three *sancti viri* address the natives on their rounds *quod lustrum dicunt*, attack them *errores eorum manifestantes*, and finally suffer *caedes crudelissima*; and (106.1f.) Maximus exhorts his listeners, *castigemus errantes*.

11 Dining with Constantine, cf. Euseb., *Vita Const.* 3.15; Theodoret., *H.E.* 1.10 (*PG* 82.937) = 1.11.1 (*GCS* p. 46); and Soz., *H.E.* 1.25; using the palace as their headquarters, see Sulp. Sev., *Hist. sacra* 2.39.4f. (*CSEL* 1 p. 92); bishops often get free travel, e.g. Theodoret., *H.E.* 1.6 and 20; and a summing up in Joh. Chrysos., *In acta apost.* 3.5 (*PG* 60.40): "Prefects and city magistrates do not enjoy such honor as the magistrate of the church. For if he enters the palace, who ranks the highest, or among the matrons, or among the houses of the great? No one is honored before him."

12 Fraudulent entry to *clerici* status, to gain exemption from the decurionate, seen in *CT* 12.1.49.1 (361), cf. the instant rush of *curiales* to that status as early as *CT* 16.2.3 (320) and 6 (326). Some examples of buying church office (alleged, but

credible, given the general corruption of the times) in *Gesta apud Zenophilum* pp. 196f. Ziwsa; Theodoret., *H.E.* 4.19 (*PG* 82.1169 = 4.22.9 in *GCS²* [1954] 252); ibid. 1.3 (889A), on Arians' venality; Synes., *Ep.* 67 (*PG* 66.1413A), a bought claque at episcopal elections, and another indication in Chadwick (1980) 8 citing Council of Serdica can. 2; bribes in episcopal courts a fixture in the earlier 6th century, Chadwick loc. cit.; and the pattern of bought bishoprics, and its instant recurrence, after being lightly pruned, in Pallad., *Dial. de vita S. Joh. Chrysos.* 48f. pp. 84f. Coleman-Norton. For a little bibliography, see Derrett (1981) 414 nn. 46f.

13 Duval (1982) 1.36, at Dougga. Note the hedera after the word *symposium* (not a proper name, surely), marking the end of the thought, as also at the end of the whole inscription. The names are in the accusative as objects of the saint's remembering. *Cubicula* = "lits de banquet." Duval's discussion seems to me needlessly hesitant. For the spirit of *do ut des*, see also p. 88, where we see that the dedicant, "loyal servant, *devotus*, of the saints, fulfilled his vow with good fortune," i.e. whatever he prayed for was to be granted *in this life*, or (134) a tablet was set up in old pagan fashion and with an old pagan style of sentiment, "Give help to someone that paid his vow."

14 Zilliacus (1963) 1, 2 p. 219, shows with good argument that the Roman catacomb tablets sometimes (not often) make conscious and thinking use of the formula, beyond its mere decorative purpose and abbreviation. For that latter, see above, chap. IX n. 21; for views on sin, chap. II n. 6, above.

15 The inscription is not of Rome, but the guild and magistracy are: *CIL* 10. 4724, with the phrase *fabente maiestate dei*. On similarly ambiguous references to the divine, see above, chap. V nn. 9f. and chap. VIII n. 16.

16 Symm., *Rel.* 3.19, the privileges requested being the setting up of a Victory altar in the senate house and the state financing of certain cults. See above, chap. VI n. 7, on some of the anti-pagan legislation lying behind Symmachus' embassy.

17 Above, chap. X n. 34 (Libanius and the law of 385); pp. 88f., on the intrigues (supposed) in Cple. re Gaza; also chap. X n. 21 on other similar intrigues re religious policy.

18 For reversal of a policy, as non-Christian force is brought to bear, see chap. X n. 30 (in Carthage), chap. IX n. 9 (in Edessa), and 10 (in Athens); in general imperial legislation, chap. V n. 41, chap. IX n. 8 and chap. X nn. 28f. It can be sensed that, from the very beginning of "toleration," Constantine and members of his circle considered a campaign of organized temple-smashing, but regretfully deferred it: "Some people, I hear, say that non-Christians have been stripped of their shrines and supernatural powers of darkness, and I would have recommended exactly this, to everybody, if the refractory violence of wicked error were not so thoroughly deep-rooted in some people's minds, as an obstacle to the general wellbeing," σωτηρία (not "salvation"). See Euseb., *Vita Const.* 2.60 (*GCS* 1 p. 65).

Bibliography of Works
Cited in the Notes

Abramowski (1976) — Abramowski, L., "Das Bekenntnis des Gregor Thaumaturgus bei Gregor von Nyssa und das Problem seiner Echtheit," *Zeitschr. für Kirchengesch.* 87 (1876) 145–166.

Aland (1961) — Aland, K., *Uber den Glaubenswechsel in der Gesch. des Christentums*,
Berlin 1961.

Alföldi (1937) — Alföldi, A., "A Festival of Isis under the Christian Emperors of
the IVth Century" (*Diss. Pannonicae*, Ser. II. 7, 1937).

Alt (1921) — Alt, A., *Die griechischen Inschriften der Palaestina Tertia westlich der
'Araba*, Berlin-Leipzig 1921.

Anawati (1973) — Anawati, G. C., "Factors and effects of Arabization and Islamization in Medieval Egypt and Syria," in *Islam and Cultural Change in the Middle
Ages*, ed. S. Vryonis (Giorgio Levi della Vida Conferences 4), Los Angeles 1973,
17–41.

Andresen (1974) — Andresen, C., "Altchristliche Kritik am Tanz," in *Die alte
Kirche*, ed. H. Frohnes and U. W. Knorr, Munich 1974, 344–376.

Athanassiadi-Fowden (1981) — Athanassiadi-Fowden, P., *Julian and Hellenism: An
Intellectual Biography*, Oxford 1981.

Aubin (1963) — Aubin, P., *Le Problème de la 'conversion.' Etude sur un terme commun
à l'hellénisme et au christianisme des trois premiers siècles*, Paris 1963.

Bagnall (1982) — Bagnall, R. S., "Religious conversion and onomastic change in
early Byzantine Egypt," *Bull. Am. Society of Papyrologists* 19 (1982) 105–123.

Bardy (1949) — Bardy, G., *La Conversion au christianisme durant les trois premiers
siècles*, Paris 1949.

Barlow (1950) — Barlow, C. W., *Martini Episcopi Bracarensis opera omnia*, New Haven 1950.

Barnes (1981) — Barnes, T. D., *Constantine and Eusebius*, Cambridge 1981.

Barns (1964) — Barns, J., "Shenute as a historical source," *Actes du Xe Congrès international de papyrologues . . . 1961*, Wroclaw 1964, 151–159.

Bastiaensen and Smit (1975) — Bastiaensen, A. A. R., and J. W. Smit, eds., [Sul-
picius Severus] *Vita di Martino, Vita di Ilarione, In Memoria di Paola* (Vita dei Santi
IV), Milan 1975.

Bauman (1980) — Bauman, R. A. "The 'leges iudiciorum publicorum' and their interpretation in the Republic, Principate, and Later Empire," *Aufstieg und Niedergang der römischen Welt*, ed. H. Temporini, II, 13, Berlin 1980, 103–233.

167

Baynes (1931) — Baynes, N. H., *Constantine the Great and the Christian Church* (Proc. British Acad. XV), London n.d. (1931).

Bell (1924) — Bell, H. I., *Jews and Christians in Egypt. The Jewish Troubles in Alexandria and the Athanasian Controversy*, London 1924.

Beschaouch (1975) — Beschaouch, A., "A propos de récentes découvertes épigraphiques dans le pays de Carthage," *Comptes rendus de l'Acad. des Inscriptions* 1975, 101–118.

Bidez (1930) — Bidez, J., *La Vie de l'empereur Julien*, Paris 1930.

Birley (1972) — Birley, A. R. *Septimius Severus. The African Emperor*, New York 1972.

Birley (1979) — Birley, A. R., *The People of Roman Britain,* London 1979.

Blazquez (1964) — Blazquez, J. M., *Estructura economica y social de Hispania durante la anarquia militar y el bajo impero*, Madrid 1964.

Bloch (1963) — Bloch, H., "The pagan revival in the West at the end of the fourth century," in *The Conflict between Paganism and Christianity*, ed. A. Momigliano, Oxford 1963, 193–218.

Bonnet (1972) — Bonnet, M., *Acta apostolorum apocrypha* II, 1, Hildesheim-New York 1972.

Botte (1946) — Botte, B., *La Tradition apostolique*, Paris 1946.

Bowder (1978) — Bowder, D., *The Age of Constantine and Julian*, London 1978.

Bowersock (1980) — Bowersock, G. W., "Mavia, queen of the Saracens," in *Studien zur antiken Sozialgeschichte. Festschrift F. Vittinghoff*, Cologne-Vienna 1980, 477–495.

Bregman (1982) — Bregman, J., *Synesius of Cyrene, Philosopher-Bishop*, Berkeley 1982.

Brown (1967) — Brown, P., *Augustine of Hippo, a Biography*, Berkeley 1967.

Brown (1972) — Brown, P., *Religion and Society in the Age of Saint Augustine*, London 1972.

Brown (1980) — Brown, P., *The Cult of the Saints: Its Rise and Function in Latin Christianity*, Chicago 1980.

Brown (1982) — Brown, P., *Society and the Holy in Late Antiquity*, Berkeley 1982.

Browning (1976) — Browning, R., *The Emperor Julian*, Berkeley 1976 (unaltered from London 1975).

Brunt (1979) — Brunt, P. A., "Marcus Aurelius and the Christians," in *Studies in Latin Literature and Roman History*, ed. C. Deroux, Brussels 1979, 1:483–519.

Bulliet (1979) — Bulliet, R. W., *Conversion to Islam in the Medieval Period. An Essay in Quantitative History*, Cambridge 1979.

Callu (1981) — Callu, J.-P., "Date et genèse du premier livre de Prudence Contre Symmaque," *Rev. Etudes Latines* 59 (1981) 235–259.

Cameron (1965) — Cameron, A., "Palladas and Christian polemic," *J. Roman Studies* 55 (1965) 17–30.

Cameron (1970) — Cameron, A., *Claudian: Poetry and Propaganda at the Court of Honorius*, Oxford 1970.

Campenhausen (1953) — Campenhausen, H. von, *Kirchliches Amt und geistliche Vollmacht in den ersten drei Jahrhunderten*, Tübingen 1953.

Camus (1967) — Camus, P.-M., *Ammien Marcellin, témoin des courants culturels et religieux à la fin du IVe siècle*, Paris 1967.

Carr (1981) — Carr, W., *Angels and Principalities. The Background, Meaning and Development of the Pauline Phrase hai archai kai hai exousiai* (Society for New Testament Studies 42), Cambridge 1981.

Cattaneo (1974) — Cattaneo, E., *La religione a Milano nell'età di sant'Ambrogio*, Milan 1974.

Chadwick (1965) — Chadwick, H., *Origen: Contra Celsum. Translated with an Introduction and Notes*, Cambridge 1965.

Chadwick (1976) — Chadwick, H., *Priscillian of Avila. The Occult and the Charismatic in the Early Church*, Oxford 1976.

Chadwick (1978) — Chadwick, H., "Conversion in Constantine the Great," in *Religious Motivation: Biographical and Sociological Problems for the Church Historian. Papers Read at the 16th . . . and the 17th . . . Meeting of the Ecclesiastical History Society*, ed. D. Baker, Oxford 1978, 1–13.

Chadwick (1980) — Chadwick, H., *The Role of the Christian Bishop in Ancient Society* (Protocol of the 35th Colloquy, Center for Hermeneutical Studies), Berkeley 1980, 1–14.

Charles-Picard (1965) — Charles-Picard, G., *La Carthage de Saint Augustin*, Paris 1965.

Charlesworth (1973) — Charlesworth, J. H., *The Odes of Solomon, edited with Translation and Notes,* Oxford 1973.

Chastagnol (1960) — Chastagnol, A., *La Préfecture urbaine à Rome sous le Bas-Empire*, Paris 1960.

Chastagnol (1967) — Chastagnol, A., "La Restauration du temple d'Isis au 'Portus Romae' sous le règne de Gratien," *Bull. Soc. Nat. Antiquaires* 1967, 47–54.

Chastagnol (1969) — Chastagnol, A., "La Restauration du temple d'Isis du Portus Romae sous le règne de Gratien," in *Hommages à M. Renard*, Brussels 1969, 2:135–144.

Chitty (1966) — Chitty, D. J., *The Desert a City*, Oxford 1966.

Coquin (1966) — Coquin, R.-G., *Les Canons d'Hippolyte. Edition critique de la version arabe, introduction et traduction française* (Patrologia orientalis 31, 2), Paris 1966.

Courcelle (1951) — Courcelle, P., "L'Oracle d'Apis et l'oracle du jardin de Milan," *Revue de l'histoire des religions* 139 (1951) 216–231.

Courtonne (1973) — Courtonne, Y., *Un témoin du IVe siècle orientale, Saint Basile et son temps d'après sa correspondance*, Paris 1973.

Cracco Ruggini (1977) — Cracco Ruggini, L., "Apoteosi e politica senatoria nel IV secolo d. C.," *Rivista storica italiana* 89 (1977) 425–489.

Croke and Harris (1982) — Croke, B., and J. Harris, *Religious Conflict in Fourth-Century Rome*, Sydney 1982.

Dauphin (1980) — Dauphin, C., "Mosaic pavements as an index of prosperity and fashion," *Levant* 12 (1980) 112–134.

Daut (1971) — Daut, W., "Die 'halben Christen' unter den Konvertiten und Gebildeten des 4. and 5. Jahrhunderts," *Zeitschr. Missionswiss. und Religionswiss.* 55 (1971) 171–188.

Decapmaeker (1961) — Decapmaeker, Rev. Père, "Le Kimbanguisme," *Devant les sectes non-chrétiennes* 31 (Semaine de missiologie Louvain, 1961) 52–66.

Delatte and Derchain (1964) — Delatte, A., and P. Derchain, *Les Intailles magiques gréco = égyptiennes*, Paris 1964.

Demougeot (1952) — Demougeot, E., "Saint Jérôme, les oracles Sibyllins et Stilichon," *Rev. Etudes Anciennes* 54 (1952) 83–92.

Demougeot (1963) — Demougeot, E., "Rome, Lyon et la christianisation des pays rhénans," in *Rome et la christianisme dans la région rhénane*, Paris 1963, 23–47.

Derrett (1981) — Derrett, J. D. M., "Simon Magus," *Conoscenza religiosa* 4 (1981) 397–414.

Deschamps and Cousin (1887) — Deschamps, G., and G. Cousin, "Inscriptions du temple de Zeus Panamaros," *Bull. de correspondance hellénique* 11 (1887) 373–391.

Diehl (1925–1967) — Diehl, E., *Inscriptiones Latinae Christianae Veteres*, 3 vols., Berlin 1925–1931; suppl. J. Moreau and H.-I. Marrou, Dublini 1967.

Dodds (1965) — Dodds, E. R., *Pagan and Christian in an Age of Anxiety: Some Aspects of Religious Experience from Marcus Aurelius to Constantine*, Cambridge 1965.

Dölger (1934) — Dölger, F., "Klingeln, Tanz und Händelklatschen im Gottesdienst der christlichen Melitianer in Agypten," *Antike und Christentum* 4 (1934) 245–265.

Dörries (1954) — Dörries, H., *Das Selbstzeugnis Kaiser Konstantins* (Abhandlungen der Akad. Wiss. in Göttingen³ 34), Göttingen 1954.

Doignon (1971) — Doignon, J., *Hilaire de Poitiers avant l'exil; recherches sur la naissance, l'enseignement et l'épreuve d'une foi épiscopale au milieu du IVᵉ siècle*, Paris 1971.

Drake (1982) — Drake, H. A., "[Review of T. D. Barnes, Constantine and Eusebius]," *Am. J. Philol.* 103 (1982) 462–466.

Duval (1972) — Duval, Y. M., "Saint Cyprien et le roi de Ninive dans l'In Ionam de Jérome," *Epektasis, Mél. patristiques offerts au cardinal J. Daniélou*, Paris 1972, 551–570.

Duval (1982) — Duval, Y. M., *Loca sanctorum Africae. Le culte des martyrs en Afrique du IVᵉ au VIIᵉ siècle*, 2 vols., Rome 1982.

Edgar (1902) — Edgar, C. C., "A thesaurus in the Museum of Cairo," *Zeitschr. für ägyptische Sprache* 40 (1902) 140–141.

Feldman (1950) — Feldman, L. H., "Jewish 'sympathizers' in classical literature and inscriptions," *Trans. and Proc. Am. Philol. Assoc.* 82 (1950) 200–208.

Festugière (1959) — Festugière, A.-J., *Antioche païenne et chrétienne. Libanius, Chrysostome, et les moines de Syrie*, Paris 1959.

Festugière (1964) — Festugière, A.-J., *Les Moines d'Orient*, IV, 1: *Enquête sur les moines d'Egypte*, Paris 1964.

Février (1966) — Février, P.-A., "Toujours le Donatisme: à quand l'Afrique?" *Riv. storia e lett. religiosa* 2 (1966) 228–240.

Février (1970) — Février, P.-A., "Conditions économiques et sociales de la création artistique," *Corsi di cultura sull'arte ravennate e bizantina* 17 (1970) 161–190.

Fontaine (1961) — Fontaine, J., "Vérité et fiction dans la chronologie de la Vita Martini," in *Saint Martin et son temps. Mémorial du XVIᵉ centenaire des débuts du monachisme en Gaule* (Studia Anselmia 40), Rome 1961, 189–236.

Fontaine (1967) — Fontaine, J., "Conversion et culture chez les Wisigoths d'Espagne," *Settimane di Studio del Centro italiano di studi sull'alto medioevo* 14 (1967) 87–147.

Fontaine (1972) — Fontaine, J., "Valeurs antiques et valeurs chrétiennes dans la spiritualité des grands propriétaires terriens à la fin du IVe siècle occidental," *Epektasis. Mél. patristiques offerts au cardinal J. Daniélou*, Paris 1972, 571–595.

Fowden (1978) — Fowden, G., "Bishops and temples in the East Roman Empire," *J. Theol. Studies*^{2} 29 (1978) 53–78.

Fremersdorf (1952) — Fremersdorf, F., "Christliche Leibwächter auf einem ge-schiffenen Kölner Glasbecher des 4. Jahrhunderts," in *Festschr. für R. Egger*, Klagenfurt 1952, 1.66–83.

Frend (1952) — Frend, W. H. C., *The Donatist Church: A Movement of Protest in Roman North Africa*, Oxford 1952.

Frend (1965) — Frend, W. H. C., *Martyrdom and Persecution in the Early Church: A Study of a Conflict from the Maccabees to Donatus*, Oxford 1965.

Frend (1974) — Frend, W. H. C., "Der Verlauf der Mission in der alten Kirche bis zum 7. Jahrhundert," in *Die alte Kirche*, ed. H. Frohnes and U. W. Knorr, Munich 1974, 32–50.

Frere (1967) — Frere, S., *Britannia: A History of Roman Britain*, Cambridge 1967.

Freudenberger (1974) — Freudenberger, R., "Die Auswirkungen kaiserlicher Politik auf die Ausbreitungsgeschichte des Christentums bis zu Diokletian," in *Die alte Kirche*, ed. H. Frohnes and U. W. Knorr, Munich 1974, 131–146.

Frey (1936–1952) — Frey, J.-B., *Corpus inscriptionum iudaicorum. Recueil des inscriptions juives qui vont du IIIe siècle avant Jésus-Christ au VIIe siècle de notre ère*, 2 vols., Rome-Paris 1936–1952.

Friedlaender (1907–1909) — Friedlaender, L., *Roman Life and Manners under the Early Empire*^{7}, trans. L. A. Magnus, 4 vols., London 1908–1909.

Fülep (1969) — Fülep, F., "Nuove indicazioni per la storia del cristianesimo in Pannonia," *Corsi di cultura sull'arte ravennate e bizantina* 16 (1969) 165–178.

Gabba (1978) — Gabba, E., "I cristiani dell'esercito romano del quarto secolo dopo Cristo," in *Transformations et conflits au IVe siècle ap. J.-C. Colloque . . . 1970*, Bonn 1978, 35–52.

Garcia y Bellido (1972) — Garcia y Bellido, A., "Die Latinisierung Hispaniens," *Aufstieg und Niedergang der römischen Welt*, ed. H. Temporini, I, 1, Berlin 1972, 462–500.

Gaudemet (1947) — Gaudemet, J., "La Législation religieuse de Constantin," *Rev. d'histoire de l'église de France* 33 (1947) 25–61.

Gaudemet (1959) — Gaudemet, J., *L'Eglise dans l'empire romain (IVe–Ve siècles)*, Paris 1959.

Gaudemet (1972) — Gaudemet, J., "La Condemnation des pratiques païennes en 391," *Epektasis. Mél. patristiques offerts au cardinal J. Daniélou*, Paris 1972, 597–602.

Gaudemet (1977) — Gaudemet, J., *Conciles gaulois du IVe siècle. Texte latin de l'édition C. Munier, introduction, traduction et notes*, Paris 1977.

Geertz (1966) — Geertz, C., "Religion as a cultural system," in *Anthropological Approaches to the Study of Religion*, ed. M. Bainton, London 1966, 1–46.

Geffcken (1978) — Geffcken, J., *The Last Days of Greco-Roman Paganism*, trans. S. MacCormack, Amsterdam–New York–Oxford 1978.

Ghadban (1971) — Ghadban, C., "Un Site Safaïtique dans l'Antiliban," *Annual, Dept. of Antiquities of Jordan* 16 (1971) 77–85.

Goodchild (1938) — Goodchild, R. G., "A priest's sceptre from the Romano-Celtic temple at Farley Heath, Surrey," *Antiquaries' J.* 18 (1938) 391–396.

Graeven (1901) — Graeven, H., "Die thönerne Sparbüchse im Altertum," *Jb. Deut. Arch. Inst.* 16 (1901) 60–189.

Grant (1977) — Grant, R. M., *Early Christianity and Society: Seven Studies*, New York 1977.

Green (1970) — Green, M., *Evangelism in the Early Church*, London 1970.

Grégoire (1922) — Grégoire, H., *Receuil des inscriptions grecques chrétiennes d'Asie Mineure*, vol. 1, Paris 1922.

Grégoire and Kugener (1930) — Grégoire, H., and M.-A. Kugener, *Marc le Diacre, Vie de Porphyre*, Paris 1930.

Gregory (1975) — Gregory, T. E., "Novatianism: A rigorist sect in the Christian Roman Empire," *Byz. Studies* 2 (1975) 1–18.

Griffe (1947–1965) — Griffe, E., *La Gaule chrétienne à l'époque romaine*, 3 vols., Paris 1947–1965.

Grimmelshausen (1965) — Grimmelshausen, J. J. C. von, *Simplicius Simplicissimus*, trans. G. Schulz-Behrend, New York 1965.

Hadot (1971) — Hadot, P., *Marius Victorinus. Recherches sur sa vie et ses oeuvres*, Paris 1971.

Haehling (1978) — Haehling, R. von, *Die Religionszugehörigkeit der hohen Amsträger des römischen Reiches seit Constantins I Alleinherrschaft bis zum Ende der Theodosianischen Dynastie (324–450 bzw. 455 n. Chr.)*, Bonn 1978.

Hammerschmidt (1957) — Hammerschmidt, E., "Altägyptische Elemente im koptischen Christentum," *Ostkirchliche Studien* 6 (1957) 233–250.

Harding (1969) — Harding, G. L., "A Safaitic drawing and text," *Levant* 1 (1969) 68–72.

Harding (1969a) — Harding, G. L., "The Safaitic tribes," *Al-Abhath: J. Am. Inst. Beirut* 22, 3 (1969) 3–22.

Harnack (1908) — Harnack, A., *The Mission and Expansion of Christianity in the First Three Centuries*[2], trans. J. Moffat, 2 vols., New York 1908.

Harnack (1924) — Harnack, A., *Die Mission und Ausbreitung des Christentums in der ersten drei Jahrhunderten*[4], 2 vols., Leipzig 1924.

Harris (1983) — Harris, W. V., "Literacy and epigraphy, I," *Zeitschrift für Papyrologie und Epigraphik* 52 (1983) 87–111.

Harrison (1963) — Harrison, R. M., "Churches and chapels of central Lycia," *Anatolian Studies* 13 (1963) 117–151.

Hefele (1907–1952) — Hefele, C. J., *Histoire des Conciles d'après les documents originaux*[2], 11 vols., Paris 1907–1952.

Heikkinen (1967) — Heikkinen, J. W., "Notes on 'epistrepho' and 'metanoeo'," *Ecumenical Rev.* 19 (1967) 313–316.

Hennecke and Schneemelcher (1963–1964) — Hennecke, E., and W. Schneemelcher, eds., *New Testament Apocrypha*, trans. R. McL. Wilson, 2 vols., Westminster 1963–1964.

Hermansen (1981) — Hermansen, G., *Ostia: Aspects of Roman City Life*, Edmonton (Alberta) 1981.

Herz (1975) — Herz, P., *Untersuchungen zum Festkalender der römischen Kaiserzeit*, Mainz 1975.

James (1958) — James, W., *The Varieties of Religious Experience*, New York 1958.

A. C. Johnson (1961) — Johnson, A. C., et al., eds., *Ancient Roman Statutes: A Translation*, Austin 1961.

S. E. Johnson (1975) — Johnson, S. E., "Asia Minor and early Christianity," in *Christianity, Judaism and other Greco-Roman Cults. Studies for M. Smith . . .*, ed. J. Neusner, Leiden 1975, II, 77–145.

Jones (1962) — Jones, A. H. M., *Constantine and the Conversion of Europe*, New York 1962.

Jones (1963) — Jones, A. H. M., "The social background of the struggle between paganism and Christianity," in *The Conflict between Paganism and Christianity in the Fourth Century*, ed. A. Momigliano, Oxford 1963, 17–37.

Jones (1964) — Jones, A. H. M., *The Later Roman Empire 284–602: A Social Economic and Administrative Survey*, 2 vols., Norman, Okla. 1964.

Judge (1980) — Judge, E. A., *The Conversion of Rome: Ancient Sources of Modern Social Tensions*, North Ryde (Sydney) 1980.

Judge (1980a) — Judge, E. A., "The social identity of the first Christians: A question of method in religious history," *J. Religious Hist.* 11 (1980) 201–217.

Kadar (1969) — Kadar, Z., "Lineamenti dell'arte della Pannonia nell'epoca dell'antichità tardo e paleocristiana," *Corsi di cultura sull'arte ravennate e bizantina* 16 (1969) 179–202.

Kaestli (1981) — Kaestli, J.-D., "Les principales orientations de la recherche sur les actes apocryphes des apôtres," in *Christianisme et monde païen*, ed. F. Bovon et al., Geneva 1981, 49–67.

Kajanto (1974) — Kajanto, I., "On the idea of eternity in Latin epitaphs," *Arctos* 8 (1974) 56–69.

Kellner (1968) — Kellner, W., *Libertas und Christogramm. Motivgeschichtliche Untersuchungen zur Münzprägung des Kaisers Magnentius (350–353)*, Karlsruhe 1968.

Kent and Painter (1977) — Kent, J. P. C., and K. C. Painter, eds., *The Wealth of the Roman World A.D. 300–700*, London 1977.

Kindler (1975) — Kindler, A., "Two coins of the Third Legion Cyrenaica struck under Antoninus Pius," *Israel Exploration J.* 25 (1975) 144–147.

King (1961) — King, N. Q., *The Emperor Theodosius and the Establishment of Christianity*, London 1961.

Klijn (1962) — Klijn, A. F. J., *The Acts of Thomas*, Leiden 1962.

Kluckhohn (1942) — Kluckhohn, C., "Myths and rituals: a general theory," *Harvard Theol. Rev.* 35 (1942) 45–79.

Koetschau (1894) — Koetschau, P., *Des Gregorios Thaumaturgos Dankrede an Origenes*, Freiburg im Breisgau 1894.

Knorr (1966) — Knorr, U. W., "Gregor der Wundertäter als Missionar," *Evangelisches Missions Magazin* 110 (1966) 70–84.

Kotula (1982) — Kotula, T., *Les Principales d'Afrique. Etude sur l'élite municipale nord-africaine au Bas-Empire romain*, Wroclaw 1982.

Kraft (1955) — Kraft, H., *Kaiser Konstantins religiöse Entwicklung*, Tübingen 1955.

Krautheimer (1983) — Krautheimer, R., *Three Christian Capitals. Topography and Politics*, Berkeley 1983.

Kretschmar (1974) — Kretschmar, G., "Das christliche Leben und die Mission in der frühen Kirche," in *Die alte Kirche*, ed. H. Frohnes and U. W. Knorr, Munich 1974, 94–128.

Kugener (1907) — Kugener, M.-A., *Vie de Sévère par Jean* (Patrologia orientalis II, 1), Paris 1907, 203–264.

Labriolle (1950) — Labriolle, P. de, *La Réaction païenne. Etude sur la polémique antichrétienne du Ier au VIe siècle*, Paris 1950.

Lancel (1967) — Lancel, S., "Aux origines du Donatisme et du mouvement des circoncellions," *Cahiers tunisiennes* 15 (1967) 183–188.

Lanternari (1963) — Lanternari, V., *The Religions of the Oppressed: A Study of Modern Messianic Cults*, trans. L. Sergio, New York 1963.

Lapidus (1972) — Lapidus, I. M., "The conversion of Egypt to Islam," *Israel Oriental Studies* 2 (1972) 248–262.

Laumonier (1958) — Laumonier, A., *Les Cultes indigènes en Carie*, Paris 1958.

Lazius (1552) — Lazius, W., *Liber de passione domini nostri*, etc., Basel 1552.

Lémant (1974) — Lémant, J.-P., "Le Cimetière du Bas-Empire de Mézières," *Rev. hist. Ardennaise* 9 (1974) 1–20.

Leipoldt (1902) — Leipoldt, J., "Berichte Schenutes über Einfälle der Nubier in Agypten," *Zeitschr. für ägyptische Sprache* 40 (1902) 126–141.

Lengyel and Radan (1980) — Lengyel, A., and G. T. B. Radan, eds., *The Archaeology of Roman Pannonia*, Lexington, Ky. 1980.

Lenox-Conyngham (1982) — Lenox-Conyngham, A., "The topography of the basilica conflict of A.D. 385/6," *Historia* 31 (1982) 353–363.

Lepelley (1979–1981) — Lepelley, C., *Les Cités de l'Afrique romaine au Bas-Empire*, 2 vols., Paris 1979–1981.

Leschi (1941) — Leschi, L., "Centenarium quod Aqua Viva appellatur," *Comptes rendues de l'Acad. des Inscriptions*, 1941, 163–176.

Lewis (1966) — Lewis, M. J. T., *Temples in Roman Britain*, Cambridge 1966.

Liebeschuetz (1972) — Liebeschuetz, J. H. W., *Antioch: City and Imperial Administration in the Later Roman Empire*, Oxford 1972.

Liebeschuetz (1979) — Liebeschuetz, J. H. W., "Problems arising from the conversion of Syria," in *The Church in Town and Countryside*, ed. J. Baker, Oxford 1979, 17–24.

Lietzmann (1908) — Lietzmann, H., *Das Leben des heiligen Symeon Stylites*, Leipzig 1908.

Lippold (1981) — Lippold, A., "Bischof Ossius von Cordova und Konstantin der Grosse," *Zeitschr. für Kirchengesch.* 92 (1981) 1–15.

Lowther (1937) — Lowther, A. W. G., "Report on excavations at Verulamium in 1934," *Antiquaries' J.* 17 (1937) 28–55.

McGeachy (1942) — McGeachy, J. A., *Quintus Aurelius Symmachus and the Senatorial Aristocracy of the West*, Chicago 1942.

McKenna (1938) — McKenna, S., *Paganism and Pagan Survival in Spain up to the Fall of the Visigothic Kingdom*, Washington, D.C. 1938.

MacLennan (1935) — MacLennan, H., *Oxyrhynchus, an Economic and Social Study*, Princeton 1935.

MacMullen (1966) — MacMullen, R., *Enemies of the Roman Order: Treason, Unrest, and Alienation in the Empire*, Cambridge 1966.

MacMullen (1966a) — MacMullen, R., "A note on sermo humilis," *J. Theol. Studies* 17 (1966) 108–112.

MacMullen (1969) — MacMullen, R., *Constantine*, New York 1969.

MacMullen (1972) — MacMullen, R., "Sfiducia nell'intelletto nel quarto secolo," *Riv. storica italiana* 84 (1972) 5–16.

MacMullen (1974) — MacMullen, R., *Roman Social Relations 50 B.C. to A.D. 284*, New Haven 1974.

MacMullen (1980) — MacMullen, R., "Response (The power of bishops outside the church)," in *Protocol of the 35th Colloquy*, "The Role of the Christian Bishop in Ancient Society" (Center for Hermeneutical Studies), Berkeley 1980, 25–29.

MacMullen (1980a) — MacMullen, R., "Romans in tears," *Class. Philol.* 75 (1980) 254–255.

MacMullen (1981) — MacMullen, R., *Paganism in the Roman Empire*, New Haven 1981.

MacMullen (1982) — MacMullen, R., "Roman attitudes to Greek love," *Historia* 31 (1982) 484–502.

MacMullen (1983) — MacMullen, R., "Two types of conversion to early Christianity," *Vigiliae Christianae* 37 (1983) 174–192.

Martin (1974) — Martin, A., "Athanase et les Mélitiens (325–335)," in *Politique et théologie chez Athanase d'Alexandrie*, ed. C. Kannengiesser, Paris 1974, 31–61.

Matthews (1975) — Matthews, J., *Western Aristocracies and Imperial Court, A.D. 364–425*, Oxford 1975.

Mazzarino (1951) — Mazzarino, S., *Aspetti sociali del quarto secolo. Ricerche di storia tardo-romano*, Rome 1951.

Mazzarino (1974) — Mazzarino, S., *Antico, tardoantico ed èra costantiniana* 1, Rome 1974.

Meeks (1983) — Meeks, W. A., *The First Urban Christians: The Social World of the Apostle Paul*, New Haven 1983.

Meer (1961) — Meer, F. van der, *Augustine the Bishop: The Life and Work of a Father of the Church*, trans. B. Battershaw and G. R. Lamb, London-New York 1961.

Meiggs (1960) — Meiggs, R., *Roman Ostia*, Oxford 1960.

Ménage (1979) — Ménage, V. L., "The Islamization of Anatolia," in *Conversion to Islam*, ed. N. Levtzion, New York-London 1979, 52–67.

Mesot (1958) — Mesot, J., *Die Heidenbekehrung bei Ambrosius von Mailand*, Schöneck-Beckenried (Switzerland) 1958.

Mitchell (1982) — Mitchell, S., "The Life of Saint Theodotus of Ancyra," *Anatolian Studies* 32 (1982) 93–113.

Mohrmann (1952) — Mohrmann, C., "Encore une fois: paganus," *Vigiliae Christianae* 6 (1952) 109–121.

Mohrmann (1975) — Mohrmann, C., *Vita di Martino* et al. (Vita dei Santi), Verona 1975.

Molland (1974) — Molland, E., "Besass die alter Kirche ein Missionsprogramm?" in *Die alte Kirche*, ed. H. Frohnes and U. W. Knorr, Munich 1974, 51–67.

Mommsen (1850) — Mommsen, T., "Epigraphische Analekten," *Ber. sächsischen Gesellschaft* 2 (1850) 57–72.

Monceaux (1901–1923) — Monceaux, P., *Histoire littéraire de l'Afrique chrétienne*, 7 vols., Paris 1901–1923.

Moreau (1960) — Moreau, J., *Das Trierer Kornmarktmosaik*, Cologne 1960.

Moreau (1963) — Moreau, J., "La Lutte entre le christianisme et le paganisme gréco-romain dans la Gaule du nord-est," in *Rome et le christianisme dans la région rhénane*, Paris 1963, 110–126.

Moscadi (1970) — Moscadi, A., "Le lettere dell'archivio di Teofane," *Aegyptus* 50 (1970) 88–154.

Munier (1938) — Munier, H., "Le Christianisme à Philae," *Jam'iyat al-Athar al-Qibtiyah* 4 (1938) 37–49.

Nock (1933) — Nock, A. D., *Conversion: The Old and the New in Religion from Alexander the Great to Augustine of Hippo*, Oxford 1933.

Nock (1933a) — Nock, A. D., "Paul and the Magus," in *The Beginnings of Christianity*, ed. F. J. Foakes Jackson and K. Lake, vol. 5, London 1933, 164–187.

North (1980) — North, J. A., "Novelty and choice in Roman religion," *J. Roman Studies* 70 (1980) 186–191.

O'Leary (1938) — O'Leary, DeL., "The destruction of temples in Egypt," *Jam'iyat al-Athar al-Qibtiyah* 4 (1938) 51–57.

Opitz (1934–1940) — Opitz, H. G., *Athanasius Werke*, 3 vols., Berlin-Leipzig 1934–1940.

Palanque (1933) — Palanque, J.-R., *Saint Ambroise et l'Empire romain. Contribution à l'histoire des rapports de l'Eglise et de l'état à la fin du quatrième siècle*, Paris 1933.

Palestra (1961) — Palestra, A., "Nuovi scavi alla necropoli romana al cimiterio paleocristiano e medievale di S. Eustorgio," *Ambrosius* 37 (1961) 33–44.

Palmer (1981) — Palmer, R. E. A., "The topography and social history of Rome's Trastevere (southern sector)," *Proc. Am. Philos. Soc.* 125 (1981) 368–397.

Parlasca (1981) — Parlasca, K., "Rilievi funerari di epoca tardo-imperiale e paleocopta," *Corsi di cultura sull'arte ravennate e bizantina* 28 (1981) 225–230.

Peeters (1941) — Peeters, P., "La vie géorgienne de Saint Porphyre de Gaza," *Analecta Bollandana* 59 (1941) 65–216.

Petit (1951) — Petit, P., "Sur la date du 'Pro templis' de Libanius," *Byzantion* 21 (1951) 285–309.

Petit (1955) — Petit, P., *Libanius et la vie municipale à Antioche au IVe siècle après J.-C.*, Paris 1955.

Pietri (1970) — Pietri, L., "La Conversion en Belgique Seconde d'un officier de l'armée de Julien, Jovin," *Rev. du Nord* 52 (1970) 443–453.

Piganiol (1932) — Piganiol, A., *L'Empereur Constantin*, Paris 1932.

Piganiol (1972) — Piganiol, A., *L'Empire chrétien (325–395)²*, ed. A. Chastagnol, Paris 1972.

Pilet (1980) — Pilet, C., *La Nécropole de Frénouville. Etude d'une population de la fin du IIIe à la fin du VIIe siècle*, I: *Essai de synthèse*, Oxford 1980

Poupon (1981) — Poupon, G., "L'Accusation de magie dans les actes apocryphes," in *Les Actes apocryphes des apôtres. Christianisme et monde païen*, ed. F. Bovon et al., Geneva 1981, 71–93.

Praulx and O'Callaghan (1974) — Praulx, P., and J. O'Callaghan, "Papiro magico cristiano," *Studia papyrologica* 13 (1974) 83–88.

Price (1980) — Price, S. R. F., "Between man and god: Sacrifice in the Roman imperial cult," *J. Roman Studies* 70 (1980) 28–43.

Rahtz and Harris (1956–1957) — Rahtz, P., and L. G. Harris, "The temple well and other buildings at Pagan's Hill," *Proc. Somersetshire Archaeol. Soc.* 101–102 (1956–1957) 15–51.

Rambo (1982) — Rambo, L. R., "Current research on religious conversion," *Religious Studies Rev.* 8 (1982) 146–159.

Ramsay (1897) — Ramsay, W. M., *The Cities and Bishoprics of Phrygia . . . , I, 2: West and West-Central Phrygia*, Oxford 1897.

Rees (1950) — Rees, B. R., "Popular religion in Graeco-Roman Egypt, II: The transition to Christianity," *J. Egyptian Archaeology* 36 (1950) 86–100.

Remus (1982) — Remus, H., "'Magic or miracle?' Some second century instances," *The Second Century* 2 (1982) 127–156.

Rey-Coquais (1977) — Rey-Coquais, J. P., "Inscriptions de la nécropole" [Inscriptions grecques et latines découvertes dans les fouilles de Tyr (1963–1974)], *Bull. du Musée de Beyrouth* 29 (1977) 1–181.

Ricciotti (1960) — Ricciotti, G., *Julian the Apostate*, trans. M. J. Costelloe, Milwaukee 1960.

Richmond and Gillam (1951) — Richmond, I. A., and J. P. Gillam, "The temple of Mithras at Carrawburgh," *Archaeologia Aeliana*⁴ 29 (1951) 1–92.

Riedinger (1981) — Riedinger, R., "Das Bekenntnis des Gregor Thaumaturgus bei Sophronius von Jerusalem und Macarius von Antiocheia," *Zeitschrift für Kirchengesch.* 92 (1981) 311–314.

Robert (1960) — Robert, L., *Hellenica. Recueil d'épigraphie, de numismatique et d'antiquités grecques* 11–12, Paris 1960.

Robinson (1953) — Robinson, D. M., "A magical inscription from Pisidian Antioch," *Hesperia* 22 (1953) 172–174.

Ryssel (1880) — Ryssel, V., *Gregorius Thaumaturgus. Sein Leben und seine Schriften*, Leipzig 1880.

Ryssel (1894) — Ryssel, V., "Eine syrische Lebensgeschichte des Gregorius Thaumaturgus. Nach cod. Mus. Brit. syr. add. 14648 aus dem Syrischen übersetzt," *Theologische Zeitschr. aus der Schweiz* 11 (1894) 228–254.

Sahin (1975) — Sahin, S., "Das Grabmal des Pantomimen Krispus in Herakleia Pontike," *Zeitschr. für Papyrologie und Epigraphik* 18 (1975) 293–297.

Sauneron (1962) — Sauneron, S., *Les Fêtes religieuses d'Esna aux derniers siècles du paganisme*, Cairo 1962.

Scardigli (1967) — Scardigli, P., "La conversione dei Goti al Cristianesimo," *Settimane di Studi del Centro italiano di studi sull'alto medioevo* 14 (La Conversione al Cristianesimo nell'Europa dell'alto medioevo . . . 1966), 1967, 47–86.

Schede (1911) — Schede, M., "Inschriften aus Kleinasien," *Mitt. Deut. Arch. Inst.*, Ath. Abt. 36 (1911) 97–104.

Schoenebeck (1939) — Schoenebeck, H. von, *Beiträge zur Religionspolitik des Maxentius und Constantins*, Leipzig 1939.

Schultze (1887–1892) — Schultze, V., *Gesch. des Untergangs des griechisch-römischen Heidentums*, 2 vols., Jena 1887–1892.

Seeck (1901–1921) — Seeck, O., *Gesch. des Untergangs der Antiken Welt*, 6 vols., Berlin-Stuttgart 1901–1921.

Sherwin-White (1966) — Sherwin-White, A. N., *The Letters of Pliny: A Historical and Social Commentary*, Oxford 1966.

Skarsaune (1976) — Skarsaune, O., "The conversion of Justin Martin," *Theologica* 30 (1976) 53–73.

J. C. Smith (1979) — Smith, J. C., "Conversion in Origen," *Scottish J. of Theol.* 32 (1979) 217–240.

M. Smith (1978) — Smith, M., *Jesus the Magician*, San Francisco, Calif. 1978.

M. Smith (1980) — Smith, M., "Pauline worship as seen by pagans," *Harvard Theol. Rev.* 73 (1980) 241–249.

Soden (1974) — Soden, H. von, "Die christliche Mission in Altertum und Gegenwart," in *Die alte Kirche*, ed. H. Frohnes and U. W. Knorr, Munich 1974, 18–31.

Ste. Croix (1963) — Ste. Croix, G. E. M. de, "Why were the Christians persecuted?" *Past and Present* 26 (1963) 6–38.

Stern (1953) — Stern, H., *Le Calendrier de 354. Etude sur son texte et ses illustrations*, Paris 1953.

Stevenson (1963) — Stevenson, J., ed., *A New Eusebius. Documents Illustrative of the History of the Church to A.D. 337*, London 1963.

Straten (1976) — Straten, F. T. van, "Daikrates' dream. A votive relief from Kos, and some other kat'onar dedications," *Bull. antieke Beschaving* 51 (1976) 1–38.

Strauss (1979) — Strauss, G., *Luther's House of Learning: Indoctrination of the Young in the German Reformation*, Baltimore 1979.

Suhl (1980) — Suhl, A., "Die Wunder Jesu," in *Der Wunderbegriff im Neuen Testament*, ed. idem, Darmstadt 1980, 464–509.

Telfer (1930) — Telfer, W., "The Latin Life of St. Gregory Thaumaturgus," *J. Theol. Studies* 31 (1930) 142–155, 354–363.

Theissen (1977) — Theissen, G., *Soziologie der Jesusbewegung. Ein Beitrag zur Entstehungsgeschichte des Urchristentums*, Munich 1977.

Theissen (1979) — Theissen, G., *Studien zur Soziologie des Urchristentums*, Tübingen 1979.

Thompson (1982) — Thompson, E. A., *Romans and Barbarians*, Madison, Wisc. 1982

Tran Tam Tinh, V., *Essai sur le culte d'Isis à Pompéi*, Paris 1964.

Twisleton (1873) — Twisleton, E., *The Tongue Not Essential to Speech . . .*, London 1873.

Vago and Bona (1976) — Vago, E. B., and I. Bona, *Der spätrömische Südostfriedhof*, Budapest 1976.

Vermaseren and Van Essen (1965) — Vermaseren, M. J., and C. C. Van Essen, *The Excavations in the Mithraeum of the Church of Santa Prisca in Rome*, Leiden 1965.

Versnel (1981) — Versnel, H. S., "Self-sacrifice, compensation and the anonymous gods," in *Le Sacrifice dans l'antiquité* (Entretiens Hardt 27), Geneva 1981, 135–185.

Versnel (1981a) — Versnel, H. S., "Religious mentality in ancient prayer," in *Faith, Hope and Worship: Aspects of Religious Mentality in the Ancient World*, ed. idem, Leiden 1981, 1–64.

Veyne (1978) — Veyne, P., "Foucault révolutionne l'histoire," in idem, *Comment on écrit l'histoire²*, Paris 1978, 202–242.

Veyne (1983) — Veyne, P., *Les Grecs ont-ils cru à leurs mythes? Essai sur l'imagination constituante*, Paris 1983.

Ville (1960) — Ville, G., "Les Jeux de gladiateurs dans l'empire chrétien," *Mélanges d'arch. et d'hist. de l'Ecole Française de Rome* 72 (1960) 273–335.

Ville (1981) — Ville, G., *La Gladiature en Occident des origines à la mort de Domitien*, Paris 1981.

Volbach (1976) — Volbach, W. F., *Elfenbeinarbeiten der Spätantike und des frühen Mittelalters³*, Mainz (von Zabern) 1976.

Waltzing (1895–1900) — Waltzing, J.-P., *Etude historique sur les corporations professionnelles chez les Romains* . . . , 4 vols., Louvain 1895–1900.

Wheeler and Wheeler (1932) — Wheeler, R. E. M. and T. V. Wheeler, *Report on the Excavation of the Prehistoric, Roman, and Post-Roman Site in Lydney Park, Gloucestershire*, Oxford 1932.

Wilken (1970) — Wilken, R., "Toward a social interpretation of early Christian apologetics," *Church Hist.* 39 (1970) 1–22.

Wilken (1980) — Wilken, R., "The Christians as the Romans (and Greeks) saw them," in *Jewish and Christian Self-Definition*, I: *The Shaping of Christianity in the 2nd and 3rd Centuries*, ed. E. P. Sanders, Philadelphia 1980, 100–125.

Winnett (1957) — Winnett, F. V., *Safaitic Inscriptions from Jordan*, Toronto 1957.

Winnett and Harding (1978) — Winnett, F. V., and G. L. Harding, *Inscriptions from Fifty Safaitic Cairns*, Toronto 1978.

Wissowa (1912) — Wissowa, G., *Religion und Kultus der Römer*², Munich 1912.

Young (1977) — Young, B., "Paganisme, christianisation et rites funéraires mérovingiens," *Archéologie médiévale* 7 (1977) 5–81.

Zaccaria (1976–1977) — Zaccaria, C., "Religione egiziana e propaganda imperiale romana," *Annali, Ist. ital. di numismatica* 23–24 (1976–1977) 161–197.

Ziegler (1970) — Ziegler, J., *Zur religiösen Haltung der Gegenkaiser im 4. Jh. n. Chr.*, Kallmünz 1970.

Zilliacus (1963) — Zilliacus, H., *Sylloge inscriptionum christianarum veterum Musei Vaticani* (Acta Instituti Romani Finlandiae I, 1–2), 2 vols., Helsingfors 1963.

Zoega (1810) — Zoega, G., *Catalogus codicum Coptorum manuscriptorum*, Rome 1810.

Index

Aelius Aristides, 9, 41, 125, 165
Alexandria, 50, 55, 59, 63, 69, 83, 90, 92, 99
Allat, 2–3
Ambrose, Saint, 53–57, 64, 75, 94, 100
Ammonius, 31
Angels, 17
Anthony, Saint, 61, 112
Antioch, 49, 64, 76, 83, 84, 157
Aphraates, 62
Aphrodite, 2, 3
Apollo, 97, 138
Apollonius of Tyana, 17, 23
Apologists, 10, 20, 21
Apostates. See Converts from Christianity
Apostles, 22, 127
Apuleius, 10, 131
Aquileia, 49, 162
Arcadius, 89
Arius and Arianism, 93, 160, 161, 164
Army: religion in, 44–47, 80, 154, enforces "conversion," 89, 93, 94, 162
Arnobius, converted, 134n15
Artemis, 18, 26
Asceticism, 8, 9, 62, 69, 125
Asia, province of, 34
Athanasius, Saint, 55, 90, 93
Atheism, 15, 110, 111, 128
Athens, 48, 54, 76
Augustine, Saint, 53, 57, 65, 71, 72, 74, 84, 95

Bacchus, 8, 78
Basil, Saint, 69, 75, 142
Bedouins (Saracens), 2, 3, 146
Bithynia, 135

Burial practices, 11, 40, 78, 80, 153, 154
Bury, J. B., 44

Caesarea, 26, 75
Caesarius of Arles, 74, 95
Callinicum, 100, 159
Carthage, 20, 30, 33, 82, 92, 94, 101, 156
Catechetical schools, 33, 136
Celsus, 14, 19, 25, 34, 35, 37
Charity: non-Christian, 54, chap. VI passim, 143; Christian, 54, 141, chap. VI passim, 143
Chi-Rho, 48, 78, 140
Chrysostom, Saint John, 64, 65, 79
Church building, 49, 53, 65, 81, 114, 142
Cirta, 49, 90, 164
Claudian, 154
Clearchus, 63
Clement, 134
Como, 64, 95
Constantine, chap. V passim, 56, 166; conversion of, 24, chap. V passim, 117, 131
Constantinople, 49, 79, 87
Constantius, 46, 47, 53, 55, 90, 96
Conversion: how defined by moderns, 3–5, 21, 124, 148; defined by ancients, 3, 52, 56, 57, 65, 123, 144
Converts from Christianity, 57, 58, 71, 72, 91, 114, 144, 145
Cybele cult, 157
Cynegius, 98, 162
Cynics, 38
Cyprian, Saint, 27, 33, 35, 36, 134

181